WE WERE GOING TO CHANGE THE WORLD

INTERVIEWS WITH WOMEN FROM THE 1970s & 1980s SOUTHERN CALIFORNIA PUNK ROCK SCENE

STACY RUSSO
FOREWORD BY MIKE WATT

Published by:
Santa Monica Press LLC
P.O. Box 850
Solana Beach, CA 92075
1-800-784-9553
www.santamonicapress.com
books@santamonicapress.com

Printed in the United States

Santa Monica Press books are available at special quantity discounts when purchased in bulk by corporations, organizations, or groups. Please call our Special Sales department at 1-800-784-9553.

This book is intended to provide general information. The publisher, author, distributor, and copyright owner are not engaged in rendering professional advice or services. The publisher, author, distributor, and copyright owner are not liable or responsible to any person or group with respect to any loss, illness, or injury caused or alleged to be caused by the information found in this book.

ISBN-13 978-1-59580-092-3

Library of Congress Cataloging-in-Publication Data
Names: Russo, Stacy Shotsberger, 1970- author.
Title: We were going to change the world : interviews with women from the 1970s and 1980s Southern California punk rock scene / Stacy Russo.
Description: Solana Beach, CA : Santa Monica Press, 2017. | Includes bibliographical references. | Description based on print version record and CIP data provided by publisher; resource not viewed.
Identifiers: LCCN 2017020339 (print) | LCCN 2017025345 (ebook) | ISBN 9781595807953 | ISBN 9781595800923
Subjects: LCSH: Punk rock music--California, Southern--History and criticism. | Women punk rock musicians--California, Southern--Interviews. | Rock music fans--California, Southern--Interviews. | Punk culture--California, Southern--History.
Classification: LCC ML3534.3 (ebook) | LCC ML3534.3 .R87 2017 (print) | DDC 781.66082/097949--dc23
LC record available at https://lccn.loc.gov/2017020339

Cover and interior design and production by Future Studio

"Tell me, what is it you plan to do
with your one wild and precious life?"

—"The Summer Day" by Mary Oliver

CONTENTS

FOREWORD BY MIKE WATT

RIGHT FROM THE START, me and d boon found something really different about this movement we stumbled upon versus the other two ways we had experienced rock and roll music up to that time: women were involved, I mean REALLY involved. it was a bags gig up in west hollywood and we drove all the way up from pedro in what became a HUGE sea change for our lives. up to that point, music for me and him was either us together in his bedroom trying to copy the licks of songs from records which was in a way happening cuz it was very personal (except for not realizing music could be actually a form of YOUR OWN expression and not just trying to imitate someone else) or arena gigs where we sat way in the back to experience something which was feeling more and more like for us nuremberg rallies, the way we felt froze out, less and less we wanted to be there.

anyway, a chance encounter w/nickey beat (he was drumming for the weirdos and was from our pedro town) provided us w/news there was a scene where people wrote their own songs (he must've heard us all pathetic trying to "recreate" someone else's recording) and that's what led us to see the bags . . . there were actually two women in the band, one was on bass. definitely the singer was using lyrics to express herself, it didn't seem like connect the dots to us—sadly, we didn't really think about lyrics as anything more than lead guitar or some kind of sound. sure, there was bob dylan but he seemed like a weird old relative at a thanksgiving chow, muttering stuff w/meanings meant for him. alice bag sang words like she meant for you to be trying to get exactly what she meant—it was profound on us. w/out thinking, my mouf fell open and out fell "we can do this" towards d boon and he shook his head—not left to right but up and down. if this lady was willing to let the freak flag fly then what the fuck were we trying to do w/music except just be together?

it was incredible and empowering. everything for us after that changed forever. we started going to gigs, all kinds of ladies were in the bands, were also gig-goers . . . pretty much it seemed like the folks onstage and those who were not were actually like taking turns playing for each other. it was all so unpredictable—this was late '70s punk for us and things hadn't been "codified" or whatever word for lamed-out that really hurt big parts of the movement . . . although that never really fucked w/us cuz luckily those ethics we found so happening we kept personal and miles from getting compromised.

people like me and d boon "weren't supposed" to be involved in what some claimed to be rock and roll and so very much we felt kindred spirits to the sisters involved—they were inspiring and balls out. it was an exciting time for us and believe it or not, alice bag is still charging hard—I heard she's gonna make another solo album soon. I was invited last year to be on a panel to talk about the "old days" at a famous university that was being organized by a lady but all the people on the panel were gonna be guys—WHAT?! I told her "thank you very much but no," cuz that's not the way it was for us, it's not what made me what I am today.

I am so glad this book is coming out, it's very important to set the record straight and let people know about the women involved in the moment in the old days cuz in my opinion it can mean a lot for younger ladies AND men these days who might be trying to figure out how to really open things up and change rusted corrupt hierarchies that do nothing but strangle genuine human spirit. punk was not just a way of dressing or even a style of music, it was for us a state of mind and hallelujah the sisters who were part of it then to make it real for some corndogs like me and d boon down in the harbor. I just can't express enough gratitude for that. let these ladies tell you in their own words—it's the best way I think to explain what I'm trying to get at here in this foreword spiel.

INTRODUCTION

IN THE SUMMER OF 2012, I attended an oral history workshop by the social justice organization Voice of Witness. I'm a librarian and professor at Santa Ana College and I participated in the workshop to discover projects I could do with students. I ended up imagining something entirely different: interviewing other women like me, now in our middle or later years, who grew up in the punk rock scene in Southern California. Did punk rock influence the rest of their lives? What attracted them to punk rock and how did they get involved? What was it like being a woman in the scene?

What you are holding in your hands is the final result of a project that took several years and countless hours to complete. How did I do it? I created a flyer about the project. I posted the flyer a few places around Orange County and Los Angeles and on Facebook. Women started contacting me to participate. I wrote up a list of questions and bought two digital recorders. I emailed some women directly and asked if they would be willing to participate. Then I started calling women and meeting them, mostly in their homes. A friend called it "punk rock anthropology."

I had no idea what an amazing experience this would be. I often say it is my favorite project of my life. Sitting on couches or at a dining room table or in a café or on a park bench while these women shared their stories with me was a powerful thing. I felt much love and a responsibility to treat their stories with care. Each story was received as a gift.

A few things were very important to me while working on this project. This book was never meant to be a who's who of punk rock. I did not want to include only well-known women

and performers. I believe that would go against the very nature
of punk rock. It was important to include women who created
fanzines and art and also those who participated solely by going
to shows. I've always believed the audience is as important as the
performer. I'm sure some readers will feel that certain voices should
have been included here, but I did my best to include a diversity of
perspectives.

Another significant part of the process was treating each
woman and her story with respect. After transcribing the
interviews, I sent each woman a copy of her interview to review and
make any corrections. It was also important that my voice as the
interviewer was as absent as possible. This is why the interviews
are not in a Q&A format. They were edited only when necessary
to provide clarity and pare things down. I wanted the readers to be
able to clearly hear each woman's voice and to keep her story as raw
as possible.

As with the stories you are about to read, growing up in the
punk rock scene was a major part of my life. Now that I am in my
late forties, many things have influenced me and shaped who I am,
and punk rock remains a big one. I was politicized through punk
in the 1980s. My eyes were opened to human rights and animal
rights. I try to live my life as ethically as possible in all aspects and
most of that is rooted in what I discovered as a teenager. I stopped
eating meat at age sixteen after getting hold of a Conflict album.
The energy of the music and the entire underground culture
surrounding it was exhilarating. It made me feel like I could do
anything. As a girl, it was empowering. It gave me grit and a way to
make it through. And it also made me feel like I was okay, because,
like many of the women I interviewed, I felt like a misfit. With
punk rock, I found my family of outcasts. I felt a lot of anger at the
time toward a world that seemed so unjust. Punk rock helped with
that anger. It still does.

I now listen to Joni Mitchell way more than punk rock, but when I'm feeling down or angry, or doubting myself, I pull out the old vinyl. I dance around the living room to the Dead Kennedys and instantly feel better. I'm so thankful for the insane times and memories, even all the times I can't remember well, because I was often completely trashed. Growing up punk rock is part of my good fortune.

I hope you will enjoy reading these stories as much as I did gathering them. Storytelling is a courageous thing. It can be an act of empowerment. It contributes to our cultural record. It allows us to be witness to voices we may otherwise not hear. Sometimes it is an act of social justice. Both the listening and the telling of the story are important. Thank you for reading this book and spending your time with the amazing voices you are about to encounter.

STACY RUSSO
Santa Ana, California

INTERVIEWS

ALICE BAG

Born in 1958 in Los Angeles, California. Played in the Bags (1977), Castration Squad (1980), the Imports (1980), Funhouse (1981), Cambridge Apostles (1982), Swing Set (1986), the Afro Sisters (1986), Cholita (1989), El Vez (1990), Las Tres (1990), Goddess13 (1993), Stay at Home Bomb (1996), Punkoustika (2002), and She Riffs (2012). Currently lives in Los Angeles and works as an author.

I REMEMBER FIRST LEARNING ABOUT PUNK when I was in high school. Seniors had off-campus lunch, so I walked to get snacks at the liquor store. The store had *Cream* and *Circus* magazines. One day *Punk* was there. I picked that up and started reading about the

New York punk scene. That got my interest. Shortly after that I got into the Ramones and Patti Smith. That is what initially introduced me to punk. It was the New York bands.

At the same time, I was really into the L.A. glam scene. I was going to see stuff like *The Rocky Horror Picture Show.* This was about '76 and I was probably seventeen years old. It seemed to me that the people who were involved in the glam scene just naturally gravitated toward punk, because both of them were innovative and edgy and challenging current forms of music. There was regular rock, which was guys in tight pants playing solos, and then there was glam, which was guys in tight pants too, but there were bands like the

New York Dolls that were challenging gender stereotypes, which was intriguing. I found Patti Smith androgynous and exciting. David Bowie introduced me to the whole concept of bisexuality. I thought, "Why do I have these feelings? What's wrong with me?" David Bowie kind of validated what I was going through.

When that transitional period started, it didn't seem like an abrupt change to people wearing leather jackets and safety pins in their ears. The music and the style and the ideas were just evolving and gradually morphing into punk. Some of the glam musicians were very proficient and it was hard for them to scale down a bit to get the rawness of punk. For those of us who had not been playing in glam, it was very easy and welcoming.

When I was in high school, I thought, "That's what I want to do. I want to be close to the music." I knew I could sing. My role models were the groupies. It seemed to me that they were having glamorous love affairs with rock stars. I tried to emulate the groupie lifestyle. Then I realized I did not want to be fawning over the rock star. I wanted to be the rock star. I started taking guitar lessons in high school. I had some girlfriends who were also learning to play guitar and we decided to form a band. This was pre-punk. We were into Queen and Elton John and David Bowie. Their musicianship was awesome. We couldn't play that stuff. We were just beginning. We played "Smoke on the Water" over and over again and struggled to change between chords. When we heard the Ramones and the Runaways we thought we could play that, so we started playing those songs.

We imagined ourselves in a band. We'd go out to places and tell people we were. At one point I saw Rodney Bingenheimer at the Starwood and my girlfriends encouraged me to go up to him and tell him about our band. So I did. He promised to help. I was living at my parent's house. I was a young girl. I was probably seventeen. My mother answered the phone early one morning. She walked in

the room and said, "It's a man."
It turned out it was Kim Fowley.
He started telling me who he
was. He said he was looking for
a band. He said he created the
Runaways and he was looking to
do it again. He asked if I wanted
to audition. Foolishly, I said yes.
I sang over the phone. He said,
"Come on down and audition."

There were a bunch of
women there who were into that
transitional scene between glam
and punk. As he auditioned
people, he would send us out of
the room. There was a group of us rejects outside. We were talking
and ended up forming a band. We found our drummer that way. So,
that's kind of how I got into a band.

The first punk show I went to was to see my boyfriend. He was a
drummer. He used to have long, Peter Frampton-type hair, and one
day he came up to me with his hair cut off. He said, "I'm playing in
a new band and they told me to cut my hair." He said, "You've gotta
come see them. They're really cool." It was the Weirdos.

My first punk band was the Bags. I was in that for about two
and a half or three years. Our first show, I think, was August '77.
We played in San Francisco, San Diego, and Portland. We opened
for Iggy Pop in Seattle. We were all sitting and listening to him. I
was just staring at him. His eyelashes were amazing. He had these
really long eyelashes. I was too star-struck to really remember the
conversation. We also played the Masque, the Whisky, Gazzarri's,

the Starwood, Hong Kong Café, Madame Wong's, the Smokestack, the Elk's Lodge, and different halls. By the end of '79, we were breaking up.

After the Bags, I had friends in the punk scene who were into drugs and dying and I didn't want to be one of them, so I decided I was going to move away. I moved back to my parent's house in East L.A. and signed up for college. I got a part-time job in a flower shop. I had been living really close to the edge. I was getting involved in drugs. I could see that it was a dangerous lifestyle. My friends started calling me. "Let's start a band." My former roommate, Shannon Wilhelm, said, "I need you to play bass. My band has a show and I don't have a bass player." She was in a band called Castration Squad. I went in as a fill-in emergency member and think I ended up playing all their shows. Then the keyboard player switched to bass and they asked me to sub. I played keyboards with them. This was probably 1980. We played in L.A., San Francisco, and Berkeley.

I've been in a lot of bands. I was in a band called the Cambridge Apostles after that. It kind of morphed out of Castration Squad with some of the same people. After Cambridge Apostles, I was in a band called Funhouse. I was in the Fire Engines. When I was living in Hollywood and still doing punk, there were bands that we would do for just one or two shows.

Shannon had named the band Castration Squad. She felt that we were beyond feminism. She felt that we not only needed to liberate women, but we needed to liberate men, because they were victimized as much by the injustice as women.

I feel that as women we welcomed ourselves to punk rock. We didn't need to be welcomed by anybody, because we were not asking to enter anybody's home. It was our home and it was ours for the taking. We behaved as though we belonged there, because we felt that we did.

Growing up, my father always treated me like a person—not like a little girl, not like a woman, but like a thinking person who was responsible for my actions. I think I've always behaved that way. When my brothers would come over, my mother would ask me to warm their tortillas. That was irritating to me. I knew if I didn't do it, she would have to get up and do it. She didn't have to, but she would make that choice. I remember at one point saying, "He's older than me. He can warm up his own tortillas." She was really upset with me. I realized I was different, but I also knew I was right.

When I was little, my father used to abuse my mother. I remember there were certain women in my life who would challenge my father and I found that really exciting. That was my sister-in-law and my aunt. When I actually felt like I was a feminist was around the time that this was happening. I remember my dad was going off on a tirade and foaming at the mouth. My aunt went up to his face. She was perfectly calm and said, "I'm not backing down." I knew that was what I was going to be like. I didn't know it was feminism. In the Bags, I didn't feel like I needed to say I'm a feminist, because I always felt like these are people who are on the same wavelength. They think like me. I don't have to say I'm a Chicana or I'm bisexual or a feminist, because it was my band. So, it was just person to person, human to human.

■   ■   ■   ■   ■

Punk gave people permission to express themselves without necessarily having the technical ability to do it. It taught me that I don't have to wait until I'm perfect at anything to do something, whether it's creative or political or any other aspect of my life. If I see something that needs to be done, I feel empowered to do it, even if I do it in a way that's not traditional or in a way that someone else would not have done it. Punk forced me to hold myself responsible for taking control of my life and not waiting for somebody else to solve my problems. If something is in my way, I'm going to figure out a way to solve it, to get over it, or get around it. I can't wait for somebody to build a bridge for me or for an engineer to come with the knowledge to build a bridge. I need to go and make it out of sticks and stones or whatever. That's how I approach my life. It's great if I can find some allies that have knowledge or better training, but if I don't, I'll figure it out the best I can. That's how I feel I keep myself in the driver's seat. Punk showed me how to take control of my life. And it's not just my life, because if I take control of my life, I influence others and I influence the world. That's how big change happens.

When I was at Cal State L.A., I wanted to do volunteer work. I had read Paulo Freire's *Pedagogy of the Oppressed* and I loved what I read. In Nicaragua, Freire was asked to create their literacy campaign. I knew there was funding through the government. I asked my philosophy teacher if I could do an independent study and go down to Nicaragua and research the literacy campaign. I'm actually thinking of writing a book based on my experiences in Nicaragua. One of the things I had to do as part of my

independent study was keep a diary. I have the diary and tons of pictures and all kinds of memories.

One of the things I learned in Nicaragua was that teaching is not one-directional. It's not only for the person in front of you, but the environment, and everything. If you're not engaged in that process, you're stagnant and not growing. Punk and my visit to Nicaragua really had an impact on the way I think and how I talk.

I think if I hadn't been involved in punk, my life could have gone in a very negative direction. I got in a lot of fights with girls and guys. Sometimes I just got drunk and picked fights. I was an asshole. I called it fight or fuck. If I didn't go home with somebody and I still had a lot of energy that I had to get rid of, I'd pick a fight. This was when I was eighteen or nineteen. I had kept in a bunch of rage that I didn't know was there until I got on the stage and started singing and became aggressive. That side of me came out. I realized I had stuff to deal with. We came from a poor family. I didn't have a therapist. My therapy was punk rock. I would go until I was sweaty and exhausted or singing and screaming and letting it all out. I think if I hadn't done that I might be a dangerous person. I really do. I will always feel connected to punk rock. It changed my life.

ALISON BRAUN

Born in 1966 in Los Angeles, California. Worked in L.A. as a photographer and writer for fanzines (including *Flipside, Maximum Rocknroll,* and *We Got Power*) and as a columnist for *Maximum Rocknroll,* and attended shows at various venues throughout Los Angeles County in the '80s. Currently lives in Seattle, Washington, and works as a program manager at an advertising agency.

I WAS ABOUT FIFTEEN YEARS OLD and I got introduced to punk rock by some people I met at school. They were into this music and I thought it was really cool. I had never seen anybody like that before. It just seemed really different and interesting. This was probably 1980 when this happened.

From the start, what I wanted to do was make a mark in the scene and put something into it, instead of just being a fan and going to shows. I wanted to give something back to the scene. Almost immediately I brought my camera to shows. Some of the first shows I ever went to, I started taking pictures.

Back in that time, nobody stopped you. You could just take pictures. I would get the pictures and do a couple of things with them. I would send them off unsolicited to some punk rock fanzines and I would give them to members of the band. I would say, "Here's some pictures I shot. If you put me on the guest list, I'll give you these pictures or I'll take more pictures." I had a darkroom, so it was really easy for me to take pictures and go home and process the film and make prints. It was a little enterprise I had going.

The other thing I started doing through my photography was getting involved with people who were publishing their own fanzines. Two in particular were *We Got Power* and *Flipside*. I started doing band interviews. I had photos in *Flipside*. I started writing for another fanzine that was based in the Bay Area called *Maximum Rocknroll*. Before long I was shooting bands, doing interviews with bands, writing a Los Angeles scene report, and then I had my own column in *Maximum Rocknroll*: "Memos from the Mousetrap." I even had a silly punk rock pseudonym. I went by the name Mouse. The column was anything I wanted to talk about. It usually had to do with my parents or school. I wrote the

column from age sixteen to eighteen or nineteen. I got a lot of correspondence. Some of it was good and some of it was weird. Anytime you put your name and your picture next to something you get a weird cross-section of people.

I would do interviews at my house. Bands would come to the house. I remember one time the Necros were over and my mother was serving them cookies. They would sit in the living room and my parents would be there. My mother knew these people. Pretty soon my dad was supplying a tie so Jello Biafra could go to court.

I grew up in Studio City, California, and that's the Hollywood Hills, so I would mostly frequent clubs in Hollywood and the Sunset Strip. In Los Angeles, if you wanted to go into a bar, there wasn't an age limit. If you wanted to drink, you had to present ID. At age fifteen, I was able to go into the clubs. The Whisky was a home away from home. The Starwood. The Cathay de Grande. I spent significant parts of my teenage years there.

The Whisky was painted all black inside. It wasn't very big. It had two levels. There was an upper lever where you could stand and look down and then there was a lower level and there was a bar on one side. It was just a typical club. It had a backstage that went up a steep set of stairs. There were some dressing rooms at the top of these stairs. It was always hot in there and not very clean. It was an extremely smoky, hot, sweaty club. Your clothes would smell like smoke. Your hair would smell like smoke. My camera bag would smell like smoke. It was not fancy at all. When it got crowded, it was very uncomfortable to stay in there. I would usually sit on the stage and take pictures. Between shows I would go backstage and hang out in the dressing room and clean my lenses.

The Cathay de Grande was much more of a dive. It had two levels. The upstairs had a small stage that sometimes had acts, but most of the bands played downstairs. It had a wickedly low ceiling and a low stage. If you were a singer in a band and you were tall and you jumped, your head would go through the false ceiling. That actually happened. It was just gross. None of these clubs were very posh, but we were all comfortable there. We knew people. It was another home away from home.

There were some bands I really liked. I liked Battalion of Saints a lot. I liked Dead Kennedys, Social Distortion, and TSOL. A lot of people in bands became my friends and I made lifelong friendships with the people I photographed.

I can't even listen to punk rock now. Every once in a while there will be a documentary on TV about punk rock, featuring people I knew. Or I'll come across some old music I have and I'll play it. I can't even listen to it anymore. This was some music that I thought was the greatest thing in the world. I was so incredibly into it. I don't know what happened. It just seems so silly.

The Dead Kennedys is the exception. I still love their music. I was just listening to *Fresh Fruit for Rotting Vegetables*. I was listening to Klaus Flouride's guitar—that sort of chunky, surf guitar—and I thought, "Wow! That will never be heard live again."

The way you look at yourself as a woman, as a grown-up, is a lot different than your perception as a woman when you're a teenager. I don't think I thought of female empowerment, but I felt empowered to be an artist, a photographer, a writer, and a journalist. It was obvious that in some cases I was the only girl in the van. There were certainly a lot of girls in the scene, but there was definitely a male energy. I didn't look at it as not welcoming or threatening. I just went about my business. I have to thank my parents for that.

My mother and father were both very supportive of what I was doing. They instilled in me values about respecting myself. I would go to questionable neighborhoods at night by myself, after I got my driver's license. I was just taking pictures. Now I see the value of it as a middle-aged woman, looking back on what I did as a teenager. It was really great as a young woman to do all this.

A lot of my friends are dead now. They had drug problems. They had drinking problems. A lot of my friends in the scene were heroin addicts. I had a couple thousand dollars of gear around my neck, so I was constantly aware of the package I was carrying. I couldn't be drunk or out of my wits. Something would happen to my camera. So, I was always acutely aware. I didn't want to be the idiot at the party drawing attention to herself. I was very aware of my surroundings. I didn't want to disappoint my parents. If I came home completely wasted or my grades slipped, there is no way my father would have let me continue to go to punk rock shows in Hollywood on school nights by myself. They allowed me to do this, not fully understanding what that meant and it was sort of a bond of trust that I was not going to break.

To put it into perspective, I had a brother in the late '70s who died of a drug overdose. I was aware of how that happened and the cops coming to our house in the middle of the night, informing my

parents that my brother was dead. I made a promise to myself after
watching that unfold. My dad was not going to bury another one of
his kids.

I really want to give a shout-out to my dad. My dad was part of
the L.A. punk scene in his own way. Before I could drive, I had to
get to these shows somehow. My dad would come to the Whisky
and pull up in front of the club. If I wasn't outside waiting for him,
he would come in. There was a club called Godzilla's in the San

Fernando Valley. Once I was
at the stage taking pictures.
No shit. The music stopped
and they said, "Alison, your
mom's outside." It was just
hysterical. I figured there
were a couple of ways I could
integrate my parents or I
could somehow work them
into my play. If I was going
to shows and I was going to
a terrible neighborhood, my
mother would say, "You can't
go unless your father goes

with you." I just incorporated him into the scene. Instead of being
embarrassed by my parents, I sort of owned it.

My dad, in his post-World War II slang, kind of endeared
himself in the most uncool way to my friends. We'd go to a show
and I'd install him at the bar. He would watch the show from the
background. He would have a beer and try to be cool, talking to the
bands and using his "Big Daddy-O" type talk. He was so funny. He
saw a lot. He saw police brutality. He saw a lot of things that I think
opened his mind. He was kind of a right-wing reactionary guy. He
met people who were gay. He met people who had blue hair. He

met musicians. He met junkies. He met all kinds of people that he had absolutely no exposure to. It kind of opened his mind that these people that look weird are actually really nice people and you can't look at them at face value. He really grew by becoming part of my scene.

It's just funny thinking of my dad sitting in the Cathay de Grande having a conversation with El Duce. This actually happened. Here's my dad. Here's El Duce. And we're sitting in a booth talking. He was such a good sport. Even when he got caught in a punk riot at Bard's Apollo. The cops were beating people up and he saw it. How weird and surreal was that?

He never pulled the plug on it. He continued to let me do it. As long as I got straight A's and kept up my part of the bargain, he was a party to this whole madness. He got me my first camera. I think he looked back on it fondly. He would always ask about people. He had an interest in it. If my dad wasn't affixed to my punk rock story, then it wouldn't be my story. He was the great enabler.

■　　■　　■　　■　　■

I think the idea of thinking for yourself and, regardless of what punk rock became or how it ended or the derivative nature that it morphed into—all of that aside, I think being a part of that music scene in L.A. in the early '80s gave me the opportunity to be independent, create things, see things that I wouldn't normally see, and meet people I wouldn't normally meet. It enabled me to grow up a lot faster. I saw a lot of things that a fifteen- or sixteen-year-old shouldn't see. I became jaded or streetwise pretty quickly. I think punk rock enabled me to be more aware of my world and more understanding of different types of people. I have certainly kept a little bit of the rebel outlook. Never bowing down to "the man." I always feel like this little punk shit at heart. There's a little part of my reptilian brain that is still a snot-nosed punk.

It was very good. It taught me to think for myself. I never
really bought into the whole labeling. I never became much of a
consumerist. The way I think is directly related to the experiences
I had. It's kind of like people who take acid. You take acid the first
time and it changes your life. The way you think after that, years
after that first trip, your mind has changed. I think that is sort of
the outlook. My mind was forever changed by being exposed to that
information and that stimulus.

I feel a connection to the memories. I don't feel a connection
to the scene. There is no punk scene. There is no L.A. punk
scene. Sure, there are people who still carry the torch. Some of
my old friends still have the band going. That makes them happy
or productive. I hold the memories fondly, but I don't think of
the scene anymore. It's like people who were hippies that went to
Woodstock. It's something you did, something you lived, and you
remember it fondly and move on.

ANGELITA FIGUEROA SALAS

Born in 1961 in Orange, California. Lived in Santa Ana, California, and London, England, in the 1970s and '80s and attended shows at various venues throughout Los Angeles County, Orange County, and London. Currently lives in Santa Ana, California, and works as a counselor and faculty member at a community college.

I WENT TO A HIGH SCHOOL that was predominantly Anglo and I was one of about twenty students of color. There were maybe one or two black students and the rest of us who weren't white were mainly Latino. Colleen, my best friend, was white. We were huge Elton John fans in the mid-'70s and that's how we became friends. We would go up and hang out at his house in Beverly Hills, because there was a little lot in front of it. We'd have parties out there. His manager took us to Le Dome one night and we were all underage. He got us drunk as lords. He walked me to the restroom, where I threw up.

It was Elton John who actually got us into punk rock, because he would talk about it. He thought it was really cool. That it was interesting. My friend and I would read all the British magazines, like *Melody Maker*. One day, Colleen had an article with Elton

John on one side. On the other side was an article about a band called the Stranglers. We thought, "This sounds really funny." This was probably '77. From reading those magazines, the British

ones, we started hearing about all these weird bands. That's really kind of how we got into it. We were fifteen or sixteen years old.

In those British papers, you'd always see ads for people wanting pen friends. I answered one of the ads. A guy wrote me. He lived in Ipswich, which is in the eastern part of England. I told him I liked punk. We used to write letters. He sent me my first mixed tape of all the British bands, so that's how I got into all these other bands. It was that combination of us liking Elton John and reading the British papers and also having a British pen friend. I would send him stuff on the L.A. bands and local bands here.

I wrote to one other kid through the Stranglers Fan Club. I was nineteen at the time and he was fourteen. We're still friends. I know his fiancée and his baby. In fact, they just had another baby and I sent a Ramones jumper, which he just loves. So, he became my other friend and then I had another person who came from the Stranglers club who is also a very dear friend of mine. I've known them since about '80.

After Elton John, I got really into Cheap Trick. That was another introduction to punk. When you talk to old punks about our musical background, we probably all liked Cheap Trick at one point. They were the first band I ever saw in 1978 at UCI Crawford Hall. The Runaways opened. I'd say my first punk album I bought was Costello. Then the Stranglers. It kind of progressed from there.

At that time, '78, '79, a lot of these bands were coming to L.A. We lived in Orange County, but we were primarily going to L.A. My friend Colleen's dad worked for one of those big aerospace companies. He worked the night shift. He wouldn't go to work until three or four in the afternoon. We'd buy tickets for shows at the Whisky. He would drop us off in front of the Whisky around three in the afternoon and would pick us up after the show. So, we'd always hit the early show. He'd be out by eleven or eleven-thirty. There was a gas station across the street. He would park there and wait for us. One time, there was a huge riot at the Dead Kennedys and Sham 69 show. The police blocked it off. They were on horses. He sat there waiting for us. He was eating an ice cream. He never said a word to us. God bless him.

I spent my youth at the Whisky. It was a cool place. Being short can sometimes be a challenge at punk shows. The Whisky stage went up to my chest. I don't think I ever sat when I went to the Whisky. We'd always try to get there first. We knew we had to get to the front of the stage, because we were short. Everything was going on behind us and we were getting pushed, but that was okay. I saw so many great bands there.

When we saw the Clash at the Hollywood Palladium, I was stuck at one point and it was hard to breathe. The drummer saw and he would stop and point at me to the roadies. I was getting squished in there. Eventually I got popped out to the side. That was probably the only time I ever felt danger and that I would really be hurt. Other than that, I didn't care. I'd go to work the next day and I'd have bruises all over me. I'd say, "I went to a punk show last night."

There were always fights, but I don't recall ever having to run from a show. You'd see people get into fights and stuff. There were riots, but a lot of them I think were caused by the police. When the Dead Kennedys opened for Sham 69 in late 1979, I think the riot was more caused by the police being there. It was the same with the Ramones at the Hollywood Palladium. They closed Sunset down and the police came on their horses. I'm thinking their presence made it more of a challenge for everybody.

■   ■   ■   ■   ■

I went to England in '81 with my other friend, Susan Sinner. I met her in '79. I was finishing high school and she was a junior at Fountain Valley High School. The first time, I just went for four months. I packed up and said, "Let's go." I saved a bunch of money

and went. I loved staying there for four months, staying in little
B&B-type places and just hanging out and going to shows. When
I came back, I worked again for another year and saved up all my
money. I wanted to go back. I had a boyfriend at the time. That is
really the reason I went back. I admit it. A boy.

The week of my twenty-first birthday in September of '81,
I left. I stayed in England until my twenty-second birthday. I
had friends at that point. I found under-the-table work as a
chambermaid cleaning hotels or B&Bs. That's what I did to survive.
The one B&B I worked at for the longest was run by Australians. It
had a pub in it. On occasion I had to go down and help them in the
pub, so I learned how to pull a really good pint.

Everybody was into the scene. There were mainly British bands
that I saw. I saw a
lot of the local ones
from here, because
they tended to open
for those British
bands. Everyone was
just there to enjoy
the music and have
fun and get drunk.
It wasn't really much

different than here. It was just easier to get around.

My two front teeth are porcelain, because they were knocked
out at some Tenpole Tudor's show in London. The singer came out
throwing a t-shirt. About three of us grabbed it. Luckily, I had my
skinhead, so they couldn't pull my hair, but I still walked out with
a bloody nose, a black eye, and one of my front teeth chipped. My
dentist just replaced both of them. I still have the t-shirt, by the way.

I transferred to Berkeley in 1993 from the community college.
The Internet was only starting. It was just text. I got my first e-mail

account when I was at Berkeley. It was kind of the birthplace in some ways with the coding, so they were a little more advanced. At that time, there were probably just a few thousand pages on the Internet. There was this one called "Addicted to Noise." It was one of the very first HTML-type pages with all the pretty pictures and articles. It was just in its infancy. They had a link for groups. There were all kinds of weird groups and clubs. Anything you were interested in, there was a group for it. I met a boyfriend through one called Bigfoot.

One of them was called the Punk List. It was out of Finland. It was just all these punks from all over the place. It had only been around about a year. Through this list, I met all these people, including my husband. We're the only ones from that group that actually got married. There were a lot of hook-ups. We're from all over the U.S. and a few are international. Someone took it over and ran it from Georgia Tech. Once he left, someone took it over from the University of Washington. Then one of my friends at Berkeley took it over for a while. And now it's a freebie user group. I'm still on it to this day.

One of the guys on the list in Seattle was finishing at the University of Washington. He started a zine. Somebody gave him a pamphlet that said *Ten Things Jesus Wants You to Know*. He decided to call the zine *Ten Things* for short. I was always posting recipes, so he asked me if I wanted to write a cooking column. For about ten issues I wrote a cooking column. It was a print zine. I still have a few. It was very well known. At one point there was some museum exhibit in New York and *Ten Things* was one of the featured zines.

■   ■   ■   ■   ■

As a woman, I'm eccentric—happily so. I never really thought about being a woman in the scene. I think it's different, because we were fans, as opposed to being in a band. So I never really saw it as anything more than going to see a band. I never felt anything about being a woman, and I've been to almost every club: the Whisky, the Starwood, Hong Kong Café, Madame Wong's, the Palladium, Santa Monica Civic, and the Cuckoo's Nest.

Being Latina wasn't an issue. We were just all people who liked a common theme, and it was the music. Nobody ever looked at the fact that I was darker or anything like that. There was a large contingent of Latinos, but that was in L.A. and mainly East L.A., because you had those local bands like the Bags and the Plugz that were Latino.

Sometimes we'd go to the Huntington Beach Pier and people would yell "dykes" at us and all kinds of things. They would spit at us and throw things at us. When I see a student now, as a counselor, come in wearing a Ramones t-shirt or some kind of punk t-shirt, I think, "Man, you don't know what I had to go through, just so you can be wearing that." We had to put up with a lot. That part of Orange County, Huntington Beach and Fountain Valley, would profile all the kids. My friend remembers being profiled once. She was waiting for the bus and the police car slowly came by.

There was that perception, because we looked a certain way, that we weren't going to amount to much of anything. I look at my friends now. They're business owners. Musicians. They've gotten an education. We're probably more successful than someone else who was "normal." But we still have that sensibility about us. It's what we got out of being in that scene that stays with us. We're still funky.

Punk rock influenced me in every capacity. My friend said to me once that people ask her what influences her politics and she says "punk rock." And I say, "Yes. I understand that." It just wasn't that we looked funny or that the music was fast and loud. There was a message in that music. Part of the reason I was a history major was because I loved history. I loved British history a lot. I learned so much about their history from bands like Stiff Little Fingers from Northern Ireland. I understood that white ethnics were discriminated against. You learn that it's not just you. It's not whether you're poor white or Latino poor. It was your socioeconomic status.

It would be rare to find a conservative punk rocker. I don't think I know any. It still influences the way I dress and act. I won't go eat at certain places. I won't buy certain things. I still want to know everything. I think we're more aware. I won't eat Domino's, because I don't like the politics of the owner or the things that they do. I may be the only person protesting, but it's still my protest. I'm still worried about Target, but I'd rather go to Target than Wal-Mart.

When I think of all of my friends, we all still have that. There's something about us that's still a shit-kicker attitude. We don't take no for an answer. With my education, I heard "no" almost throughout the whole time I was in school, from kindergarten through college. "No, you're not going to go to college. You're going to be in remedial classes." But I knew I wasn't stupid. My counselor told me to go to trade school. At the community college, I'd hear, "Don't aspire for the highest institutions. The local school is just fine." It was always you can't do this and you can't do that, but they couldn't keep me down there. Just because I'd always been working class didn't mean I had to stay that way. It still goes back to that attitude. The punk rock comes out every now and then.

■   ■   ■   ■   ■

I have no regrets. I talk about that with my friends. It's interesting how much of us are still friends from the '70s or '80s. I think it's because we had that commonality of being just a little funky. A little weird. Some of us were too smart for our own good, or we became smart. In certain ways, punk rock heightened your own

wanting to know more. A lot of us, whether we have an education
or not, are voracious readers. We have to see movies. We have to
read articles. We have to keep up on things. Education was what I
wanted for me, but some of the people I know who are some of the
smartest people in the world just have a high school education. We
can have huge discussions, because it has nothing to do with going
to school. This opened up the world for a lot of us and we still take
advantage of it. We continue to encourage each other now. I think
all of us are still learning. Our priorities may change, but we still
want to learn. We still want to explore. We still want to hear about
other things. I really think it was punk rock that did that.

It can be challenging at times, because I work in a more
traditional field. I still feel like an outsider sometimes. I still feel
kind of weird. But I have to be honest. I'm the most popular
counselor at the college and I know that's why. When I was at the
four-year university, the students loved to see me. They said, "You're
more fun." We could sit there and talk about punk rock bands or
shows. I'm still funky. I hope that never goes away.

ANN SUMMA

Born in 1950 in St. Louis, Missouri. Worked as a freelance photographer in the 1970s and '80s, attended shows at various venues throughout Los Angeles County, and lived in Beloit, Wisconsin; Freetown, Sierra Leone, West Africa; Los Angeles and Berkeley, California; and Tokyo, Japan. Currently lives in San Miguel de Allende, Mexico, and works as a freelance photographer.

I WAS BORN IN ST. LOUIS, MISSOURI. As a child we lived in an apartment building, but then we moved to a suburb called Kirkwood. I think I had a pretty normal suburban upbringing. I have an older sister and younger brother. My father was an artist until the children were born and then he had to take a straight job, so he became a surveyor. He built our house. He did really abstract paintings. They were beautiful watercolors of towns. During World War II he was a cartoonist for one of the papers, but then he progressed. He was really more of an abstract expressionist. He had showings at galleries and a show at the St. Louis Art Museum. He would always be painting in the basement. As a kid, I would go downstairs and he'd say, "What do you see here?" and I'd go, "Well,

I see a town." He would say, "Yes, that's right. It's a town. You got it."

My mother became a teacher. She raised us most of my life. She was at home when I was a young person, but then she started

teaching seventh grade. She taught her entire life. We lived in a suburban American existence of riding bikes, being wild Indians, running around, throwing rocks at each other, and having tree houses and a creek. It was a different world then. I think we were really free and my parents were pretty loving parents. My mother had been abused as a child, which effected all of us in some way or another, but I had no actual experience of that myself.

When I was in college, I spent a year in Sierra Leone. When I came back I felt quite alienated by the United States. I was only twenty-one or twenty-two. When Nixon got reelected, Jeff Spurrier, my partner, and I were very disenchanted, so we moved to Tokyo. We were in Tokyo during all the glam rock of that period. Even though that was happening, we were unaware of it. We were just listening to jazz and we never really liked the mainstream Western music that was happening during that decade like Steely Dan, Fleetwood Mac, etc.

When we were in Japan, Jeff started working for *Rolling Stone Japan* and I started shooting. I was a sociology major, but I didn't really like it that much. When I discovered photography, I got very much into it. I'm a very social person. A camera gives you permission to kind of invade somebody's life. At the time, I had a couple of mentors in Tokyo. At some point we realized that in order to have our careers, we had to move back here. We couldn't figure out where to settle. I had an interview at *New West Magazine* in Los Angeles, and the art director said, "Yes, we can use you." He gave me three assignments total. That was it. On the strength of that, we moved to L.A.

We came back to the States and decided we wanted to be journalists. We were living in a small apartment on New Hampshire, at the corner of Vermont and Santa Monica with our two cats that we brought with us from Tokyo. It cost around $160 a month. We were not that into L.A. It took a long time. We didn't meet people we really liked, but then I met this woman on the bus. It turned out her duplex was empty, so we moved over to Silver Lake. Then we were in this duplex that was magical. Lari Pittman and Roy Dowell were on one side and Cathy Opie was on the other side. There were four apartments. Robert Lopez, who was in the Zeros, lived there for a while. Jon Bok the designer, and later Ron Athey the performance artist were also there. There was something about that area that attracted artists.

In the later '70s, we somehow went to a show. I cannot remember what the first show was, but our minds were blown by the whole scene. For me as a photographer, I was always looking for something that was visually interesting. Up until then, I felt like the things I was shooting were boring and I had to make them look interesting. All of a sudden I realized, "Wow!" This was something new and different and exciting. Visually it was really amazing. It was pre-Internet. It wasn't like one person put a safety pin in their cheek and then the whole world would have it. Each different little facet took time to develop.

We would go everywhere—the Whisky, the Roxy, the Starwood, Club 88, Madam Wong's, the Vex, the Anti-Club, Cathay De Grande, Ukrainian Culture Center, the Masque. There was the ON club, which was kind of a punk reggae club. I liked the energy, the music, the passion, and the general vibe of it all.

In '79, I had to get a job. I worked at the *L.A. Times* as an administrative assistant or something for a year. I hated that job so much that it actually gave me vertigo and I was hospitalized. The good part about that job was that one of my bosses was Robert Hilburn. As a perk, I used to get passes to the shows. I would go out until five in the morning and then I'd go in to work at nine in the morning. It was really crazy.

I always had my camera at the shows. The camera gives you a reason to approach and start talking to people. The punk thing was different, because people weren't as approachable. Part of it was the "fuck you" mentality. "Don't take my picture." I think in general, though, people like being photographed and it kind of gives you permission to do that.

I worked a lot for the *New York Rocker*. I had covers with them. The *L.A. Reader* was published at the same time as the *L.A. Weekly*, but the *Weekly* kind of trounced the *Reader*. The *Reader*, in a way, was almost more alternative. One of my editors was Matt Groening, the *Simpsons* creator. The editor/publisher, James Vowel, was a

former *L.A. Times* staffer, and he believed in me. Jeff and I started doing a column for them that was similar to Pleasant [Gehman's] column in the *Weekly*. We would go out four or five nights a week, and it was kind of this music/gossip column.

Jeff also started writing a weekly column for the *Times*. I would often shoot photos for that, too. That's how I started building my portfolio.

I eventually worked for *Rolling Stone*, *Cream*, and others. I didn't really work for the little fanzines at all. I started my career as a photographer very late, because I didn't find it until I was in my mid-twenties, but I felt like I was really learning how to shoot and so I was very loose and spontaneous. I think it also gave me an absence of fear. I'm not afraid at all to approach people and I think maybe I kind of got trained to not have fear by the punk rock experience. I find my students get scared to actually get in somebody's face, because they don't want to invade their space or whatever, but I always tell them, "If you ask somebody to take their picture, then they're going to say yes or no. If they say no you just got to move onto the next person."

At one point with my career, after I left the *Times* around 1980 and I freelanced for the alternative press for a couple of years and worked in labs and other odd photo jobs, I realized that I needed to start working for magazines. I don't even know how I actually survived that time. I always considered myself a journalist. That was my focus and my goal. I put together my portfolio and took it to New York. It was really lame, but I got work out of it. I don't know how. Eventually I started shooting for *Guitar World*, *Guitar Player*, and some of those more established rock and roll magazines. Then I started working for Conde Nast and Hearst and Time and all those bigger publishers.

Through my late- or my mid-thirties through my fifties, I was working steadily as a magazine photographer or editorial photographer. I also worked for Getty Images and then I started working for Corbis. It all just kind of mushroomed and I started teaching at Otis [College of Art and Design] in '95 when they were still in MacArthur Park. They needed a professional to teach editing and lighting. I've been teaching there yearly up until this year.

■　　■　　■　　■　　■

I think in a way punk rock influenced my politics. It's like the absence of fear thing again. I'm a very political person and I've always been really involved in politics. I was a member of the Women's Action Coalition (WAC), which was created after Anita Hill. It was a group of artists that formed in New York and then in Los Angeles. We had three or four hundred members in L.A. We used to do what we called "actions." We would go out and

protest. It was mostly built around sexual harassment, because of
Anita. I don't know if I would have had the ovaries to do some of
the things we did in WAC if I hadn't been involved in the punk
scene. We did some really outrageous stuff. I was the "Minister of
Information," which was fun.

In terms of feminism, I was a feminist before punk rock. I
became a feminist in college, reading Betty Friedan and Gloria
Steinem. That's a battle we're still fighting. To me, that's kind of
what's going on right now with the presidency. Women are still not
equal. We make seventy cents on the dollar, and there's still all this
abuse and harassment. It's like a war against women and I feel like
that should be the most important issue, because we're the majority.

In the beginning of the punk rock scene, women were welcome.
When it got more hardcore, it became less welcoming. I remember
being at the Anti-Club with a girlfriend, and she was pogoing in
ballet shoes. Later you had to wear jack boots or you would never
get anywhere near the stage. Her feet would have been mauled. In
terms of being female or male, the men were a lot more aggressive,
but I never felt anything against me personally. One night a bottle
almost hit me in the head onstage, but I don't know who threw it. It
was almost more anti-photographer than anti-women.

I would not say I'm traditional in any way, except for being
monogamous. I don't really think about it much, but sometimes
I do, especially living in Mexico. You feel like a lot of people that
end up here are kind of off the beaten track. I didn't grow up in
Kirkwood. I didn't stay in Kirkwood and have kids. I feel like that
might have been more because of feminism than anything else.
Maybe feminism and my experience living in Africa for a year
and then Japan really kind of informed who I became. I just never
wanted to be a suburban housewife. My career was always really,
really important to me.

When people say, "Why don't you have children?" we say,

"Oh, we forgot." The reality is, we did kind of forget. We were so busy with our careers and just traveling and going out, and having children was never a priority for me. I just didn't feel that maternal urge to have children, and I feel like the life I have now I would not have had if I'd had children. It's not like I didn't have children so I could have a career, it's just that it was never a priority to have children. It's fine. It's kind of a relief in a way.

My connection with the punk rock scene sort of comes and goes. Recently, there was the publication of the John Doe book [*Under the Big Black Sun*]. My photo was on the cover of that book, which was super cool. John and Exene did readings and all of us photographers showed up for book signings at the Central Library in downtown Los Angeles. They also did a reading at the Grammy Museum, and then we all went out afterwards. It was very weird, because we're all old now and everybody is sort of mellow and settled. It was just great to see everybody. It really made me feel more of a connection than I've felt in a really long time. I mean, it's been forty years, right? Thirty years or forty years?

CANDACE D'ANDREA
AKA LOLLY POP

Born in 1956 in Glendale, California. Lived in Los Angeles, Glendale, and Tujunga, California, in the '80s and worked as a booking agent at the Cathay de Grande. Currently lives in Cottonwood, California, where she works as the chief operations officer for Mystic Records and is the owner of Candy Land Starr Productions and Cathay de Grande Hollywood Records.

I WENT TO L.A. VALLEY COLLEGE in 1981, after my husband passed away one year prior. I took a two-year occupational certificate for stage as a theater arts major. I married young at eighteen and had two children and suddenly needed an education to gain employment. I dated my husband for two years before we married. When he died, I was devastated.

I liked modern dance, and I grew up playing keyboard. I have fourteen years of classical music behind me, and at nine years old, I was in the studio performing Franz Liszt and heavy classical music. To cut loose, my friends and I would go to the Odyssey in Beverly Hills and the Palace in Hollywood, and we would dance until, I don't know, four or five o'clock in the morning. We also went to Seven Seas and danced a lot. We were really into the new wave scene. I'd never heard any punk rock.

One of my friends, Scott Mayer, was an actor. He was in the movie *Savage Streets* with Linda Blair, and I received screen credit for doing his makeup and many others. One day he said, "I found this really cool club! You've got to go there with me." So we got to the Cathay de Grande and there were cops in full riot gear. They weren't letting anyone in and I was really aggravated at my friend, telling him, "Why did you bring me to a place like this? This is terrible! People are getting beat up by the cops." It was just a really

bad scene. So, we left, and I was never going to ever go there again.

And then, my friend that I grew up with and went to Valley College with around the same time, Dawn McKennon, told me that she had found an old friend of mine, a neighbor named Dobbs. He was a really good friend. She told me he was bartending downstairs at the Cathay, and I told her, "Well, I will go there only because Dobbs is there." If it weren't for him, I never would have stepped foot in the place. So anyway, we went, and I reconnected with my old friend Dobbs. He was also booking shows.

That night that I went with Dawn and reconnected with my friend Dobbs, Bad Religion and X were playing. I fell in love with the music. The whole scene downstairs at the Cathay was so fun. I became a regular. I started meeting a lot of the different performers. We would go backstage and party and meet people. I got to know everybody there so much that when English Frank, the booking agent at the Cathay de Grande, was fired, Michael Brennan asked me if I wanted a job. Everybody knew, even Dobbs, about my history in music. So I was hired, and I worked there until they closed, sometime between '86 and '87. If I hadn't worked there and known people like Dobbs who worked there, I would have been intimidated really bad. You had to be tough to hang out with those guys.

One of my favorite bands I worked with would have been the Red Hot Chili Peppers. Anthony Kiedis was always very nice. I knew Flea pretty well. A couple times we went to his apartment with Scott Mayer and hung out. Suicidal Tendencies was also one of my favorites and Bad Religion, Social Distortion, Decry. El Duce and Top Jimmy became two of my best friends. El Duce would say that I was the only true lady in Hollywood. He wouldn't even let anyone cuss around me. If people were talking really filthy, he'd yell at them to clean it up and watch it because there's a real lady in the room. If I hadn't known him personally, I would have thought he was completely disgusting and he was a horrible person. I would have thought the worst. But knowing him and the kind of person he really was, I understood that it was an act while onstage.

I loved Monday Night Blues at the Cathay. Top Jimmy & the Rhythm Pigs had a standing gig there every Monday night. We went to some private parties that they were hired to play at down in San Juan Capistrano for the Fourth of July weekend every year. We would leave the Cathay after we closed up and drive down to San Juan. This guy who hired them, I don't remember his name, had this great big huge piece of property on the beach, and there were several homes that sat around a big swimming pool. One of them was set up for the performers. When you got there, everything was ready to go like you were home. Everyone had their own separate rooms, and there were clean sheets on the beds, and the bathrooms had clean linens. I mean, it

was like a high-class hotel. Hundreds of people would come, and the band would play on the tennis courts.

■　　■　　■　　■　　■

I've always been able to identify with women in the mainstream. I grew up in a nice neighborhood. My grandmother lived on Clifton Way in Beverly Hills, and we spent a lot of time there and in North

Glendale. I was always around professional women. My mom had a lot of tea parties. I had to transition between high-society women and punk rock. I found it easy to go back and forth between the two. Women can be pushed around in society quite a bit, and they're told to be seen and not heard like a little house mouse. I could stomach that for so long, and then I would go down to the Cathay and let out all my aggression. Punk rock was a good release. It's the freedom that women in mainstream society don't really get. I could relate to people singing songs about oppression and wanting to get somewhere.

Punk rock teaches you to be tough and strong. It teaches you that you can speak out and hopefully you won't get your head bashed in. It prepared me for what was to come. The last twenty-three years have been a very hard struggle to make it in a society in Northern California that's male-dominated and run by the sheriffs and crooked corruption. If I didn't have that foundation of learning from punk rock, I never would have made it these last twenty-three years.

My work in the music business has continued all these years, even despite the trials and tribulations. It's really nice that I started out in punk rock. I lost touch for a couple of years until I moved up here. Now I network with about 2,000 musicians. Punk rock has helped to keep me in a good frame of mind.

I started writing my memoirs about my work at the Cathay and working the last five years as a volunteer at Mystic Records. I've put new life into Mystic Records, and it's because of the people I met thirty years ago. It's because of the reputation I built for being honest, a person of my word, and someone you can depend on. I feel very close to these people, and when we see one another, it's like a family reunion. In fact, I had a reunion for friends at the Cathay de Grande in 2012.

I am now in a partnership with Mystic Records and have my own record label: Cathay de Grande Hollywood. This year, I have released and published sixty-five albums in punk rock and four releases for country singer-songwriter Dickey Lee on my label Horseshoe Records. Music is very inspirational, giving young and old the platform to speak what is on their mind. We are fortunate to live in the USA and enjoy the freedom of speech to take a stand and speak our mind. Punk rock is the platform to sing away your troubles. As I have heard: "Do something wonderful people may imitate."

My involvement in the scene was wonderful, because the people I met are so nice. I mean, I'm still friends with them thirty years later. We're like a big punk rock family. They're honest. They don't pretend to like you. If they don't like you, they say so, and I like that. They are down-to-earth people, street people, people who have formed a bond together, and our bond can never be broken. It can't be bought. It can't be paid off.

CATE GARCIA

Born in 1965 in Torrance, California. Lived in Los Angeles and San Luis Obispo, California, in the '80s and attended shows at various venues throughout Los Angeles County. Currently lives in Rancho Palos Verdes, California, and works as a pet groomer.

I WAS SIXTEEN. I think it was freshman year in high school. I was held back a grade, so I was a little older than everybody in my class. This was at South High in Torrance. I distinctly remember that I wasn't in the scene at all. I am one of seven, and I'm the second to the youngest. I had older brothers and sisters that were very actively involved in high school projects and such.

One of my older sister's friends was trying to find a band for the prom. They were talking about going to Hollywood to check out a band. I don't know how it happened, but I ended up going with a guy named Kevin Shorter. I think it was six dollars to get in the Whisky. We were checking out the girl band the Go-Go's. We put a bid in, but another high school put in a higher bid and got them that year.

That was my first exposure to anything like that. I had very frizzy curly hair. I think I was in a jumpsuit that was straight out of the '70s, with a big belt. I was lucky I didn't get myself killed. I almost did. These girls were like nothing I've ever seen before. At the time, the Go-Go's were truly more punk than when they became more commercialized. Belinda was spitting at the crowd and there was a pit. I was scared, but I loved it.

Growing up, I had a few things happen to me at school that made me a little edgy and a little angry and it was a very easy slide into the punk rock scene where that kind of edge wasn't necessarily bad. It was expected and it was part of the scene. I had a kind of date rape thing happen. The guy was everybody's friend and people knew I was angry. He had a girlfriend. They were very popular people. I wanted to beat him in front of everybody. I was squished down a little bit and I think that fueled my involvement in the scene. This is retrospective. I could have never put that together back in the day, but punk rock kind of gave me the fuel—a little fire in my belly.

I've got kind of a hair trigger and a little fiery temper anyways, so all these things made the perfect storm. I have a space issue even to this day. Don't crowd me. I don't like crowded elevators or anything like that, and it tends to trigger me pretty quickly. I did not do close contact sports. I would fight.

Fighting within the scene was all very easy. You'd get in the pit and get black eyes and broken feet or whatever. It's expected, and that's what happens there. I fought guys. I employed steel-toed boots after breaking my foot once. Unfortunately, I enjoyed it a little too much. I'm like that crazy little Irish person in the bar— she's small, but she's crazy. I think the key to fighting is you just don't hesitate. If there is a moment of hesitation, it's over. I haven't gone to see any of the bands again now. I'd love to, but I tell you, I could be brought back to thinking I'm seventeen again really quickly and I just don't want it. I don't need to fight any more.

That Black Flag crowd was tough. If you were going to have a crowd that would just fight for the sake of fighting anybody, that was them. The Dead Kennedys crowd was comparatively mellow. People loved the music and were there for the music. I have a really good story from seeing the Dead Kennedys. I think it was at Godzilla's, but I'm not positive. They had these huge speakers on the stage. My boyfriend at the time took to climbing up and diving into the crowd. About the third time, they got wise to this. The crowd split and he hit the ground. I remember having to go in there and drag him out unconscious. He kind of ruined it. We had to leave to go to the emergency room and get his head stitched closed.

■   ■   ■   ■   ■

I don't think gender made one bit of difference in the scene. I never felt unwelcome. It was genderless. I loved my involvement in it. If I could have changed anything, I probably would have tried to make myself be a little more aware of who I was seeing and what I was doing. I was a little fragmented. I don't have the names and the places exactly and I wish I would have paid a little more attention to some of that, but outside of that, I loved it.

I remember I would walk down the street and be harassed because of the way I looked. I'd have bottles thrown at me. You could be curing cancer or Mother Teresa in a wig and they'd still hate you. I found some of the punkers to be far more passive people than people would have expected. Even though they loved to physically engage in the pit and all that crazy stuff, it didn't mean they were necessarily aggressive human beings. People really will just hate you for the way you look and have no inkling who you are. It was an interesting thing for me to discover as a sixteen- and seventeen-year-old, and I think it made me a bit better of a person.

One of my big beliefs is that our society has a lack of rites of passage. I wasn't raised with any kind of faith where there was a rite of passage or a celebration of communion or anything. I almost feel like punk rock, for me, was a self-imposed rite of passage, because we lack it in our society. It was my self-imposed rite of passage into adulthood. I think a lot of tattooing, scarification, and piercing is like a rite of passage. It's trying to push yourself to a point and seeing that you can take it and still come through whole. Surviving youth is really an accomplishment. Some Native Americans will have a rite of passage where they take the young man out to the forest. They have to survive for a period of nights and maybe eat some crazy stuff that makes you hallucinate. There's something to be said about that. I see a lot of kids trying to find that. A challenge. Push me hard. Make me survive it. Make me believe what you have to say. Like an awakening. I think we did it amongst ourselves.

CECILY DESMOND

Born in 1970 in Santa Barbara, California. Lived in Long Beach, California, in the '80s and attended shows at various venues throughout Los Angeles County. Currently lives in Long Beach and works as a self-employed silk screen printer.

I WAS PROBABLY TWELVE when I first started listening to punk. I had a cousin who was in the Suicidal scene [influenced by the band Suicidal Tendencies]. He was friends with the guys in the band. He introduced me to the music of Suicidal Tendencies, the Cramps, Black Flag, and bands like that. I had a friend in junior high who was into all kinds of music. He introduced me to the Subhumans, Crass, and Stalag 13. From there, I met other people who were into the scene. We were mostly twelve or thirteen years old. The scene was already going. There were so many good bands with many views I related to. I was anti-social and a lot of the bands were articulating what I was thinking. I didn't like society at the time.

I also grew up listening to Secret Hate, the Grim, Kraut, and Die Kreuzen. I would listen to them over and over, because they

hit that chord. It made so much sense to me. There wasn't just one type of punk that I liked. There were bands I liked for the political aspect and there were bands I liked for just the music.

My favorite band

was and still is Rudimentary Peni. That's my heart right there.
And Crass's *Penis Envy* album. When Eve Libertine sang, I think
she spoke to all the women. I liked the Subhumans. Another one
of my favorites was the Dead Kennedys. Just hearing Jello Biafra's
voice and the lyrics. They were so astute, smart, and well-spoken.
Combined with the energy and the voice, it was just, wow. He
blew me away. I liked 7 Seconds's *The Crew* album, because they
really spoke for everybody's rights: women's rights, anti-racism, and
anti-bullying. That spoke to me. And MDC, because [singer Dave
Dictor] was honest, very well-spoken, and knowledgeable. I liked
Minor Threat. While I wasn't straight-edge, all of the other stuff
was so right-on.

I didn't start going to shows until I was thirteen. I remember
listening to 7 Seconds and Minor Threat records before. The
cool thing is that Zed Records was close by, so there was access
to all different kinds of punk. It wasn't just a local scene. It was
everywhere.

I went to every single show I could. Being thirteen, my mom
didn't want me out every night at all times, but as often as I could,
I would go to Fender's. There was a little place called the Melody
Dance Center. I think that was over on Atlantic. There was
Emerald Hall. It was on Redondo and Seventh. They only did a
couple shows before it got closed down. Some of the bigger places,
like the Olympic, the Palace, and the Palladium, I didn't go to as
often, because they weren't as accessible as getting on the bus and
going to Fender's. That was more of getting everyone together and
finding someone with a car. There were also some friends who put
on cheap shows, dollar shows, at the Filipino Community Center
and in backyards.

I recall going to some protests, such as anti-war protests. That
was the time of the nuclear arms race and the big bombs. It was
the Food Not Bombs era. There was the [Big Mountain Elders

Relocation Resistance] that MDC was very much about. I think the government was moving [Native Americans] off their land, because there were mineral properties that the government wanted. I did People for the Ethical Treatment of Animals protests and handed out flyers.

I wanted to do a lot, but I was more of a supporter. Along with that, I was doing drugs. That prohibited me from doing a lot more than I could have and would have if I wasn't so involved in getting, using, and finding ways to get high. I did everything I could get my hands on, except for heroin. The only reason I didn't do heroin was because I saw friends do it and OD. They would either die or never be the same. I started out with LSD. I did spray paint, White-Out, mushrooms. Then I got into speed and PCP. It progressed. If I liked it, I did more. Alcohol was always in there. Alcohol was obviously the first thing because it was the most accessible, and then it just progressed.

■　　■　　■　　■　　■

Growing up, I never felt like I belonged anywhere. I always felt like an outcast. I didn't speak girl talk. I wasn't the popular kid. I got along with the nerds and geeks or the people who didn't even get along with them. That was where I felt the most comfortable. With punk, that's where it was for me.

I fell in love with punk rock at a show. It was 7 Seconds, the Abandoned, and Suicidal Tendencies. There were a whole bunch of other bands playing, too. I think I was thirteen. I was on the edge of the pit and I was watching the crowd slamming. A guy came around and he just socked me in the arm. It didn't matter if I was a girl or a guy or anything. I was one of the crowd. He didn't do it to hurt me. He did it, because he was dancing. And he wasn't saying, "Oh, you're a girl, I'm going to be careful with you." At that point, I felt a part of it. That's when I realized, this is my home.

I think that in the earlier scene, with the people that I hung out with, it didn't matter if you were a guy or a girl. Whoever wanted to put something into the scene or create a zine, it was all good. It was all accepted. That was my crowd of people, my friends, the people I went to school with and the people I went to shows with.

As years went on, I've been in bands. In the 1990s and 2000s, I've run up against a lot of guys who dismiss women. It's the boys' club. It's, "Oh, you're a woman who's saying something. It can't mean that much." But in the '80s, I didn't run into that. I saw friends that were girls doing stuff. I never thought it was an issue. Just like in my group of friends, being black wasn't an issue, being gay wasn't an issue, and being a woman wasn't an issue. Now, if you had long hair, that was an issue [laughs]. "What's this hippie doing here?"

Punk rock absolutely influenced the rest of my life by who I surround myself with. I have a kinship with other punks. They understand me. I wouldn't date a guy if he wasn't into punk, because he wouldn't understand going in the pit or why I want my hair short. He wouldn't understand that unless he was a punk. So my husband is from the scene.

Politically, I'm further than left. I don't believe in a government. I don't believe in being controlled or in capitalism, but it's the world we live in. I like it here better than I would in a lot of other countries.

I'm an atheist. I don't think I'm spiritual. I have my views and I have my values. I live a life. I consider other people, my pets, my husband, my family, my friends. Some people would say I have morals, but they are not other people's morals. I've been vegetarian since about '84. I've had a couple of ventures back into eating meat, but shortly after, I came back. I don't believe we should be killing animals for food when there is absolutely no reason why we should. I love animals. I'm not vegetarian for health reasons at all. I'm vegetarian for ethical reasons. I don't live my life for an image.

I have people say, "What difference does it make?" It's like Minor Threat says: "At least I fucking try."

* * * * *

Punk rock inspired me to learn bass. I've been in four bands. The first three bands were fun. We called it splunge rock. The first band was the Caltransvestites. I joined around 1996. We were all about having fun. There were politics in some of the lyrics. We had a song called "White Trash" and songs about lesbians and songs about your mom, but it was about having fun and doing what you want to do. It wasn't serious. If someone fucked up, it wasn't like, "You fucked up that song! That was the wrong key!" It was ridiculous. We dressed up and in drag. To me, it's really important to be in a band where the views are alike. You have the same ideas in mind and the same direction.

The last band I was in, the Vaginals, we were more a traditional punk band. We didn't throw out toys into the audience or dress up funny. We had more of a political view, but songs that affected us as people, as women. There was one guy in the band who was open-minded. I wasn't in that band until around 2002.

It was something I wanted to do when I was twelve, but I didn't have the money and I didn't have the resources. I didn't have friends who wanted to put a band together, and I was using drugs.

I absolutely feel a connection to the scene. There are still so many good bands out there. I don't go to shows nearly as much as I used to. Life changes. There are considerations. But I think that there's still a great scene out there. The majority of it is underground and people don't know about it. And people say, "Punk's dead. There's nothing going on." Well, there is. There are a ton of bands all over the world, including this country, that are putting out great stuff. You just have to look for it. That's fine by me. I don't like when punk is exploited and the media and parts of society trivialize it. They dilute it and take the power out of it. Like when you see little girl bondage pants at Target. I don't think that changes anyone who is punk. It doesn't dilute actual punk. It just dilutes peoples' perceptions of it.

My musical tastes have grown. The older I get, the more I listen to. I listen to rockabilly. I listen to ska. I listen to world music. I listen to all kinds of music. I definitely have my preferences. I don't like contemporary country. I don't like any metal. There's some punk that has a metal overtone. It depends on the band. Sometimes I'll tolerate it, but usually I can't listen to it.

My overall views continue to be punk. My overall ways in everything I do. How I treat people. The way I look at things. It's always going to be because of my experiences with punk.

My involvement in the scene was absolutely good. It's made me the person I am. It's given me fulfillment in life. I don't regret anything that I've done. I mean, there are minor things that, if I could, I would do differently, but on the whole I take them all as experience and I've grown from them. I've learned from my experiences. I wouldn't change. If I had the chance, I probably would be more into the scene. I'd do more. I'd be involved more.

D.D. WOOD (GRISHAM)

Born in 1965 in Long Beach, California. Lived in Long Beach and Seattle, Washington, was a solo recording artist with Hollywood Records in the '90s, and is the lead singer and rhythm guitarist for Gypsy Trash (1985–present). Currently lives in Long Beach, where she works as a writer and a teacher in the Long Beach Unified School District and is the lead singer and rhythm guitarist for Gypsy Trash (1985–present).

WHEN I WAS GROWING UP, the cool thing about my house was the huge time span between siblings. My sister is now sixty-five, and I'm forty-eight. My brother Mark is in his early sixties, my brother Don is in his mid-fifties, and my brother Jack is in his early fifties. It became this very interesting and eclectic library of music we were listening to. My sister was taking us to the love-ins in Los Angeles and San Francisco in the '60s. I was listening to Janis Joplin and Cream before I was even five years old. Mark was also into the '60s scene. My parents were into Charlie Pride and Dolly Parton: country in the '70s. Don was really into the Tubes and ELO in the '80s. And Jack was into hardcore. Because of this span, I moved through music as a fluid entity, and I didn't believe I had to pick or choose one particular category to embrace.

Even though Jack is considered a hardcore artist in the punk scene, he was, and is, the same way. He turned me onto music like Kraftwerk and Adam Ant. We were all into Duran Duran when they first came out. I listened to the Bee Gees because I loved their catchy hooks and harmonies, and was madly in love with Billy Idol from Gen X. Every morning on the way to high school, my best friend and I would listen to Stiff Little Fingers and the Dead Kennedys. We'd go to school all mad and angsty, but that didn't stop me from coming home and listening to Al Green.

When I was about thirteen, Jack was already pretty notorious in the punk scene for being in a band called Vicious Circle, which later morphed into a band called TSOL. It was the late '70s, like '76, '77. I looked up to them in a way that a young thirteen-year-old looks up to an older sibling. You idolize them without realizing that what you are idolizing might be trouble. I can't lie. At that age, I liked the rebelliousness of it. My family had always been rebels in their own right.

My sister left home in the late '60s, when I was quite young, to live in a commune in England with a crew of her hippie friends. She taught us about Beat poets and took us to the Glide Church in San Francisco and, of course, Ferlinghetti's bookstore: City Lights. So, you can see, we were already into counterculture before the punk movement began. As children, Jack, Don, and I already had this subversive lifestyle. So when Jack started doing the punk thing, it just seemed like the next step in the whole musical evolution.

Everyone in my family plays music. It didn't seem strange that hardcore came into our home. People always ask, "What was it like?" Well, it was kind of violent and crazy in the beginning. Punk was different from anything I had experienced. It was intense and interesting, and it seemed like I would become "tough" and accepted by my brothers if I liked it, too. That's how it started for me. I wanted to be grown-up. I wanted to be what I thought, at thirteen, was cool. I liked the sound of the music, the anthems, and the beat. It made me feel wild and on the edge—willing to take risks and step outside traditional boundaries.

When I first starting listening to punk, I still had my long hair. My mom and dad could be lenient about things, but that didn't always pertain to me. They weren't going to let me buzz my head at thirteen or dye it crazy colors. I was the baby of the family. I was a very young girl in a scene that wasn't particularly kind to very young girls, and my parents were wary. But it's hard to keep a sibling away from other siblings.

I started sewing my Levi's in and making peg leg tight jeans and wearing Chucks. I got into new wave first because I loved the sound of the music and it was melodic enough to keep my mom from coming down hard on me. So I would listen to Gary Newman and Devo and the B-52's and the Cars and the Tubes and brag about my brother being in a punk band, and I thought I was just tough shit. It's funny looking back on this now, at my age, as a parent and a teacher telling this story. I was such a dork trying to be cool.

So Jack was doing Vicious Circle, and mom didn't want me involved. Even though Jack and I don't always get along, he did have a tendency to be protective of me during that time period, and he didn't want me hanging out with some of the guys in the crew. I was attracted to my brother's friends, who seemed so mature and tough and scary and exciting in all the wrong ways. I was thirteen.

They were eighteen, nineteen, twenty-year-olds. It makes sense that my mom was concerned. The punk world moved very fast.

What people need to understand about the music is

that it was kind of like a criss-cross in Southern California. There were hardcore people, but there was also this thing that was surf and skate culture combined with punk. I remember wearing a Sex Wax shirt in middle school and being sent home because it was considered too subversive. Seems silly now. But it was a big deal back then.

■ ■ ■ ■ ■

I was thirteen the summer I went to England with my mom and sister. That was when things really changed for me. Of course, that's because hardcore punk was happening in England, and trust me . . . it was nothing like anything I had seen in America. This was '77. I remember we were on the streets of London and there was this huge group of skinhead punks with Mohawks and black leather. Just Sex Pistols on steroids. There must have been fifty to seventy-five of them. They had taken over the street. They were rocking cars and climbing the street poles, screaming and chanting punk lyrics, and I was watching like, "My God!" Terrified but also super fascinated and excited by them. I remember being stunned by it. When I came back from England, I started advancing into the scene. I was now this really tough little girl. I chopped off my hair, dyed it, began the multiple piercings and heavy makeup, and listened to all the British imports from the Sex Pistols to the Clash, no matter what my parents said or did to try to stop me.

I became more active in the scene and involved through my brother Jack. I went to hardcore shows on a pretty regular basis, listened to the music openly at home, hand-scrawled lyrics and punk artwork all over the walls of my room, and basically settled into it. Our house was the house to be at. Jack had band practice in the garage and built this huge skate ramp in the driveway, and all the skaters would come over and skate the ramp.

I was constantly thrown into this heavily male-dominated

environment, and I was quite impressionable. The girls that did come around, of course, wanted to have sex with the guys. There were very few women in my world at that time who were choosing to be equals to the men. There was one girl, Denise Fleming, who was an amazing skater—still is—but she was the only one. My father did not condone pot smoking, drugs, or any of those things, but it was happening all the time. Boys were my mom's favorites, so the boys got away with a lot.

Being Jack's baby sister, I became privileged into this punk world. Frank Agnew and Rick Agnew were coming over to the house, and the Dickies were stopping by. Crews were coming in and out constantly and staying on tours. You never knew who would show up, and that was always a lot of fun.

For the first few years, that's what my involvement was. I laughed and joked with the guys and was the baby sister of the crew. Then, when I was about eighteen, I married my punk sweetheart, Greg Holtz, and had my daughter, Lex. I moved away for a while and lived in the Seattle-Port Orchard area. Then I came back, got divorced, and met Joe Wood, the new lead singer of TSOL, and a whole new chapter in the punk world began for me. My mom watched Lex while I worked or went to college, and at night I was in O.C. going to Spatz, Duke's of Huntington, or Raji's in L.A.—that whole thing. College and work and baby during the day, shows and partying at night.

When I first met Joe, he was playing in his blues band, Cisco Poison, with Drac Conley on guitar and Frenchy on harmonica—both L.A. scene guys. Even though my brother Jack and I don't always get along, I was always loyal to my brother and a bit flippant about the whole TSOL lead singer thing. People can argue about who did it better as much as they want, but the honest answer is that both Jack and Joe brought something interesting and unique to the band. I love the songs Jack wrote for TSOL, and I love the

songs Joe wrote. They both have a great ear for melodic music.
You can't compare the two. But I was young, and when I saw Joe,
I was snarky. He came up to the bar after the set and said, "You're
D.D. Grisham." I said, "And you're Joe Wood." And he said, "So,
the rumors are true. You're as beautiful as everyone said you are." I
said, "You know, your blues stuff is really good, but my brother is
still better at TSOL." He turned to his best friend and said, "Man,
I'm going to marry that girl. Buy her a drink." And we immediately
started dating. I'm not sure I made the easiest choice by choosing to
be in a relationship with the guy who took my brother's place in his
band, but you love who you love, and I've never regretted it.

So, Joe started coming back to the house. Now, prior to dating
Joe, when I was about fifteen I had a little thing with Ron Emory,
and Mike Roche liked me for a little bit after that. So I'm sure
my brother was pretty sick of his little sister messing with guys in
TSOL by the time I brought Joe home.

Joe would always wear long sleeves when he came over, to hide
his tattoos. Jack wasn't tattooed at all at the time, and my father
was never tattooed. My uncles, my grandfather—they were tatted
and had that subversive thing that all the World War II guys out
of Long Beach had. They were tatted at Bert Grimm's and worked
at the shipyard. But not my dad. It's not that he wasn't wild, but he
was more conservative.

Of course, Joe and those guys were doing heroin. My brother
tried to warn me about this, but I didn't listen. I never did heroin,
and I didn't realize what that entailed at the time. I was still so
young, even though I had a baby of my own. So there was Joe,
coming to the house in his long-sleeved shirts, probably not only
hiding tattoos but also any track marks. I remember the first time
he came and he had on this red-and-white gingham, button-down
cowboy shirt. He looked like the devil had gotten dressed for an
occasion [laughing]. We were sitting on the front porch when

he left, and my mom said, "He doesn't fool me with that shirt! I know he's covered in tattoos. He can't hide it from me!" Despite the warnings from my mother and brother, we fell hard in love. It was really passionate. We clicked. Joe's really charismatic. Great storyteller. Amazing musician. Very funny. Super witty. Literary. There were a lot of things I really loved about him, despite the downside of the addiction.

I've always been a writer. I wrote poetry, and I was writing lyrics. I was always sitting on the front porch and playing guitar. I'd play a lot of Patsy Cline and Loretta Lynn and folky stuff, and by this time, I was back to being this little earthy thing, which always surprises people. There was a dual side to me. I was raised a hippie. Then I was the punk when I was hanging around TSOL, and Jack before Joe. I seemed really hard and strong. I don't think people would have thought I was afraid of anything in any way. I really carried that persona. But in the time period I was with Joe, I had begun to soften again and really settle into motherhood.

The punk scene of my youth, from the time I was thirteen to sixteen, was very misogynistic, and I found that very unappealing as I grew up. There was a huge dark side to it, so I had already started moving away from that by the time I was eighteen or nineteen. I liked being earthy, hippie, country, and folky. Right after that time, Robbie Allen, who played with Jack in Tender Fury, started coming to the house. Robbie just came in one day to get a drink of water and heard me singing and said, "I want to play with her."

I remember when we first started practicing, I had to sneak out to go to rehearsal without Jack seeing me because he didn't want to share Robbie with me. It was pretty funny. One time, my mom saw me climbing out the window of my room with my guitar case, and laughed at me for being such a chicken. But Jack, like everyone in my family, has a temper, and at that time had a real problem with being irrational. I didn't want to deal with it.

Robbie and I started playing in Gypsy Trash, and through that I was in the scene in a different way. I was now a performer, and we were really the only cowpunk, rockabilly band in Long Beach. You had X in L.A. and the Red Devils in Huntington and us in Long Beach. That was when I started seeing the scene from the stage perspective.

I have always been a performer. I performed my whole life in dance competitions, plays, and musical comedy. But this was different. I felt more pawed over in the scene. There are some fans of music that are really good at understanding that you need some space sometimes when you're performing, or after you perform. Some people are not very good about that and will climb right on top of you and get on you. They are excited about your music and very intense. That's lovely, but it takes a lot out of you when you perform. When I started performing onstage and playing with Gypsy Trash, guys started liking me, because I was D.D. from Gypsy Trash. I didn't like that. It was no different than me idolizing my brother at thirteen. People see the stage presence, the persona, and they fall in love with the fantasy.

It's not an ego thing and it's not a conceit thing, but I can't sit here and act like I wasn't attractive, because I was. Beauty gets you to a lot of places in those scenes, and being Jack's baby sister immediately put me in a position to be accepted. I had been raised by this group of boys who were playing in these bands, and had been around them so much in my life that I was part of the crew.

Ron Emory gave me my first stage guitar, an old, beat-up acoustic with a horse head on it. I loved that guitar. Mike Martt and I would sing duets. Mike Roche had the Electric Chair at that time, and was always finding perfect stage clothes for me. They came to my shows and supported my music and later, when

I had my solo record deal with Hollywood Records, they were all really proud of me. I was a girlie girl but also kind of a tomboy and a band girl, and I think that served me well at that time. Steve Soto always likes to say I was the Shirley MacLaine to their Rat Pack, and I think that says a lot about what it was. I was privileged. I was part of the inner dialogue. They liked me because I was intelligent and quick-witted. I hate saying it like this. It sounds like I'm egotistical, but I'm not. I'm just really realistic when I look at it now.

I think what is hard for me, looking back, is seeing that many of the boys in the crew (none that I've mentioned here, but many others) would be one way with me and so abusive to other women. I won't say who said it, but one of the guys in the scene said, "I got into punk rock so I could do all the fucking drugs I wanted and fuck all the chicks I wanted to fuck." I was like, "Wow, that's really why you got into music?" I'm into music because I love to play music. I mean, despite the attraction to boys, I always wanted to play music and never looked at performing onstage as a way to get sex or drugs. So it was odd for me to hear that statement.

Even with strong self-esteem, it was still hard to not fall prey to that world—a male-dominated, misogynistic world. As a woman being in it, you had to use your wit and your intelligence to navigate it, so you weren't destroyed by it. I saw so many girls who were used and spit out, and I hate that about the punk scene of that time. For years, I was very loyal to many of those men, but at the same time, the stories I've heard and the stories women have told me since really upset me. I have created more and more distance from many of the people in the scene, both men and women, who still look back at that time period with great affection and, in my opinion, blinders as to how much harm was done and how many people we inevitably lost.

I performed. I became established. I proved that I had talent, and I got my record deal. I did these things on my own merit and suddenly, my opinion as an artist now mattered to all of the crew I grew up with. But the boys, even now, still all play in bands together and keep women a bit outside of their circle. Ask any of the women in the scene that play with a band of all guys, and I'm sure you will hear it—from Texacala, to Exene, to me.

What's funny is that my son, Dylan, who is an amazing musician, won't have anything to do with the punk scene. Jack asked him to play drums for TSOL, and Dylan said, "I'm not going anywhere with them." He sees it because I have raised him. He's in this new group of musicians. He plays with all these female musicians, and they are amazing artists. He does not have that misogynistic quality at all. It's lovely. Whenever I would get upset about my past with the guys in the crew, Dylan would say, "You don't need their approval, Mama. Not anymore. You need to just do your own thing." He keeps me on track about that. But it still hurts sometimes, because it's your tribe and it's your group.

■　　■　　■　　■　　■

There have been negative and positive influences from being a punk in that scene. One negative influence was the sexuality that was accepted in that time period. Women were made to feel like they had to put out to get something in return or be accepted. I don't like that. I don't like some of the things I did sexually, thinking that I was being cool. Now I look at it and maybe it was my self-esteem being fragile when I was young and vulnerable. Of course, there were drugs and alcohol. I'm very fortunate that I did not party very long. I only dabbled in things from ages thirteen to fifteen. People around me were offering. It was around all the time. By the time I was sixteen, I got hard into heavy partying, but I got bored of it so fast. I'm not an alcoholic or addict. I'm not a partier. I might drink once in a while, but it's not my thing. I like going through life straight. I was so done with that.

I regret the violence. I was a total fighter. I was a brawler. I had no problem with it. My family was built that way. We're brawlers. It's not like I would just pick someone to brawl, but there was one time when I got in a violent situation with someone and it is one of my biggest regrets today. It was a woman in the scene. We were all drunk at a party. I was about sixteen. My friends were mad at her about something and they wanted me to beat her up, because I was such a strong fighter. I beat the living daylights out of this girl and she just kept trying to walk away. She didn't even throw a blow. I kept hitting her and hitting her like a total idiot. I remember that having such a profound effect on me. That was the last fight I ever got into. We are good friends now, though I don't see her often. I still have a hard time looking her in the eye, because it is something I regret to my core. It is so not what I am as a teacher or what I would want for any of my children. It makes me want to cry just talking about it. I apologized to her and she said, "Don't bring it up again. I've forgiven you. It's over." This is great for her, but it's never going to be over for me. I think carrying that shame is a good lesson to share with my students. I talk with them about how you can't take things like that back.

I often think about the violent acts I committed: arson, vandalism, stealing cars while I was trying to be cool or under the influence. I was bad. I went to jail three times before I was sixteen in this one-year period when I got crazy into punk. I'm thankful that I'm not a felon, because I couldn't be a teacher. I can't imagine my life not being a teacher for the last twenty years, because I see it as my true calling.

The positive things about the scene were music, my art evolving from my childhood, and my friendships and connections. As a teacher, my punk roots so influence the way I teach. Although it still hurts and there are triggers and dark places that really bum me out, I don't regret any of those things, because it made me who I am today as a person and a teacher. I have a tendency to be able to see all sides of things and not judge students rashly, like ones who may be abrasive, alcoholics, or addicts, or come from a gang or punk environment. All of this colors my teaching. I'm able to influence their future through it. When I talk about things and tell them, "I wouldn't do this, and this is why," there is much more weight coming from someone who did it and knows why. They are always shocked when I tell them I was arrested three times and I tried to set the same school on fire where I now teach. There are teachers who have not been through that experience who influence just as well, but for me, I'm a storyteller and my life is so much out in the open through my music and my writing and my community and connections.

So many of my friends are dead from overdoses, violence, or accidents. I talk to my students about it. I think those experiences keep me aware of how precious things are and how one unkind word can change everything. This is such a core of my teaching and a message that I pass. It has become a positive thing in my life, and a way for me to influence a new generation.

EWA WOJCIAK

Born in 1952 in Lodz, Poland. Lived in Los Angeles and San Francisco, California, in the 1970s and '80s and worked as the art director for *L.A. Weekly,* the creative director for Cannon Films, and in the art direction, content creation, and distribution departments at *NO-MAG.* Currently lives in L.A. and works as a professor of art design.

I WAS BORN IN POLAND when it was still a Communist country. My mother was a survivor of the Holocaust. My father saved her life. He rescued her. My father was Catholic; my mother was Jewish. It was a very black-and-white time. I remember standing in line for food that was rationed when I was a child. The first year of my life, my father was in jail for refusing to join the Communist Party.

We were one of the early families to get a TV. My earliest memories were of seeing Disney's Tinker Bell once a week. It really changed my life, because I thought it was magic. I wanted to be an artist after that.

I came to America with my mother in '61. We lived in the Fairfax area. I was the only non-English-speaking student at my junior high, almost all the way to high school. I don't remember it as being hard, but I remember it being odd. I

had nothing to compare it to. When I first got here, I remember children coming up to me. I didn't understand that they spoke a different language. I thought they were somehow making fun of me. I remember crying and having my mother explain to me that we were in another country.

One of the first places we lived in Los Angeles was a hotel on Sunset Boulevard, which is no longer there. It was a giant transient hotel where we paid by the night. My father stayed behind, because the Communists would not allow a full family to go at the same time. He was supposed to come later on, but he passed away from a heart attack. He never arrived. When we got here, we were pretty much on our own.

I lived with my mother all the way through college. She was a singer and studied opera before the war and had recorded some songs. After the war, she was weak. She took care of me and couldn't do anything. When we came here, she got a job working at a dry cleaner. Somebody taught her how to sew buttons. She supported me. That's pretty much my early years in L.A.

My first job was managing the Hot Dog on a Stick at Muscle Beach. One of my early friends that I made in Los Angeles in junior high was Diane. Her father started Hot Dog on a Stick. I used to go down there with her a lot and I would also work the county fairs. I became the manager of Hot Dog on a Stick. All the way through college, I would go to the beach in the morning, open the stand, make lemonade, and then go to college and come back and sit on the sand and lock the place up.

I went to Cal State Northridge as an undergraduate in art and then I went to Mills College in Oakland for graduate school in fine arts. I moved to San Francisco and that was a huge change. There was never any doubt about art. From the time I was little, I knew I wanted to make art. There was never a plan B.

When I came back from San Francisco to L.A., I worked at my

first job at A&M Records. At that time they had Peter Frampton
and a lot of music I wasn't interested in. Bands like Blondie were
just starting to come up, and I was listening to that. I worked for
about two years there. I was part of the first record company lay-
offs. They laid everybody off and I was without a job. Through
a friend of a friend, I heard that there was a business that was
starting. I didn't even really know what it was, but this person said,
"Well, go down to this place and check it out." I went to what was
the *L.A. Weekly*, but at that point, it was only maybe six people
sitting around and trying to talk about what the paper was. They
hired me. They hired me to be an assistant designer. Within the
first two weeks that I was there, the art director had a horrible fight
with the publisher and I wound up replacing him. I designed the
prototype for the paper and I was the art director for the first three
years of the paper.

It went from nothing to about a hundred and some pages.
There was nothing like a guide to L.A. or what was happening
in L.A., so the *Weekly* was the first paper to do that. There was a
tremendous amount of activity and I was in the center of it. I hired
all of my friends to work for me. We went from a department of
two people to a department of about twenty-five people putting out
the paper weekly.

I really had a passion for all of it. I started going out and getting
to know what bands were playing and where or what new gallery
was coming up. I remember going to the Masque really early on
just by word of mouth. There would be maybe fifty people there
for a show. I have a really vivid memory of that. I had already gone
to many clubs, but the Masque was different. It was right below
Hollywood Boulevard. You walked down a grungy alley to get into
the place. The closest thing I can compare it to is when I see the
early stuff of the Beatles and they were playing in subterranean
clubs. It all felt very super alive and it would be really, really

crowded. Everybody was excited to be there. It wasn't a negative environment. It was really energizing. When the band played, it felt important. It felt like you were at exactly the right place where you were supposed to be. It was like that was the center of the world. In the early days, it felt like everybody in the clubs was your peer in some way. You may not have known who everybody was, but it felt like you knew who they were.

At the same time, I met Bruce Kalberg. He was working temporarily in the accounting office at the *Weekly* in a different room, and I would go back there to talk to the accountant every so often. Maybe a week and a half after meeting Bruce, he moved in with me. It was very quick. The first time we met, he took me by the hand and we walked down to his car. It was a VW bug and it was filled with his magazine: *NO MAG*. He said, "I make these." We looked at them and I thought, "This is really interesting." This was late '78 or '79.

Literally another week later, the magazines were being made at my house in the living room. He was my partner for thirty-two years until he died. He started *NO MAG* in '77. I came in on issue three. He started the magazine with Mike Gira from the Swans. They went to art school at Otis [College of Art and Design] and were friends from that time.

I became really involved with Bruce's life and all the bands. We would shoot bands at the house and build sets at the house. We went to shows almost nightly. I was still working at the *Weekly*. All the different people from my day life would intertwine with my night life, plus new people that we were meeting. Then Bruce got a studio on Hollywood Boulevard in Las Palmas. We started doing more elaborate shoots there. I was involved with a lot of the selling of the ads, the printing of the magazine, and the layout. A lot of the people in the magazine were people that came in to show me a portfolio, maybe at the *Weekly*, but I thought, "Well you can't work

here, but you'd be perfect to work for us." Nobody was getting paid.
None of this was about money.

We would find a band or an artist we were interested in and
we'd go see them at a club or their house. We just said, "Okay.
You come with us." It was a lot of fun. Bruce would have his tape
recorder and his camera. We'd build a lot of sets and we'd put the
magazine together. This was pre-computer, so it was all done by
hand.

Bruce would transcribe the interviews or stories that he
would write or that somebody else wrote. I would go get the
typesetting and then we would glue it on boards, which is called
"paste up." It was an old way of doing things. We would do it with
rubber cement and pieces of paper. We worked obsessively to
get them done. When they were done, the problem was getting
them printed, because nobody would touch them. A lot of people
saw the magazine as pornography. They saw punk in general as
pornography. It was really difficult. The person that typeset the
articles was one of the early publicly gay typesetters. He had a small
business in North Hollywood and we would go to see him, because
he had no problem typesetting the work.

We would take the photographs to labs where we knew they
wouldn't look at things. Even though there is no pornography
anywhere in the magazine, it was seen as some sort of subculture
and dark threat. This was during the Reagan and Jimmy Swaggart
years. There was actually an incident where Bruce and I were in
bed on a Sunday morning and somebody called us and said, "You
got to turn on the TV." We flipped on the TV and Jimmy Swaggart
was holding a *NO MAG* and preaching with it in his hand. He was
saying that it was the sign of the devil and all this stuff. We were
labeled very early on. We were also audited twice, which I'm fairly
sure came right after that.

I think there was a lot of fear, and people didn't see the humor.

NO MAG is a very funny magazine. People saw it as very serious. There was a dinner party that *NO MAG* threw. It was a fake dinner party. Everybody dressed up and we documented it. It was called a cannibals' dinner party. Obviously nobody got eaten, but Tower Records refused to carry the magazine, because they actually believed that we were eating humans.

When it came time to get a printer, we couldn't find anybody to print, so we tried to figure out who was printing pornography. We would drive the boards, the paste up boards, to a place south of San Francisco. There was this older Mexican guy who printed all of the stuff that was semi-illegal in California. We would spend one or two days and watch him print and then we would rent a car and drive everything back. I still live with some of those magazines now. We moved them from place to place and we would distribute them just by going up and down the street. I'd go up and down Melrose or I'd call record stores or record distributors that were working with new bands and see if they would buy an ad.

We tried to get legitimate. We opened a bank account at the Bank of Beverly Hills and we would try to go there once a week, so we would be like business people, but it never really made any money at all.

■　　■　　■　　■　　■

I think punk was about not being part of a traditional society. It was about inventing your own voice and your own persona. When I was in college, the feminist art really hit with Judy Chicago, Mimi Schapiro, the Woman's Building, and all the stuff that was happening. I was in consciousness-raising groups. I came out of the hippie thing and went into the feminist movement. I don't think I was ever hardcore feminist, other than that I certainly believe women have equal rights and are probably smarter than men. Other than that, I'm not a political person that way. I'm more interested in pushing art forward than pushing womanhood forward. I never thought about what it meant to be a woman in punk. That's not a way I would think, but it was an exciting time to be a person that was making stuff and having a voice. I'm a 100 percent believer in all of that. I don't know if a woman's voice is more important than a man's voice. I'm not even sure I care. My dog's voice is pretty important to me, too. Still, if somebody told me I couldn't do something, I would be pretty darn pissed and take them down.

I never had kids and didn't marry. There was never any time for it and it was never a priority to me. I don't see marriage and children as being enough. It just never happened that way. That's not to say that I don't believe in love or having kids. What was important in my relationship was work. Our connection was our work. Now that Bruce is dead, that's still where I'm at. I've never been part of a world where a man would take care of a woman anyway. I've always had to think on my feet a little bit. I came from a home that didn't have that much, and then my mother had cancer for a long time and I took care of her. I didn't see that marriage cures things or makes things any better. It's just a different direction, so it was never a priority in those ways at all.

My mother never really learned English fully. When I was twelve years old, I was already doing the bills and taking care of things. When she got sick, I took care of things, so I've always been an adult. At this time in my life, I feel like I don't want to take care of anybody or anything. It doesn't seem to pay off for me, so I think taking children and marriage on is like signing up for something I've already done all my life.

What's important to me is my work. I had a fairly big career in entertainment design. I did that during the '80s and the '90s. I've owned my own business. Bruce and I published the book *Sub-Hollywood* in 2005, which is about the punk scene. We started a

distribution company. I oversaw the printing and the layout of that.
There was a point where we also owned a place called the Beatnik
Bookster in Silver Lake, which was a store of books and odd art
objects. It was really fun. Then Bruce got sick, and I started to teach.

I've been at USC for years. I also taught at Art Center.
Teaching has become a second career. At Art Center, I taught
portfolio development for professional photographers. At USC, I
primarily teach in the design department with graduating seniors
doing design classes. We deal with things like publications,
entertainment design, and graphic design. I also teach something
called special projects, which is where students work with
professionals outside of the school environment. We produce
something with a real client. For example, one of our clients for
several years was the Grammys. For three years, my class produced
the Grammy campaigns and got to attend the Grammys. We did all
the posters and the billboards.

I love teaching. It's incredibly great to be around young people
that are interested in making stuff. In many ways, it's kind of a
perfect storm. These days, I am super involved with teaching and
I've become really involved in publishing again. Part of it is due to
the interest in the punk stuff. I put on two major events at USC
called *Shelf-Life: A Big Day for Small Press*, which had guest speakers
and vendors and a carnival-like atmosphere about small press.
Through that came Printed Matter Los Angeles Art Book Fair,
which I've been pretty involved with. I'm a major exhibitor at the
MOCA Print Fair ever year. This year, I spoke at MOCA about
publishing. This January, I published a personal project that uses
old and new photographs. I'm working on another book. I just did
a show of Bruce's work called Void California in San Francisco and
I'm putting together a show in Hamburg, Germany, for 2017 that
is going to be about some of the people that worked in *NO MAG*
along with me. It's a bridge between the old stuff and the new stuff.

Punk rock changed the way I look at everything, 100 percent.
There isn't anything that happens where I don't think, "What
would the punk rocker do?" Then I do that. I try to really listen
to myself and trust myself and not give in to any kind of norm. I
still go see music. I don't go out quite as much because I work all
the time, but I feel like I am still connected to music. It's still an
important part of life. I think seeing live music is really important.
The group experience is really important, which is a shared
experience.

I go to art openings once or twice a week. I go out more than
I should. I'm not a young person, but I try to stay current and also
support other people that make art. I really think it's important
to do that and to keep everything moving forward, not only
personally, but culturally. To me, that is punk rock. I didn't retire.
I feel like I'm the same person, with the same curiosity for new
things. There are tons of great new things happening.

There was a period of time when Bruce passed away where I
felt like I wasn't as outspoken. I'm not a loud person, but I feel like
I was more inward, because I didn't want people to see me. For
so many years, punk rock was not considered a good place to be
from, so I didn't really talk about it. I felt like I kept a lot of my lives
separate. There was my work life, and then there was my other life.

The people I work with knew I was interested in things, but
they didn't really know to what extent. I have different groups of
friends that know me for what I do with them. I feel like in the last
few years, this has become an impossible, stupid thing to do. Now
I just figure I'm going to be who I am and put it all out there and
make stuff. If somebody doesn't like it, I don't care. In some ways,
I'm more punk rock now. I think part of that is also getting older.
You feel okay. You're aware of time and you know that you only

have so much time to do what you have to do, so you have to do it.
If you're going to do anything, the time is now. For a while there, I
felt I was too tired or old. Now I feel like there is not enough time
or energy to do all of the things I need to do. It's not just that I
want to do these things. I need to get shit done. Every moment is
accounted for.

EXENE CERVENKA

Born in 1956 in Chicago, Illinois. Lived in Sandpoint, Idaho, and Los Angeles, Santa Monica, Venice, Sherman Oaks, Mount Washington, and West Hollywood, California, in the 1970s and '80s and played in X (circa 1977–present) and the Knitters (circa 1980–present). Currently lives in Orange, California, and works as an office manager, singer, artist, speaker, and poet.

WHEN I WAS ABOUT SIX WEEKS OLD, my parents moved me and my sister, who was about a year and a half older, from Chicago to rural Illinois. It was a town called Mokena about an hour and a half south of Chicago. My dad built a house and it was on land that had once been part of a farm. There were houses here and there. It wasn't a suburb like we would know them now. There was a church in my town called St. Mary's Church, and they had a school. That's where I went to school. I could walk to school.

When I was thirteen, we moved to Florida. I lived in St. Petersburg, San Antonio, Dade City, and eventually Tallahassee when I was twenty. I quit high school on my sixteenth birthday in St. Pete and I started working. When I lived in St. Pete, it was just fantastic. My sister and I shared a house and we would go to junkyards and thrift stores. This was in the '60s and '70s. We just had a feast of everything in the world. That's where I really got my education.

I had a bunch of different jobs, as you can imagine. My first job was selling cemetery plots over the phone. I did that for two

weeks, and one day I went to work and the doors were locked. I
realized I had just sold a bunch of cemetery plots to old people and
somebody had just stolen all that money.

My second job was working for the Leukemia Foundation
Society. I was a phone solicitor, because that's what you could get
as a girl. When I would get a job as a waitress or work in a mall in
a jewelry store, I would get sexually harassed to death. Back then,
you couldn't really say anything about it. You'd just have to quit or
they'd fire you if you wouldn't have sex. Eventually, my sister moved
to New York with her husband. You know, you get to the age where
you're nineteen or twenty and you say, "St. Petersburg's great, but let's
move to New York. Let's move to San Francisco. Let's move to L.A.
Let's have a life, you know?" I wish I could go back there now that I
appreciate that world more, but I just wanted to live in a big city.

I was a visual artist and a writer. I was dressing crazy in amazing
vintage clothes and having fun and going to gay bars in Tampa. My
sister's ex-boyfriend was moving to California. He needed someone
to help pay for gas. I sold my 1950 Cadillac for $300 and ended up
paying my bills off with $180. I got into a car with a tweed suitcase
and a paper bag and came to Santa Monica to live with my friend
Faye. I didn't know that two girls from Texas had just moved there
and her boyfriend had been living there with her and I was the
fourth girl and the fifth person in this place that was a studio. I had
a single kid's bed in the kitchen. There was an earthquake the first
night I was there. It was pretty interesting to me.

I came to California just to get out of Tallahassee, because
someone offered me a ride. I would have gone anywhere. If he
would have gone to Chicago, I would have gone to Chicago.

There was a program in California for people like me. I was a
high school drop-out and a woman. I could get free job training
and then get placed at a non-profit. Taxpayers would pay for it. I
would work there for six months, and by then I would be on my

own. I could get a job. I would have training. It was getting people not on welfare, but off. It was getting people into society. It was a great program. I learned typesetting and typing back then, and I got placed at Beyond Baroque in Venice, which was the biggest literary thing in the world. I asked to go there and they said yes. I was twenty at the time.

I rented an apartment at West Washington Boulevard. It's now Abbott Kinney. It's now the richest part, but then it was a terrible ghetto. I was living in a little crappy apartment above a liquor store next to a jazz club and across the street from a women's gay bar. I had it made. I had some really bad problems then with drinking and stuff, so I was always in trouble, but it was great. It was fantastic.

I would work in the day at the library at Beyond Baroque, which was incredible back then. It's the biggest small press library in the world. We helped typeset things and mimeograph. It was really old-fashioned.

After work, I would get the old clock radio and the typewriter out. I would listen to Wolfman Jack on KRLA and I would write and type and make up songs and poems. I had a mattress, a kitchen table, and chairs. I had a couple of plates and a pot and a pan or something. That's all I had. One night I said, "Well I got to go to that poetry workshop." So I went down to Beyond Baroque.

I was really scared. I was awkward socially. I never fit in and I never will in this world, so it was very weird for me. I went into this room and there were people that I thought of as poets. Everyone was older or weirder and I just didn't know. There were probably thirty people sitting in chairs. I sat down and this guy sat next to me. They were always having assignments. They said, "Everybody

write down your top favorite ten poets." I was like "Boy, that's going to be tough," because I didn't know. I was looking over at that guy's list next to me, but I didn't steal from it. I just thought I'd write what I know, but then I saw that he had written John Lennon twice on his list. I just poked him and said, "You wrote John Lennon twice." He went, "Oh, okay." The guy was John Doe. He was super literary. He was from the East Coast and he was the opposite of me. I had never heard of a bagel. I guess I probably brought a poem to read and he did, too, and we listened to some other people and realized we were the coolest people in the room that night. There were some amazing people there.

After that, we went to the jazz club next door. We each had enough money for one glass of wine. I forget what it was called, but it was a really famous club. We went back up to my apartment and he smoked those really smelly French cigarettes. We sat at that little table and I think maybe we had a beer between us. We talked and then we became friends. I was not into that relationship at all. I was going out with Vietnam veterans and getting in trouble. I was hitchhiking down to Watts to get into all kinds of weird stuff. I was just wild, wild, wild.

■　　■　　■　　■　　■

What happened was the punk scene was starting. John told me about the Masque. He had a car, so we drove there one night. John had already met Billy Zoom and they had started playing together. One day he brought me to rehearsal and Billy was like, "Oh, great.

He's got a girlfriend. Never been in a band, can't sing. Great." I started singing with them and goofing around. You didn't have to be able to sing or play. The scene was full of kids. Some could play great and some couldn't play it all. It really didn't matter how great or terrible you were. Everybody was great in their own way.

I couldn't do anything so I fit right in, but I wrote well. We were driving down the street one night, me and John, and we were passing this place and there were a bunch of band names on the front. I went, "That is so stupid that bands have to have names. Why do they even have to have names? Why do they have to be this or that? If I had a band, I'd just put a big X up there." Then he went, "Why don't we just call it that for now?"

We started playing when I was twenty-one. We never thought of it as performing. We never thought of it as audiences and fans. It was like everybody would get together and just do what they wanted to do. I remember when we played the Masque, because you really couldn't play clubs. You had to rent halls. We'd rent a large front hall or some weird hall and you'd play there for a couple of shows. Brendan Mullen would put it on. He'd take the money and then the band would get the money, and then it would get closed down and we would never be able to play there again. Eventually the Whisky and the Starwood and some places like the Troubadour started letting us play, but chairs would get broken. It would be a mess and then nobody could play there again.

I think the thing that we didn't realize, that I realize now, is the power of youth that we had. We were a bunch of kids tearing up the whole town and everything we did was starting to make news. People looked at us was with a mixture of fear and awe and respect. At that time, you didn't have blue hair. If you did, you couldn't even go out in public or you'd get killed. You couldn't have straight-leg jeans in public. You couldn't have anything. There weren't tattoos. It was before tattoos. It was before piercings. It was before everything. There were bikers and there were punks and everything else was normal and we were just hated. It was pretty tough. There were as many girls as boys. Nobody knew if anybody was gay or straight. Nobody cared, nobody talked. Back then, we were just human beings and we were young.

I think it must be so hard to be a human being that age now, because you've got to pinpoint your gender. It's like fascism now, and we had none of that. We could say anything we wanted to. We were just like bratty kids having a great time and I don't know if people can still do that or not. It was very free. Life was so great back then.

Around 1980, or maybe '82 or '81, the Knitters started. The band pretty much started the whole alternative country thing. We still play. We started out as a band to do benefits. Then we started playing for ourselves a little. We put out a couple records, but it's kind of a thing we come and go with.

■   ■   ■   ■   ■

Poetry used to be something that you did if you were really weird and just wanted to die in obscurity. I just like writing. I didn't want to be a beatnik. I didn't want to be a poet. I wasn't a poet like Patti Smith. I didn't want to make a myth out of my life. I just wanted to write. I was actually a very successful poet. I worked with Lydia Lunch and a bunch of other people. Henry Rollins used to open for me. Life was just good, because everything was art and everything was fun. You'd get in your 1955 car and you'd drive down to the car wash and get a bunch of tacos at two in the morning and drunkenly drive back home to Mount Washington and wake up the next morning and work on songs. It was just a great life. It really was. We knew we were doing important stuff, so the poetry was part of it and that kind of became more after X had been around awhile.

The Zero One Gallery started then. It was an after-hours club. People brought their own beer and we started doing art shows. Raymond Pettibon would exhibit. I would exhibit. Everybody would exhibit. It was really amazing and kind of like guerilla art. Of course, there wasn't really an audience for that at that time, so that was just kind of underground stuff.

I didn't really ever do much with my visual art until about ten or fifteen years ago. I started having a real career at it. So far it's all collages, although I'm thinking of doing other projects now, but I don't know if I will.

I started doing collages from the time I was a teenager. Then, whenever we were on tour, any city I was in, I would find trash on the street that was unique to the city. If I was in New York or Philadelphia or Texas, I'd find anything from a local place or any kind of candy bar wrapper from that town. And I'd find really great stuff in thrift stores. Everything was just so interesting and bizarre. Southern menus. I'd go into a restaurant and they'd have the old place mats with a hobo on it or something. I'd say, "Oh my God. That's beautiful," and I'd keep it.

One day, much later in life, probably fifteen years ago, I thought of how I was just going to drag this stuff around from house to house. I've moved a hundred times. I just didn't want to let go of it. Then I said, "What if I combine them together and make art out of them?" I finally started doing that and that's when I got my art career together. I had my show, *America the Beautiful*, about twelve years ago. It was at the Santa Monica Museum of Art in conjunction with an amazing show that Kristine McKenna did. No one has ever heard of it, because L.A. never gets credit for being artistic. It always gets made fun of.

The late-'70s and '80s scene has influenced my life less as time goes on, because there's more stuff that's come after it. It's influenced more people's lives than it's influenced my life. I've been a bigger influence on other people. I look back on my life  and I say, "I wish I would have worked harder. I wish I would have taken things a lot more seriously." I had no idea that those records would ever come out. I didn't think [the 1981 punk documentary *The Decline of Western Civilization*] would ever see the light of day. You're a kid. You don't take things seriously and no one's really paying attention, and then suddenly you start getting famous.

Early on, we would get these reviews. We were the number-one record of the year in the *L.A. Times*. We were just so wild and renegade and we got so big so fast. I saw reviews that said, "X wouldn't be so bad if they'd get rid of that horrible girl who can't sing. Why she's in the band, we don't know, because the other musicians are so accomplished. John's a great singer and songwriter. She's ruining the whole band. They'll never make it, because of her." Some reviews said, "X, the worst band of all time" or "This is the genius band the world's been waiting for. This is the best band since the Doors" and "Exene is the star." I realized they can't all be true. They cancel each other out. Somewhere in the middle is the truth. We're a pretty good band that came exactly at the right time. We created something out of nothing, worked really hard, and had a unique style.

■   ■   ■   ■   ■

I'm the least feminine woman I've ever known. I'm such a tomboy. I always have been. I really don't get any of the social things with women. I never get my nails done. I never go shopping. I really think it's all terrible. I don't flirt. I don't know how. I don't understand social cues. I've missed out with many guys possibly liking me, because I just have no idea why they're even talking to me and I never could get it. I never tried to look pretty. I just tried to look like what I thought was a silent movie star or like a Depression Era housewife. To me, that was the epitome of beauty. I never tried to flaunt my sexuality or act cute or be like a girl. I paid the price.

When Madonna came along, that ruined everything for everybody. Of course, it's been further ruined ten thousand times worse since, but she really ruined it. We thought we were going to change the world. I thought we were going to revolutionize the way men and women reacted with each other in politics, art, culture, and music. Everyone was going to be liberated like we were. They were going to see the punk thing and go, "Oh, that's so cool. I don't have to act like a stupid girl anymore. I don't have to have big feathered hair. I don't need frosty lips. I don't have to pander. I

don't have to look stupid and we don't have to play bad music." We
thought we could show everybody how great things can be. No,
that did not happen. Eventually it just got buried, pretty much.

My life is different now than how I expected it was going to be.
I think you create a foundation for yourself, whether you know it
or not. Everything you do is building the foundation for the rest
of your life, whether it's going to school, getting married, having
kids, becoming a junkie, going into the military, or becoming a
stock car racer. Whatever it is that you do, you're going to build
on that forever and it's never going to go away. It's not like you fix
it—you just pick up and move or you do something different—
but all that stuff is a foundation. Maybe it's internal, or maybe it's
your reputation. Whatever it is, it's the stuff upon which you build
the rest of your life, and so when you get older, you have to see
how solid that foundation is and what you've built on it and how
much you've torn down and how much has been abandoned and
neglected. Where you are is how solid you are as a person.

I think that I've slayed most of my demons that I started out
with in life. The things that were the disadvantages of what I was
born with, my social awkwardness and my fears, I've gotten rid of
most of that. My anger and my resentments—all that stuff seems
to be gone. I'm very much at peace with myself.

However, what's around seems like it's not as much of a life as
I would like to have. I think that's true for everyone. I think we all
live in a horrible, horrible age of narcissism, sociopaths, criminality,
and corruption. I think that the best you can be is a really good
person. I think there's really no point to life like I used to think.
When you're young, everything is hopeful, because tomorrow
you're going to get a new idea for a song and next week you're going
to meet some amazing people. Someone is going to ask you to be
in some weird, underground film and you're going to meet this
amazing guy and fall in love and have kids and then you're going

EXENE CERVENKA

to move to this other town and
you're going to meet these great
kids and you're going to start a
band together and it just goes
on and on.

Then one day, that ends.
There isn't a future and it's kind
of hard and you're kind of sad
but really, when you get into
your sixties or seventies, there
isn't a future. You might have
grandkids and all that, but it's not like you're suddenly going to
move to another country and start a whole new life and get married
again. It's not going to fucking happen. You're done and I'm sorry,
but it's true. It doesn't mean you can't have a great life. It just means
those things are not going to happen.

When you're young, the whole thing is limitless. Possibilities
are endless and that's great and that's the way it should be.
What I don't like is that young people now haven't taken their
responsibilities very seriously. They haven't fixed the world or
changed the world. They're just marching along into some kind of
brave new world order, which is basically where I see it going. It's
kind of sad to see that and it's kind of sad to see what's happening
to the country, but I do think that, if my personal job in life was to
be a better person, I think I got there. I'm proud of what I've done.
I wish I could have worked harder. It's my only regret. I will tell
you a quote by a woman that we should all love and respect, as the
women in this book should. It's Bette Davis. She said, "Getting old
isn't for sissies." That is true, but neither is punk rock for sissies.

HEATHER L. GRIFFIN

Born in 1969 in Redondo Beach, California. Lived in Redondo Beach in the '80s and attended shows at various venues throughout Los Angeles County. Currently lives in Torrance, California, and works as a graphic designer.

I WAS BORN IN REDONDO BEACH, CALIFORNIA. My dad worked for Northrup as an aircraft engineer, and my mom worked for Pacific Telephone as a budget manager or something related to budget. My early family life was good for me, but not so good for my older brother. He was seven years older. My mom and my father got married when my brother was five. He was from my mom's first marriage. There was always weirdness between him and my dad. There were complications, uneasiness, and abuse later on. There was a lot fighting around my brother and how they were raising him. In many ways, I kind of played the adult.

I first started getting into punk when I was eleven, which sounds really young in retrospect. My parents weren't around, so it was easy to go hang out with friends down at the park who were into it. That's really where I got my first real taste of punk rock. The kids at the park, mostly boys, were all a little bit older and they were listening to music. I'd go down there after school. I can remember my first taste of Minor Threat and my first taste of Generation X and Stiff Little Fingers. I started dating one of the boys. His older sister was one of the most "hardcore chicks" of the time. We'd kind of raid her record collection. The music definitely had a different energy.

Going back, even before this, probably in '80, I was at my grandma's house and there was an article in the paper about this big gig that had happened. I told my grandma, "That's what I want to be. I want to be a punk rocker." She looked at me like I was out of my mind. I already knew I was different. I was a little chunky. I never felt like I fit in.

When I started to hang out with these guys down at the park, they just accepted me for who I was and they didn't make any qualms about what I looked like or what I didn't look like. At school, it was all about fitting in with the rich girls. I just never got into that.

Comparing the boys at school and the guys in the scene, the guys in the scene were more mature. They were older. Essentially, they weren't exactly more mature emotionally, but for some reason they thought I was cute. In a lot of ways, it was a self-esteem boost. Then there was the sex element, which I think played a pretty big part in it. It was real easy. Promiscuity was okay and made me feel good about myself. For sure I wasn't going to do that with the guys at school. It was so tightly interwoven. The interesting thing, though, is that the more punk rock I got, the more tough I got, the more I noticed the guys in the circle that I was hanging out with were starting to go for the cheerleaders and the girly girls. They didn't really want to be with the girls who were close to them and were in the scene. We used to give them shit for it, but I think that was about the extent of the conversation. It was more a conversation that the punk girls had amongst themselves.

My first shows I went to were at the Vex in East L.A. We would catch a ride out there somehow. I remember my first show out there was the most fun and amazing time. I think that was what really hooked me—going to shows and just feeling the music,

being around everybody, and watching the bands. There was
something so dynamic and so powerful about that for me.

The Vex was a building in a dirt lot across from a freeway.
There were three phases of the Vex, because there was the first
Vex that I was too young to go to, but the second Vex was the one
where I really started seeing bands. You'd walk in and there was a
smoking section. There was an outdoor patio and the room where
all the bands would hang out. I remember seeing Social Distortion
there. I think that was my first show. It was Social Distortion and a
band called Conflict from Phoenix with a girl singer. I just thought
that was the bee's knees. I was like, "Wow! She can do it. That's so
cool." I remember feeling welcomed there. I think that was probably
the best part of it. It was just a dirty, rough and tumble, scummy
little place. The music was super loud, and there were a lot of cute
boys. I remember having a lot of fun there.

I went to shows at the Olympic and a ton of other places. I have
so many memories. There was something about going somewhere
collectively where you would meet people from all over the city
and from Orange County. Everyone ended up at the same place for
much of the same reason: because you love the music. We would
have a couple of beers, and that was about it. I was pretty young, so
it wasn't too much about getting buzzed. There was a buzz that you
got just from being there and from just the excitement of it.

Finding the scene made me feel more of an outcast, but it also
made me feel more okay with being an outcast. At the time, there
were a lot of things going on at home that were weird. Running
around with friends who had colored hair and leather jackets,
shaved heads, or whatever was like my family of choice instead of
my family of birth. Probably a lot of people ran away. I did when
I was around twelve, for a couple of weeks. I lived in a tent with a
punk boy at a golf course. Like I said, it was the family of choice.
Having that identity just helped me feel okay out in the world.

Before that, the world was not an appealing place.

The scene definitely influenced the rest of my life. I remember painting political things on my leather jacket in high school. It was about standing up for people who didn't have a voice. That's something that I still believe in and still root for and get actively involved in, like participating in rallies when we invaded Iraq and Afghanistan. The Subhumans is one of the political bands that always comes to my mind. Questioning my beliefs around things all stemmed from punk rock.

Unfortunately, there was violence, especially towards the end of the Olympic years. It got really bad when the gangs got involved. It wasn't a peaceful thing, but that was part of the attraction. You would see a lot of fights happen. I was always the one in the middle saying, "Hey, why are we fighting against each other and not fighting against the bigger outside picture? It's supposed to be them that we're fighting against, not us that we're fighting with."

The violence and the drugs got to be a real drag and turnoff. I think towards the end of the '80s, I went through a stage where I thought maybe I needed to try and be normal. That was a depression for me. It wasn't until I chopped all my hair off again that I felt like myself. My attempting-to-be-normal phase that I failed at was probably for a year and a half. I've worn my hair short since I was twelve. I was never really into doing my hair unless I was spiking it. Sometimes I wonder what my husband thinks about that. He knew what he was getting into when he got the job as my husband. I'm not the most feminine. I've never been a girly girl.

On a personal level, there have been a lot of choices, good and bad, that stemmed from punk rock. I used to always say, "There's punk rock in the best way and punk rock in the worst way." We've lost so many people, because part of their identification process with punk rock was the drugs, and it was self-sabotaging. I've been there. I've been in that state and made those choices, but I've always thought that punk rock in the best way is that you're actually working within the system, but against the system. You have to be a part of it to fight it. That goes back to my punk rock upbringing. Here I am at forty-seven with blue hair.

■   ■   ■   ■   ■

I've always been an artist. My mom tells stories about me building sand castles, but not out of sand. I made them out of yogurt and birdseed on the living room carpet. Being involved in the scene, it really helped bring out some of that artistic desire. I did t-shirts for bands and learned how to silk screen. I remember the first time I did my own silk screen. It was the best thing ever. I got one of those kits where you just read the directions. I thought, "I can do this." A friend's band, the Detonators, needed t-shirts done, so I just started doing them and it all worked out. At that time, I never had the compulsion to create flyers. In retrospect, I really wish I had, because that's more along the lines of what I do for a living now in graphic design.

I got my AA in visual communications, which is graphic design advertising. On the career side, I do a lot of advertising. I work for a company that employs 242,000 people around the globe. It's kind of scary, because part of my punk rock anger in my belly questions it. I think, "Okay, now you're working for the man." I wonder, "Am I doing the right thing?" I've done the freelance thing. Sometimes being punk rock in the best way is working for the big company and making decent money. It's not really a bad thing, but I get conflicted about that.

The punk rock scene has been such a huge part of forming who I am and the choices that I've made and just everything that I've come to be. I wouldn't be who I am without it. It's really my heart.

I still go to shows. The music is my connection. I still have a ton of friends who make music and are very deeply involved in the scene. We're still connected through years and years of friendship, and all those friendships are due to punk rock. It's been such a wild ride. There's a spiritual element to it, too.

When I was younger, I went to Christian school. Then I got into punk rock and moved about as far away from my spiritual base as you could go. I got into different forms of spirituality. I don't think I would have gotten any awareness of those had I not gotten into punk, because it opened my eyes in so many ways and it opened my heart in a lot of ways. I put myself through some crap. It brought me to a place where my heart was opened.

JAMIE LURTZ

Born in 1969 in Long Beach, California. Lived in Long Beach in the '80s, attended shows at various venues throughout Orange County and Los Angeles County, and worked in publicity at I.R.S. Records (1989–1990). Currently lives in Anaheim, California, and works in sales for a liquor distributor.

I WAS ABOUT FOURTEEN OR FIFTEEN. I was in junior high. A girl who was a little bit older than me was into punk rock, and she kind of got me into it. I stayed with her and we talked about bands. She had a bad attitude. I had a lot of problems at home, so I kind of had a bad attitude, too, so our bad attitudes went together. I remember she was the first one that had FTW, Fuck the World, as her motto. That kind of got me into it. Also, I used to get picked on a lot in junior high, so I befriended the punk rock tough girls. They stuck up for me.

We went to a lot of shows. My first gig was the Toy Dolls and the Adicts at the Olympic Auditorium. My first actual concert was Billy Idol. I was fourteen at the Toy Dolls and I was fifteen at Billy Idol. I would ditch with anybody who wanted to ditch and we went to shows pretty much every weekend. Mostly we went to Fender's in Long Beach, and sometimes we'd go up to Hollywood to some fetish clubs. I don't know how we got in. We were like fifteen. I remember my friend stole, or joy rode, another one of our friend's mom's car and we went up to the fetish club one night and talked our way in. I remember Stiv Bators was there from the Lords of the New Church. He was sitting in a booth. It was really dark. They played a lot of death rock music at the time: Bauhaus, Siouxsie, Sisters of Mercy. I just remember being, "Wow! I'm in Hollywood and all these people are really cool." Everybody was wearing leather jackets and black. It was fun.

I really liked the Dead Kennedys and Suicidal Tendencies. My friend, Trish, and I had this little tiny tape recorder we used to carry around. We had a mixed tape that I made. It was the Cure, Wasted Youth, and Suicidal Tendencies. We'd carry that on the bus and we'd sing and harass people who weren't punk rock. I liked a lot of those darker bands like Sisters of Mercy, the Damned, Bauhaus. They were considered punk, and then they became death rock.

My family thought I looked ugly. I didn't live with my mom. She had various boyfriends and they just thought I was weird and they didn't like me, so I lived with my grandparents. I think, because they were my grandparents, and I was an only child, I kind of got to do whatever I wanted. I had a car. They didn't like the way I looked, but they put up with it. I think they hoped I'd grow out of it, but it didn't really happen.

At Fender's, there was an all-ages room and then the bar in the back. There was no way to get in the bar. I never saw the bar, because I wasn't twenty-one at the time. We'd always get really close to the stage. It was just one big room with bathrooms. It was kind of like an ugly gymnasium, but it was the best club in the world [laughs]. I remember lots of mohawks, leather jackets, people throwing up. It was really fun. Going to Fender's was just super exciting. My friend's parents would drop us off and we'd find a ride home from some willing stranger. We were probably at Fender's once a week, at least. There were always shows and they were cheap. Eight bucks. I think we saw Nina Hagen for eight bucks. Vandals. Bad Religion. 45 Grave. Sisters of Mercy. Yeah. All those shows were super, super cheap.

We saw Bad Religion so many times at Fender's. And the Vandals. TSOL. I lived right around the corner from Jack Grisham of TSOL, so we'd go see TSOL all the time. Circle Jerks. Fear. UK Subs. None of them really stand out as being the best show. There were so many great ones.

People would be in the pit. They called it a slam pit. I remember I was at Bad Religion and 45 Grave at Fender's and I was sitting on the stage and I took a boot to the face. Somebody was stage diving. It wasn't like they kicked me. It was like, "Ah! A boot's coming." I was like, "That's cool! I've got my war wounds." I don't remember any violence really pertaining to any of the shows. I mean, I went to the Dead Kennedys at the Olympic and that was in a really bad area, but I don't remember it being scary or being worried. Everybody was pretty cool. I think it was one of their last shows. It was crowded. Packed. It was amazing.

We'd go to Zed Records in Long Beach by the traffic circle, and we'd get tickets there. Zed's was the best—the premier record store. I had a friend, David Delucca, and he used to hang out there every day and they got tired of him hanging out, so they gave him a job. He had every record, every flyer, anything punk rock. You'd go to David and he would know.

We used to take the bus to White Slug. White Slug was an independent record store, kind of like Zed's. I think it was in downtown Long Beach and then it moved to Seal Beach. I remember the guys from Christian Death were there. We'd go and see bands and the police would harass us 'cause we looked all crazy, but it was fun.

■   ■   ■   ■   ■

I got into punk 'cause I was a weirdo and I didn't relate to the normal people at school. Punk rockers were always really friendly and welcoming. You could be different and it was okay. All the outcasts fit into the punk rock scene, and then everybody just kind of accepted you. Nobody gave me a hard time because I was a girl. If I wanted to go in the pit, I went in the pit. If I wanted to stage dive, I did a stage dive. Everybody was cool about it. Because I was small, I used to go up to big guys and tap them on the shoulder and ask them to put me on their shoulders, so I could see. People would give us rides home. We didn't know any of those people. I don't know if they were trying to hook up with my friends or if they were just being nice, but we always got rides home.

It was an awesome scene to grow up in. It was really welcoming. I felt like I could be an individual and I was accepted. I loved it. Even though I didn't like my teen years—I had a lot of conflicts in high school and I ditched a lot—I had so much fun. I look back and think of all the shows I've been to and all the bands I've seen and it amazes me. I'm impressed with myself. I think the scene made me accepting of differences. If people look different, I don't really give a shit. If I want to have a purple mohawk, I'm going to have a purple mohawk. I don't care what people say. And it kind of made me have a more eclectic mix of friends, 'cause there were a lot of misfits in the scene. I'm independent, non-conformist, and a little crazy. I never wanted kids, but being married was fine. I wanted to be a good person and nice and friendly, but if people didn't like me, I didn't really care.

I'm still really involved in music. I still like Bad Religion and X. They're my favorite bands. I pretty much go to all their shows. If I'm kind of grumpy, I'll put on the Dead Kennedys. A lot of the darker stuff—Bauhaus and 45 Grave—I still love them. I've grown and I have broader interests, but I still love those bands I grew up with.

I just got really into music, especially any kind of alternative music. I guess that's how the scene influenced my life. I got a degree in recording engineering. I worked at Tower Records for almost ten years, from 1991 to 1999. From around 1989 to 1990, I worked at I.R.S. Records. They put out Concrete Blond, the Cramps, some Police stuff. They had some punk bands. I worked there in publicity.

I have a lot of friends from that time. I think I developed really strong friendships. I'm still friends with some of the people that I went to junior high and high school with. We all went to shows. We still occasionally go to shows, so I think I made long, lasting lifetime friendships with those people. I think that's important.

JANIS OLSON

Born in 1971 in Los Angeles, California. Lived in Huntington Beach, California, in the '80s and attended shows at various venues throughout Los Angeles County and Orange County. Currently lives in Anaheim, California, and works as a legal assistant.

I RECALL BEING VERY YOUNG. I believe the year was 1983. I was only twelve years old and in the sixth grade. This is when I had my very first encounter meeting somebody who was punk rock. During this time, I was living in a foster home in Huntington Beach. I was an only child, as my foster mom had no children of her own and no other foster children she was parenting. I had been living with her for several years before she decided to bring another ward-of-the-state into our home.

I will never forget the day I met my foster sister. Prior to her arrival, I recall being somewhat worried about whether or not I would like her, and I wondered if we would get along well together. I had mixed emotions about someone new coming to live with us. Would she even like me? I had absolutely no idea what to expect. Then, the day came when she arrived. Still, to this very day, it is a memory so vividly clear to me. The doorbell rang and we opened the door and there, standing before us, was this tough, bad-ass chick wearing ripped-up jeans and a black leather jacket with all these unfamiliar buttons and patches sewn onto it. She had a mohawk,

too. A mohawk? I was clearly her opposite. I really hate to say it, but I was the epitome of a Miss Goody-Two-Shoes. I was a plain and simple kind of girl. I was mousy, quiet, and I got good grades. But this girl, she was different. She was a presence.

I could tell just by looking at her that she had way more experience than I did. I had never smoked or drank, and I certainly didn't know anything about punk rock music. However, this was all about to change. I was on the precipice of something new. I was definitely captivated by this introduction, meeting my new foster sister, especially considering I had never met anyone quite like her before. I don't recall there being anybody at my school, either, who looked or dressed this way. Admittedly, I was somewhat afraid, but what I was afraid of, I wasn't exactly sure. All I know is that I was amazed by this new girl standing there on our doorstep. It was as if a gust of wind had hit me. I was totally blown away.

Being that I was so young, I didn't have the wherewithal—namely the money—to change my style or appearance, but I definitely had an interest in the music and what the style of punk rock was all about. There was a sense of danger to it all, too. It struck me that one had to be resilient to be punk rock. I mean, let's face it, it's not as if a person wearing mostly all black with crazy spiked hair and a studded collar fit into the mold of the classic cookie-cutter image that most kids my age had during this time period. It was the '80s, no less. However, for me, it wasn't so much about the way punk rockers dressed as much as it was the attitude that a person who looked and dressed this way exuded.

One of my best friends from grade school had an older brother and he was into punk rock music, too. I remember he drove a blue VW Bug with surf racks on top, and he had wild hair and was a bit of a rebel. My friend and I would go down to the beach and we would see her brother hanging out with all his friends. They were punk rock boys, and we developed crushes on some of them. As far as being involved in the punk rock scene, I was just too young. It's not like I could go to bars or clubs to see bands play. I wasn't old enough, but I certainly had a curiosity and a desire to know more about what it meant to be punk rock.

A few years later, during the summer of 1985, the courts decided that it was time to send me back home to live with my real parents. This was an extremely difficult time for me, because I was leaving behind the security I felt I'd had living with my foster mom, not to mention that I would also be leaving behind all the friends I had made while living and attending school in Huntington Beach.

The courts removed me from my foster family, but before sending me back to live with my biological parents, I had to first move in with my older biological sister, to whom guardianship had been given temporarily while the courts were conducting their routine processes to ensure that my transition would be a smooth one. During this interim period, I had just started my freshman year at Whittier High School. Having left all my friends behind in Huntington Beach, I had to start all over again at a brand new school, not knowing a single soul. I had no idea where I was going to fit in and who my new friends would be, but I see now how I gravitated towards a certain group, and they were a group known as the "punks."

Looking back, I still cannot believe how relaxed the rules were at Whittier High. There was the main quad area that was located smack dab in the middle of the school's campus. This is where all the kids would gather during short breaks and the lunch period. It was like a scene from a movie, seeing all the adolescent cliques and their respective corners to which they belonged. In one corner, there were the sports enthusiasts, also known as the jocks and cheerleaders. In another corner, there were the brainiacs, known as

the geeks or nerds. Then, of course, there were the metalheads and
the punks. I am sure there were other stereotyped groups, but these
are the ones I remember most clearly.

Still, to this day, I find it rather amazing how students were
allowed to smoke cigarettes on campus. Literally! The principal
could walk right by you and see you smoking a cigarette, and he
wouldn't say or do anything. Smoking was totally allowed. I recall
very distinctly hanging out every lunch break in the quad with the
punks and smoking cigarettes. This is where I seemed to fit in the
most. I felt accepted despite the fact that I was still struggling with
feelings of not fitting in anywhere. I think this is pretty typical for
most kids this age. It's just a part of growing up. However, in my
particular case, I really do feel that I was drawn and attracted to
this group because everything I was going through emotionally at
the time was weighing very heavily on me.

To me punk rock meant being rebellious. It meant being tough
and kick-ass. If ever I felt weak, I had to rely on these concepts to
get me through. I had to be tough. I had to be kick-ass. I had to
be punk rock all the way! Despite the fact that I didn't look punk
rock on the outside in terms of my style or the way I dressed, I was
still very much accepted by this group of people, and it is where
I seemed to have fit in the most. It was all these experiences that
piqued my interest in not only the music, but the people and the
scene.

I think my involvement ended up being a really good thing for
me. As I got older, my experiences with punk rock music and all
that it entailed influenced me in different ways. I think it left an
imprint, as far as how I think politically. I definitely feel that people
should live their own lives, be independent and free to make their
own decisions and choices, and not have government dictate every
aspect of their lives. I'm glad that I've had the experiences I've had.
I have great memories of the past and all the people I met along the

way. I'm glad that I at least felt like I could fit in somewhere.

Driving down the street nowadays, I see kids who are all dressed, wearing their tight black pants, leather jackets, crazy colors for their hair, and their Doc Marten boots. Being a forty-two-year-old woman now, I drive by and I nod my head a little bit. I think to myself, "Yeah, that's pretty cool. That's kick-ass cool." I like those kids. If I was young, I'd want to be friends with them. They're my kind of people and I appreciate them for who they are and what they represent.

JENNIFER PRECIOUS FINCH

Born in 1966 in Los Angeles, California. Worked as a photographer in L.A. in the '80s and played bass for Sugar Babylon (1984–1986) and L7 (1986–1996). Currently plays bass for L7 (the band reunited in 2015) and continues to work as a photographer in L.A.

I GREW UP IN SOUTHERN CALIFORNIA, in Los Angeles. My father used to take me to a bookstore as a treat on Sundays and let me pick out my own books to read. I gravitated to the music section. I was ten or eleven. That's when there was sort of a popularity of punk rock books coming from the U.K., which I think influenced a lot of people who were in Los Angeles and were older than I was.

Later on, I had a babysitter who took me to a Ramones show when I was eleven. Then, when I was twelve or thirteen, I started to go to shows in Los Angeles. I was a minor, so it was very difficult to get in. I think there was a big divergence that happened in '81 between what we can call punk rock and what we can call hardcore. When hardcore started, when I was about fourteen or fifteen, that was what I was truly more interested in, because it was a suburban youth movement as opposed to punk rock, which was almost like an urban art statement movement. It was really sort of the aggressive nature and actually the masculine nature of hardcore that I was ultimately attracted to and a part of. The hardcore movement combined a lot of outdoor sport-type activities, like skateboarding. I think that there were a lot of women that participated in it. It was just in this more traditional perimeter role.

My initial involvement in hardcore was going to shows in Hollywood at places like Madame Wong's, the Starwood, or the Whisky. I was always interested in photography, so I took pictures.

It was part of how I got in for free and met people.

I participated in helping with hardcore fanzines that were in Los Angeles. Eventually, I started to play music. For me, music came much later. Now that I'm older, ten years isn't a big deal. Back then, year to year was a big deal. I didn't really start playing music until around '84. Punk had already gone up and gone down. Hardcore had already dissipated in Los Angeles by '84 and moved back to the suburbs. The Olympics came to Los Angeles. There were curfew laws. It was harder to throw shows. That's when I started playing music.

■   ■   ■   ■   ■

As far as being female, for me, punk rock almost seemed fifty-fifty with participants. When we talk about movements or cluster movements in pop culture and art, we are looking at the influence of not just bands, but people who did fanzines, who did radio shows, who promoted shows, who promoted parties, and who had art surrounding it.

Because I grew up through punk rock, I saw bands like Alice Bag, Castration Squad, 45 Grave, and the Cramps. There were women that were playing music, so it didn't bother me at all to pick up an instrument and play hardcore or to listen to Black Flag, the Circle Jerks, or Bad Religion and think I could play that or be in a band like that.

My tastes started to change. I met Courtney Love and I met some other very strong, interesting, funny, diverse women that were involved with hardcore and punk rock. I formed a band with Courtney and moved to San Francisco. I played there for a few years. It was called Sugar Babylon. This was the same time as punk rock and hardcore were happening in Los Angeles and where all that divergence happened. I still have this thing in me where music was sort of this athletic sport at the same time that it was movement and performance and not a contained craftsmanship, but it was explosive and big feeling. I got that directly from Black Flag and the Circle Jerks and all these big, masculine boy bands. It was going out and being physical and experimenting with your body as this form of expression outside of traditional, trained sports. And also from watching skaters like Jay Adams, who just passed away. We dated for a while and he was a big influence in the skate scene and what was happening.

I think that there wasn't a mechanism back then to get a fucking girl on a skateboard. I hate to say it like that, because it sounds like I want to say that my life was just super open and not stopped by anything. I look back and the men in my life were positive. They weren't saying, "Oh, you girls can't skate." They weren't like that at all, and especially the guy skaters. They actually gave me skateboards and they were supportive. They wanted me to play guitar and gave me amplifiers. I got a lot of that kind of support. It's interesting, because music ended up being something I had to fight for after a while, so I always wonder about that.

There is a difference between an academic middle class and growing up as a woman in the academic middle class. If you were becoming an attorney or you're getting into medicine, you're going to face issues because that's a world dominated by men, but I grew up in a working class environment, so there wasn't anywhere else to go other than where men go. I would've been expected to, even in the late '70s or '80s, to create a partnership with a man with a dual income. There wasn't anything pushing me back. There was only support, because the only way to survive was with a dual income. I'm grateful that I never went to college, because I don't have this riot girl mentality about repression of women and music. I'm often criticized for not having it.

I was always encouraged to do everything that I could do, and that's what I think that the biggest influence that punk rock had is. I think that there's a certain time in a woman's life, when she's like fourteen to twenty-one, where she thinks she can do anything. She can do anything, and punk rock and hardcore encouraged that mentality. It was that DIY-you-can-do-anything-in-this-scene.

In 1986, I joined L7. I played bass. I sang. We're doing a documentary with L7 right now. I was a visual person and I started videotaping very early, so they asked me to start to go through this 150 hours of home video, which is just me holding a camera in a tour van while we're making jokes. It's like the worst nightmare an editor will ever have.

My experience now dictates how I felt then, so it's very hard to create a narrative over it. I came from a really harsh background of child abuse. I started doing heroin very young. The drugs just stabilized me so I could go forward with my dreams and just be able to do it and climb onstage. I didn't worry if I was good enough or bad enough. Didn't worry if I was pretty enough or fat enough or too skinny or whatever. I just didn't worry about anything. It's a complete relief of self. So it's very difficult for me to tell my story, because it also coincides with a drug that supports it.

I didn't drink. I didn't smoke weed. It was just this small, continuous amount of this one drug that helped with whatever my issues were at that time besides addiction, like ADHD, focus issues, insecurities, self-esteem. It's really hard to tell people, "Hey, here's how I did it!" I get sensitive about talking about that. The other girls in L7 have different experiences. I know people drink to relieve self-esteem, but that's the whole challenge when you're a young woman. It's being relieved of that sense of self and not taking anything personally.

I got clean before L7 became popular. It was in the '90s, so right when we started picking up and going forward with larger shows, not club shows, like hall shows. We toured a lot. We all had day jobs and pitched in to get a van. This was like '87. Because of punk rock, I've been a booker. I knew what it would look like for a booker in, say, Cincinnati. You were sitting there with phone books, looking up record stores and saying, "What are your venues? Do you have phone numbers?" We were just calling them up and booking tours like that ourselves. That all came from punk rock.

I really just wanted to be onstage, so that I could have access to sex and drugs and be able to see shows. There isn't any freeing statement beyond what probably any dude wants when he sits in his bedroom and plays guitar, because he just really wants to get laid and he has a good hyperfocus on how to play. I didn't have an experience much beyond that or a statement beyond that based on my gender or sexually or identity or anything. I just wanted to play music, so I was blessed without people in my ear going, "What's it like being a girl in rock?" Thankfully, no motherfucking feminists were around me at that time to ruin my fucking experience.

Being involved in the music scene and the punk-to-hardcore transition influenced every aspect of my life. It influences my perception any time I enter a collaborative situation that might have a goal. I know how to be a part of the group. I know how to be a leader. I know how to be a support person. I think that, sexually, it influenced me too, because I really do prefer guys that came up through that scene. I'm single. I have a lot of access to sex, and there's a certain male I prefer, and it's somebody who came up through that also. I don't want to be laying around in bed after sex and having to explain how weird it is to see Henry Rollins on TV. I don't want to explain that to somebody. I want them to just look at the TV and we both snicker and we both know.

I think my involvement in punk rock, which bridged into

what we'll call grunge and what we'll call riot grrrl and scenes
that came right after, were really the last true eras of that style of
collaboration. The last era of the written fanzine, the last era of the
radio show that you had to tune into in block time. Kids today have
a different experience and are having their own and awesome cool
experience, but our generation was the last. Anyone who continued
music through the '90s definitely experienced the last of that. I love
the Internet. I think it's done great things for music. Things are just
different.

I think that what I learned from punk rock and hardcore and
rock and roll, whether it's Chuck Berry to the Beatles to the Stones
to Black Flag, is you write about your experience. This type of
music is experiential. So, I wrote a song called "Everglade" about
a girl's experience about going to a show. I sat there thinking, I'm
going to create a story about my experience, because I don't know
what it's like to be in your shoes when you go do what you're doing.
I can empathize, but I can't talk about or try to create what I think
people are going to relate to.

As an adult, I feel so honored that as a fourteen-year-old I was
able to have a voice in the movement with other fourteen-year-olds.
There's just so much work to do around the world. When I hear
women in the Middle East got ahold of L7 tapes, that's where it
really is. I think younger women see me as somebody who has done
something with her life that's admirable. I've lived a life worth living.

JENNIFER SCHWARTZ

Born in 1965 in Newport Beach, California. Lived in Santa Monica, California, the '80s, worked as co-editor/co-creator of *We Got Power* fanzine, sang for the Lovedolls, and attended shows at various venues throughout Los Angeles County. Currently lives in L.A. and works in Internet product development.

THE PROGRESSION INTO PUNK ROCK didn't start from one day. I wasn't listening to Journey and then I heard Black Flag and that was it. It was more of a longer progression, starting in '78 or '79. I was like, "What is this? This is a new sound." This was something I'd never heard before, and I responded to it. So that was just the first entrée into something that was out there that was different.

My brother and I grew up in Southern California. At that time, '78 or '79, we had just moved to Santa Monica. There were a couple of record stores around there at the time, and they had a new wave section. It was just about a bin of records with maybe twenty that you'd flip through. It was that curiosity and that emerging style that started to bubble into a presence, not in any major media, but at a record score or by picking up a weekly.

There was a little store there called the Village Muse, which was a new wave store, and Madness and Berlin played there, so it was just that kind of bubbling up. Then KROQ came on the air sometime around then and they were playing things. My brother and I kind of discovered things together like ska and Madness and the Specials. My very first show when I was fourteen was the Selecter. They played the Whisky with the Plugz.

The first time I heard Black Flag, the Germs, the Adolescents, everything was on *Rodney on the ROQ*. We'd huddle around the radio on Saturday and Sunday nights and listen to these songs. You would sit there with your tape recorder and tape these songs to listen to. It's all you got. That's exactly how it started and I'm sure I'm not the only one who tells this story. It's sad because on KROQ they make fun of Rodney a lot, but he was very important to the development of the scene. I don't know how it would have been without him.

It was scary. We were very young. None of us had cars, and when I say "us," it was me and my brother, Jordan, and our friend, Dave Markey, who lived half a block away. We met him running around the neighborhood. We were just like little kids at the time, so we started and built up courage. We rode our bikes to the Pacific to see X, the Gears, and the Blasters. After a while, we got comfortable and started going to more and more shows. We'd take the bus to Oki Dogs or the Whisky. You could take the bus from where we were and go to almost a show a night, so I started going out a lot. The Minutemen would play probably twice a week and we would go to each show, and each show would be amazing. It was just an unbelievable moment in time.

Everything was a work of art. It was a group of people at this weird storm of culture, ability, and some sort of freedom. We were all kids of the '70s, where our parents were like, "Go do your thing. Leave me alone. Let me do my thing." We were out on the streets from twelve years old, creating or destroying. It was a very open time. There was a lot of sex. There was a lot of drug use.

Dave was a very productive young teenager who had already done little fanzines in the neighborhood. He'd already made films with a Super 8 camera. So as soon as we got into this, we started the fanzine called *We Got Power*, which was me and Jordan and Dave and another friend, Allen. It had band interviews and photo galleries and games. The goal for Dave and Jordan was to get free records and get on the list, so having a magazine was the perfect entrée into all of this stuff. With a silly little fanzine we could get interviews with Hüsker Dü, the Misfits, Black Flag, anybody.

We did that for a couple of years, and then Dave and I started working on a feature film called *Desperate Teenage Lovedolls*, which was a story about an all-girl band that rises to stardom. As Dave would say, fucks and kills their way to the top. We would get all of our friends and bands to be in it. Red Cross is in it. Black Flag did music for it. Jello Biafra is in one scene. Minutemen were supposed to do a song, but they unfortunately didn't. We actually did two feature films, *Desperate Teenage Lovedolls* and *Lovedolls Superstar*. From that movie then, I started a band called the Lovedolls, which was supposed to be sort of the real-life, but fictional version of this movie band. That was an all-girl band, and we would play around a lot.

■   ■   ■   ■   ■

In some ways, in my own experience, the scene was welcoming to women, because the people that I gravitated towards, the bands and the scene, were more artsy and eclectic. I didn't hang out in Orange County, so I don't know what that was like, but if you hung out in Hollywood or the South Bay, or any of the Westside Santa Monica scenes, those are the people who were misfits and drug addicts. They came from broken homes or were gay, but didn't know it. Those people tend to be less gender-oriented, so it didn't matter. But if you jump out of that scene and go elsewhere or go to some more hardcore shows, it wasn't that open to women in that kind of environment. The dancing, the smells, the sound—it was a dude thing for sure.

I don't feel like I fit in as far as the typical gender identity. I never did, so I don't know what other women do and behave like and I certainly don't follow any rules like that. I just couldn't, and I realized that a long time ago, thankfully. I don't even try. I own a dress—just the one.

Being in a band, being on the stage, the condescending bullshit was rampant. You got shit about how a girl couldn't play and didn't know how to play. I got it all the time—the household "Show your tits." I remember one show at the Scream, probably more later '80s. There were guys standing in the front row and I got so fed up with them. I didn't lift up my shirt, but I basically gave one a lap dance in a very sort of angry way right in his face. He shut up and walked out. You could just stand up to any of these guys or say anything to them and they got very quiet all of a sudden, so you could shut them down, but it was always there. Yet, at the same time, it never stopped us. We were all tomboyish and tough and didn't think, "Oh, I'm a girl. I can't do that." That never ever crossed our minds. It wasn't even part of our vocabulary.

When you meet people who love music, whether it's punk rock or metal or whatever they love, there's always that common connection, so being in the scene influenced me to a degree that that's the path I followed. I never got off that path. It's still what I do. It's still who I am. I've never gotten far from it.

My involvement in the scene was definitely good. I had to put myself out there in front of a lot of people all the time and entertain and perform, and I had to overcome a lot of issues of self-esteem or shyness and just do it. I do it every day. I do it all the time. I don't know how to be a mom or design a mobile app. I just do it. That spirit of that time was "just do it," and that didn't exist before then. You didn't need a contract for a record label to be in a band. You didn't need a publisher to start a magazine. I talk to Dave all the time. He still makes movies. My brother just did a book. We're still creating. It's still happening.

JENNY LENS

Born in 1950 in Los Angeles, California. Worked as a photographer in the '70s and attended shows throughout Los Angeles County. Currently lives in Santa Monica, California, where she works as an educator and disrupter, sharing life, work, creative secrets, and power tips for creative entrepreneurs online and in real life.

I REMEMBER IT VIVIDLY, as if it were yesterday. I was twenty-five, living in the Valley. I earned my BA in art from Cal State University, Northridge, and my Master of Fine Arts in design from the California Institute of the Arts. I was living in a little house in Granada Hills. While buying groceries and looking at a fairly new magazine called *People*, I saw a photo of this strange-looking woman who referenced Rimbaud. I don't know anything about French Symbolist poetry, but you want to talk about Symbolist painters? I can talk for days. I knew of Rimbaud because of references in art history books I repeatedly studied. I bought *Horses*. I put it on the turntable. My life was never the same again.

I was a nice Jewish girl hearing somebody saying, "My sins my own, they belong to me." I said, "Whatever that's about, I want more." I was and am one angry, frustrated, abused woman. I was beaten from a small infant till I was fourteen. Verbally abused till I was forty-eight. I was aware that the world is hostile if you looked a little different. Dark curly hair was cool for Annette Funicello, but not when straight blonde hair was in vogue. I was nothing. The outsider. Anybody who knows me, knows I live in my head—my own world. I just say what's on my mind.

I was raised minimally Jewish in a very anti-Semitic country. Jews don't believe in sins. Our trespasses against others, hurting people and mistakes we've made, whatever you want to call it, are

JENNY LENS

not sins. They are "errors and omissions" in a legal term. Heaven and Hell are *now*. You have to deal with it *now*. I really loved Patti Smith's statement of taking personal responsibility. Very personal and very political. The political is personal. From the Sex Pistols to the Clash, Ramones, Bags, X, Screamers, and so many early punk releases, people were saying vital statements.

This was November or December 1975. Patti Smith was playing at the Roxy in January 1976. I stood outside in the cold for a long time. I saw people get out of their cars and walk right in. I channeled Scarlett O'Hara from *Gone with the Wind*. I said, "As God is my witness, I don't know how, but I'm going to be part of this. I can't play, sing, write, or dance. I'm not pretty, so not a groupie. I don't know what I can do, but I'm part of this now."

In August, I saw the Ramones the first night. I sat at Dee Dee's feet. His pronounced cheekbones inspired me to take photos. I had to take pictures of that man. He was gorgeous! The second night, I grabbed my camera. I met them. My life was changed forever. If I ever forget how I got into punk, take me out and shoot me. That is the most important memory in my life. Like being born.

■   ■   ■   ■   ■

It's a strange contradiction that I was photographing rock and roll, but I never looked at rock and roll magazines. I grew up on *Look* and *Life* magazines and some others. Certainly those photos made an impact on my life. As a young teen, I started collecting movie history books. We had no access to DVDs, videotapes, cable, net, or anything beyond pizza on demand, if we had that. We simply

could not see these films. I had no idea who these people were. I
wanted to know why they were worth mentioning or remembering.
I really wanted people to have that reaction when I took pictures.
I wanted them to get lost in my photos as I got lost in early movie
photos. I didn't know much about photography. I didn't go to rock
shows much as a kid, because I didn't drive till I was eighteen. I
hate cars and don't drive now. I'm not safe behind the wheel. I'm a
daydreamer!

I was not then nor now much of a live rock and roll show
fan. I don't spend money on rock and roll. I spend it on my art.
I listen to Broadway more than anything. I'm this famous punk
rock photographer whose heart isn't punk, but Broadway. That is
what I wanted to do: photograph Broadway and ballet. I wanted
to be Martha Swope. I grew up seeing her photo credits in the
magazines. Color. Broadway. Ballet. I couldn't imagine that as
reality 'cause I heard it snows in New York. I'm a sunny Southern
California girl.

We didn't have photography in my art history books. I came to
photography late. I had to teach myself how to develop film, make
proofs, and make prints. I learned from articles in photo magazines.
I'm lifelong DIY. I had no background in photography, dealing with
the press, live rock, or rock magazine photos.

I studied art like nobody's business. I compose like a painter. I
always told people I was a photojournalist. I was very pure about
that, because I wanted honesty. I lost some licensing for records,
because I don't have a lot of group shots backstage like the other
photographers. Boring. I captured spontaneous real life. My goal
was to photograph what I saw. I wanted people to see what I saw
through my eyes. I succeeded. My intention was to document
this cultural revolution unfolding in front of me. I set forth my
intention before ever stepping foot into the Roxy.

I always called the Whisky my home away from home. I'd stand on the stairs at my favorite step. I'd photograph the stage. I got a little zoom lens. I could focus on an individual or the group. Now you can't stand on stairs, because of all the stupid fire regulations and crap.

I would be standing there, with people constantly going up and down and up and down. The steps were always vibrating. I'd be jumping up and down, pumping one fist in the air, the other hand holding my camera, and singing along. Then I'd run upstairs to the backstage door, then up the backstage stairs. Then party time! I took so many fun and wonderful pictures backstage. It was just marvelous. Many great shows.

I even got pregnant in the upstairs backstage bathroom. Not too many people get pregnant backstage at the Whisky. I had an abortion November 11, 1978. It matters little to me. I never wanted children. I have no regrets. I'm grateful to the free clinic and easy access. Doctors and my mother always told me I couldn't get pregnant. I didn't have my diaphragm with me that night. But at the Whisky, anything can and did happen.

The Starwood was an interesting place. A lot of rooms. A lot of good pics and stories. X, Go-Go's, Dead Boys, Damned. It was harder to shoot the stage there. I danced upstairs a lot at the Starwood.

I didn't go that often to the Masque, 'cause I was working! I was shooting elsewhere or in my darkroom. I didn't get paid. I didn't have money to keep shooting L.A. bands. I wanted to document bands from New York, England, San Francisco, etc., but I took classic Germs photos and other photos at the Masque. The Masque was not my favorite place to shoot. The stage was too close to the ground. There was nowhere to set my camera down to change lenses. You couldn't even pee there. Oh, the bathrooms were scary filthy! I sometimes left my camera home when I went to the Masque. Sometimes I got drunk like everyone else. But usually

I took pictures. Many are in the *Live at the Masque: Nightmare in Punk Alley* book.

Alice Bag started her blog in 2005 or so. She had a page on the genesis of the song "Violence Girl." I'm so thrilled Alice used my photos for that. It really means a lot to me, because I think the photos are shit. Bad exposure. Camera problems. I appreciate that people have brought value to my work. They see beauty in my work that I don't see. Alice has always been the best friend to me. Alice saved my life in major ways. I love what she's done with her life.

■　　■　　■　　■　　■

Some in L.A. punk do all they can to defame me because I share my stories and those of others, and my photos have been published since 1976. People think I've had it so easy and made lots of money. I wish! I've risen above a lot of abuse, neglect, lies, and crap. I'm still here. Artists must be strong and resilient. Especially women.

I was stunned to realize New York photographers actually collaborated and cared about each other. Not in L.A.! One woman photographer, whom I introduced to my punk pals a few years ago, goes on and on about how famous she is, while doing all she can to take me down. I've helped a few who stabbed me in the back, but I'm still here. L.A. punk was not one happy family, but that allowed us to do our own thing.

I believe there's room for all of us. All who want to share stories and photos. There's no best or single voice or vision. We all have something to contribute. Sadly, few share my point of view. I have more important projects in my life than rehashing all that. Not my loss. My life is full and exciting.

Sisterhood and punk don't belong in the same sentence. I've met many amazing women, but, each of us were and many still are working on our own lives, which puts walls between us. I've helped photographers, writers, performers. Some have been so vitriolic to me. I'm stunned. I mourn the loss of friendship and misunderstandings but really, fuck it. I've got a lot more to give the world than worry about people who tell tall tales about me. I only mention this 'cause no one is immune to this stuff. You gotta just get on with your life.

There would not be a scene without the women. Anybody who says differently needs to look at photos, fanzines, and magazines— *Back Door Man*, *Slash*, *Flipside*, and smaller fanzines. Strip out the women, and there is not much left in L.A. I love early punk. Hardcore punk is a whole different animal. Hardcore punk was not female-friendly.

In early punk, women booked and produced shows, managed bands, wrote songs, wrote music criticism and reviews. There were the visuals: hair, makeup, clothes. Women were graphic artists, PR, and marketing. They worked at magazines, fanzines, record companies, management, and, yes, photography. And anything and everything else. Muse, fan, lover, friend. Who was gonna stop us? Punk was underground. As Patti Smith says, "We made it, take it back." Women were always involved in art, music, culture. Ever see art credited to "Anonymous"? That's women. Many men took credit for artistic and scientific discoveries that women created. No one could do that during early punk. Men have tried, the press believes them, but we know the truth.

I could talk for hours of the women in L.A. and their influence from being in the audience, onstage, and backstage. I have not read about other cities. We women are left out of the equation. L.A. and San Francisco are at the bottom of the punk coverage.

The story that's not been told—not in documentaries, books, or movies—is how L.A. punk influenced the world and L.A. women were up front and center. I can say, with total conviction, that L.A. women took command. We did whatever the hell we wanted, when we wanted, the way we wanted. This doesn't mean we got our way or became rich and/or famous. But we sure gave it all we got! And we changed the world.

Every day, I see in real life and online tons of Millennial women, Gen X-ers, and Boomers, male and female, with blue or purple or pink hair. I see black fingernails. I see deep, blood-red lipstick and dark eyes. I see hair, clothes, makeup, jewelry, accessories, and boots, all that we found and made and wore. I see punk influences everywhere—at Whole Foods, the farmers' market, YouTube, business videos, ads, everywhere. It would be easier to list where punk hasn't made a dent.

I don't care what it is, you can do it. That is how punk really influenced the world in so many ways. When people say they missed out or wish they were me or alive then, I say, "Shut the fuck up." There are all kinds of wonderful opportunities and things happening now. L.A. is alive with world-class art and growth. Things are hot here and so exciting. I've been closely following art communities and traction since I was a teen. L.A. has never been such a hotbed for artists.

I knew I needed to get my punk pictures into the computer and into the world. I embrace whatever technology tools to accomplish my goals and manifest my dreams. I built websites. I built computers. I taught computer programs and digital art, page layout, and web design at colleges. It was all in the service of others and art and built upon punk. My lifelong goal, starting when I was maybe four or so, was to leave the world a better place than I found it and to be around other artists.

Back then, I was looking for an art community, and I still am. My whole life. You have to constantly have an open-minded and open-heart attitude, or something great can be under your nose and you'll miss it.

JOHANNA WENT

Born in 1949 in Buffalo, New York. Lived in Seattle, Washington,
and Los Angeles, California, in the 1970s and '80s and worked as
a performance artist. Currently lives in Los Angeles and works as a
lecturer, performance artist, and spoken word performer.

MY FAMILY WAS REALLY POOR. We moved to Seattle from
Kansas, thank God. We were lucky to do that. My dad worked for
Boeing in Seattle. He was a flight engineer. My mom was really sick
all the time. I had two older brothers and a younger brother and
sister. I had to take care of my younger brother and sister, because
my mom was constantly hospitalized. I always took care of those
kids. I was like a mom at a really young age. I learned to cook when
I was around four years old. I would stand on a chair and make
scrambled eggs. My mom died when I was around eleven, but she'd
been hospitalized almost the whole time since I was five.

We didn't always have a TV, and half of the time it didn't work.
We would have sound or picture,
but we rarely had both. I used to
watch the *Mickey Mouse Club*. I'd
dance around. I really felt like I was
somebody. Nobody in my family
did. They thought I was somebody
who was supposed to clean up after
them and take care of things, which
was okay. I did it.

My mom, my dad, everybody,
would say, "Don't sing. Don't sing.
You sing off-key." I didn't listen
to it. I didn't care. I would sing as

loud as I wanted to. I would make crazy costumes for my dog or my little brother or sister. I never went to an art museum until the eighth grade when I went one time. I never went to movies, except something like *The Three Stooges*, if I was lucky. I didn't have any cultural background.

I went to Catholic school and hated it. I used to hang out in the library and read mythology. I always loved horror and really scary stories. I didn't believe in what my parents believed or what anybody believed. I tried to just keep going, keep surviving. I was a really wild teenager, because my mom died. I started smoking and drinking at a young age. I didn't do great in school, but I wasn't stupid, so I did okay. I never did homework, but I got decent grades.

After I graduated from high school, I went to beauty school and I started hanging out in theater. Seattle has a big theater scene. There were all these little theaters where they would do Chekhov plays. I would just hang around and try to get a role. Most of the time I was doing set stuff or stage management or makeup. Anything I could do, I did.

I was at this party in 1974, and I met this guy, Tom Murrin. I was working at a pharmacy in Seattle. I met him and it was like one of those moments where I went, "Oh, God. I just met somebody who was amazing." I think he thought the same thing. He had just gotten to town on that day. He was a lot older than me—about eleven years older. He grew up in Los Angeles, became a lawyer, and at twenty-two years old he was the youngest lawyer who ever passed the Bar in Los Angeles. He met Ava Gardner in a Beverly

Hills law office where he worked. She said, "Come to Spain with me." Because he was kind of a boy toy, he went to Spain with her. They were great friends for his whole life, until she died.

He went to Spain thinking he was going to be Ernest Hemingway or somebody. He was trying to write. Then he tried to paint. Then we went back to New York, and started hanging around the theaters. He wrote some plays. He traveled with these plays, and did these plays, and lived in Paris for a while. He moved back to New York and went, "Oh my god, I have to stop using drugs, and drinking too much, and smoking." He was probably in his early thirties.

He moved to Humptulips, Washington, to work with some guy he had met in Paris. He was doing these weird plays in this strange little town called Humptulips, which was basically a truck stop. I think it had a bar and maybe a store or something. He lived in a little tiny trailer. He was trying to do these plays in this bar for lumberjacks and their girlfriends, and a lot of drunk people. That didn't work out for whatever reason. He went to Seattle.

That day, I met him at this party in the evening. We just clicked. He said, "Come over to my apartment. I'm going to do Balloon Theater." It was sort of a thing that was made up. I said, "Okay, do I have to audition?" He said, "No, no, you're perfect. Just come." So I showed up, and we went out on the streets. We went to Pioneer Square—the big, huge farmers' market there. We were dressed up and we had all this glitter on our faces. We had some balloons and we were moving in a sculptural way. Who knows what the hell we were doing. He had worked with the Theatre of the Ridiculous and the Theatre of the Absurd in New York. It was pretty intense. People were interested, and it completely changed my life. I got my picture taken right away and was on the front page of the *Post Intelligence* or something. I was like, "Okay. This is it. I can do whatever I want to do and it's my performance. If anybody doesn't like it, they don't have to like it."

Tom said, "Okay, we're going to take this show on the road." A few of us left town, and we started traveling. We went down to Los Angeles, and then most of the people left. We started doing shows wherever we could do them for a couple of years. In '77, his dad passed away. His dad was here in L.A. We used to stay with his family. All of a sudden, he wanted to go to Asia. He wanted to go to India and Japan. He wanted to go to Hong Kong. I didn't have any money to do that, so I stayed here.

I started playing at this little tiny coffee shop which was right down the street from Los Angeles Community College. I lived in this apartment with one little tiny bedroom, which was as big as a closet. I was really poor. I didn't have a lot of money. I worked three jobs sometimes. I did window dressing. I worked at a wallpaper warehouse. I did all this stuff. I dug in the garbage for props and things. People would give me their old clothes. I'd make dummies out of them.

I had my props and costumes, and I just said, "I'm going to go down to that coffee shop. It's the closest thing." The guy who owned the place said, "Okay, I want you to be a regular." Every week I performed there. I kind of taught myself how to perform. We had already performed all over. We'd performed in Europe, New York, and Baltimore. We traveled the whole United States performing, but it was street theater, so it was just flying by the seat of our pants.

I started doing it there at the coffee shop. Then I wanted to do music. I wandered into the Masque in late 1978. I saw the Mau Maus play. I was like, "Okay, I think this is where I want to be." I was already making my own blood and my own costumes. I'd gotten to the point where I had a solid visual presentation. I really wanted music. I wanted some kind of backup. I wanted the band.

I ended up going down to the Hong Kong Café and talked the guy who managed it into booking me. He put me on the bill.

I think the Plugz were on my first bill. I performed and got fifty bucks or something. I was like, "Oh my god, this is great." I had a drummer who I had just met three days before. He didn't even show up on time, which really looked bad for me.

Afterward my friend, Z'EV, a percussionist from San Francisco who was originally from Los Angeles, came up to me. He was a really well-known, avant-garde percussionist. He said, "Get rid of that guy. That drummer. He's no good." I said, "Believe me, I'm getting rid of him. He didn't even show up on time." Z'EV came to my apartment the next day. He said, "I'm playing with you." He played huge pieces of junk—a car fender, any kind of piece of metal

or shit he could find. He was amazing.

I became a regular with Z'EV at the Hong Kong. We would drive up to the Mabuhay and play in San Francisco. Dirk Dirksen, who ran the Mabuhay, was the greatest guy. He loved my show. He always put me on. He always paid me decently. I became a headliner there. I started playing more shows in L.A. I got on the cover of *Slash* magazine. It snowballed from there.

■   ■   ■   ■   ■

The West Coast scene was totally different from New York. It wasn't a copycat scene. In New York, there was a lot of stuff going on. A lot of really great music came out of there, but I felt like the West Coast energy was grounded in the West Coast. There's more space. There's more room.

When I performed in
New York, it was always
difficult. Here, I threw all this
crap in my car, or a friend's
car, or whatever, drove down
to the Hong Kong, did my
shows, packed up, threw it
back in my car, and drove
home. In New York, it's a
different landscape. It's always
harder. That's why I didn't go
to New York.

It's easier here. I was able to give a bigger presentation. I'm
a West Coast gal. What can I say? Once my family moved from
Kansas to Seattle and I saw the ocean, I could not believe the
power of that water. That air. The breeze of all of that. I am not
somebody who can be crowded or feel contained.

My performance art came from my feeling that I could do
whatever I wanted. I used to write my dreams down every single
night. When I was lacking inspiration, I would go to my dream
book. I would try to make a costume or a prop or something that
represented that vision that I had when I was asleep. I really felt
that whatever I did was a direct inspiration from the collective
consciousness of my audience, and my community, and my world.

I could not believe how I was embraced by the punk rock
community. Most of them were quite a bit younger than me. It
wasn't as censored as things are now. Kids used to come to these
shows. They were moved by it. Quickly, I moved to headlining. I
had a full band. I played with Fear a lot. I played with the Dead
Kennedys up in San Francisco. I played with the Mutants. One
time, I played with Black Flag. I played with the Germs.

Around 1980, Z'EV decided that he wanted to move to

Amsterdam. Mark and Brock Wheaton, brothers from the Seattle band Chinas Comidas, came down to Los Angeles and played some gigs. The band split up. Mark Wheaton called me, and then Mark and his brother started performing with me. I said, "Look, these are the rules. We don't practice. We play. You do what I do. Which is, you key into the consciousness of the audience, and you improvise. Like jazz. Like anybody who is disconnected from the rules."

I tried to make a little script, like how a band has a playlist. It was usually from my dreams. Sometimes I would follow it, but if I didn't feel like following it, I didn't. Once the blood came out, once the really gooey, messy shit came out, I tripped on it and I fell down and I slid, and it was messy and impossible to keep going.

My idea was to create a different show every time. One of the things that always bothered me about regular performance art, or performance in general and even dance, is they play a set list. They play the same song. They play it over and over. They play it each night they play at a different club. For me the idea was, how do I mix it up? How do I break that string of consciousness? How do I make some kind of explosion happen by cutting through the expected reality and going into a more cosmic, confused state of being?

A lot of the performances were very trance-based. I would go into a state where everything I did was sent to me by the collective consciousness. I had these ideas and I put them out there, but if during the performance I didn't feel that it really jived with the moment, then I didn't do it. I'd go to something else. I prepare the props, and the costumes speak to me. They tell me what to do, and I follow.

■   ■   ■   ■   ■

In the early '80s when I was performing, I was not a part of the art scene. In fact, I was pretty much rejected by any kind of art scene. I did not know what performance art was. The first performance art

I saw was a Robert Wilson production at the public theater. I saw this guy, Christopher Knowles. He read the phone book. Actually, he didn't read the phone book. He knew the phone book. I thought, "Okay, I get it. This is performance art? I think I'm a performance artist." I started calling myself a performance artist. There's no other way to explain it. I'm performing in a moment, in a time, and this is my art form. It's certainly not a play. It's certainly not a piece that's going to be repeated. It is a performance, in a space, time, and place. I try to be as honest about what I put out there. I try to connect as much as I can with some kind of unconscious. If that's not pure enough for people who want theater, or they want a music set, or they want something that's been rehearsed, or whatever, I don't care. This is what I have and this is what I have to give.

The first time I started using blood was in '74. I learned to cook when I was younger, so I cooked up this blood recipe. I can't remember all the shows where I used it, but I remember in '74, I was in New York. It was summer, and it was really hot. I made these weird nipples under my bra out of balloons and blood that I cooked up. I was in Washington Square Park. I learned some magic tricks, too. So I would do this thing where I would cut my nipples off. I got a little bit of flack from certain feminists about that. I understand. I agree. It's kind of weird. From then on, I used blood and I made my blood recipe.

After a performance, I was exhausted. Then I had to clean up. The clean-up was a mess. A huge mess. Sometimes if I had a band play after me, I had to clean up the stage really fast. My costumes were ruined. I'd have to throw shit away. I'd save some pieces and use them for something else. I turned them into a new thing, but I always felt that they had the power from that last performance. I also have this strange connection with objects and things and textures and colors and movements. The way I move my arms. The way I move my body. If something comes to me, I trust it. I trust that is the expression that I am supposed to put across. If I destroy a costume I really love, I say goodbye to it. I sacrifice it. I say, "Okay I'm good with this."

■   ■   ■   ■   ■

You can't walk through life as a woman without experiencing sexism. What woman doesn't experience that? But I got to tell you, there were so many inspirational women back then! There were so many voices, and they were so powerful. And they kept coming. It wasn't just a short period of time. I was just unbelievably inspired by the women in the scene.

Being a woman artist is like being able to own your sexuality. It's being able to own your sex. Being able to identify with your core being. My core being is feminine. That's it, man. I have a pussy. That's what I have, and that's what I like, and I'm good with it. I can't say that I don't like the penis, 'cause I do. I like all of it. I think it's authentic to own your sexuality and also your animal self.

I always say I am an animal first. All that brain pudding is so

confusing. When you look at a dog or you look at a cat, their animal core is the driving force. I trust that more than the deepest, most philosophical thought. Most people don't. I feel that it grounds me to the earth. I really believe it's important. Many people have told me that I am anti-intellectual, but I've always been fascinated with thought, and with different people's opinions, and I listen to everything. I don't have to believe what other people believe. As a really young kid, that was my breakthrough.

When my parents used to take me to church, I would see the Holy Communion wafer and I'd go, "That's the moon." I couldn't believe what they did. I knew that they were lying to me. I knew that there was no truth there. I knew, and I trusted that they believed it, but I also trusted that they had some questions that they were not courageous enough to face. I had to face those questions, and I had to ask those questions. I always did. I was punished. I was punished to the point where sometimes I would just shut up about it, but I didn't lose my own self.

I live for art. I love art. Art has given me everything that's good in my life. I live in the Hollywood Hills in a really nice house, and I came from the projects in Seattle with nothing. Art will give you everything you need. You always have to trust that. It really will. It's magic. It's the magic power. It really is.

KARA NICKS

Born in 1964 in California. Worked for SST Records and as a
roadie for various bands including Black Flag, Minutemen, and
Meat Puppets in the 1970s and '80s, and lived in Tucson, Arizona;
Galveston, Texas; and Norwalk, Hollywood, Torrance, and San
Pedro, California. Currently lives in Nashville, Tennessee, and
dabbles with computer code, bugs, and whatnot.

I DIDN'T GET INVOLVED IN THE SCENE, because of where
I was living, until I moved to Tucson in October of '82. I was living
in Norwalk, California, before, which explains why there was no
scene. In Tucson, my mom worked at a pool hall called Troy's
Billiards. That cat was from Torrance, California, and he would
have bands play on the weekends. One of the bands was a '60s type.
I was talking to those cats, and they told me I would probably be
better off hanging out at a place called the Backstage, which was a
dive bar on Fourth Avenue. I started going there and hanging out.

Tucson had an awesome scene. The punk rock scene was very,
very open. Long-haired people and skinheads would show up, and
everyone would get along. It was not that way in Cali. Everybody
went to shows in Tucson no matter what kind of music the band
did. It was kind of like the Nashville scene. So even if you might be
into rockabilly or punk rock or some kind of noise fusion, you went
to shows. Of course, the bigger shows drew all the crazy people
from the college.

The first violent show I saw was Black Flag. When I would
go to shows at the Backstage, people would slam in the pit and if
you fell, people picked you up. It was fun. Black Flag was different.
It was *wow*. All these jocks showed up, and they thought it was
cool to punch people in the face. It was hardcore. I don't know if
that's how Black Flag always was or if Henry brought that kind of

mentality. You know, the way he sang songs compared to how Dezo
[Dez Cadena] or Keith Morris did it. I'm not sure if that's true.
That's just what people have told me over the years.

I believe Dezo was playing a show in Tucson in December of
1982, and that was the last [Chuck Biscuits] show. While Dezo was
in town with this show, I ended up meeting him. Dezo told me he'd
be back in May and, if I came to the show, he'd put me on the guest
list. In May 1983, I went to that show with my friend Anita. Davo,
the roadie, was the first one I met. Mugger was the second person I
met. They wanted me to hang out. So we ended up getting in free.
I thought it was cool as shit. We got there really, really early, like
five in the afternoon. We ended up talking and chilling. I learned all
there was to learn about merchandise and what the merch person
does and what the sound dude does. I just kind of followed him
around and was learning shit. I was taking it all in. I thought, "I
want to do this. It's cool." As the night went on, me and Davo hung
out. He said, "You should go to Phoenix with us. But how are you
going to get home?" I was like, "We'll figure it out. Don't worry. I got
this. I got this." So we ended up getting in the van with Black Flag.
There were a bunch of people in that van. There were altogether
ten people: Davo, Mugger, Spot (he produced *Damaged* and stuff),
Joe Carducci, Chuck Dukowski, Greg Ginn, Henry Rollins, Bill
Stevenson. There were just the random people who worked for
SST, the roadies, and Black Flag. It was weird.

So, we went to Phoenix. When we were loading in, I helped
roadie. Carducci said, "You're our guest. You don't have to." I told
him, "I don't ever want anybody to call me a groupie." I helped
Davo load gear and the merch and set up the table. I also helped
set up all the mics. It was pretty cool. It was at this place called
Mad Gardens. That show was bizarre, because it was a wrestling
ring with a chain-link fence. It was awesome. It was a trippy show
to say the least. I remember climbing the chain-link fence and just

hanging up there.

After the show, we had to hitchhike home to Tucson. Davo took us to the last exit out of Phoenix. He was really nervous and scared for us. We panhandled at this store and got enough money to buy a twelve-pack. We were at this on-ramp and started drinking. Who knows how we ever survived it. Carloads of strange, random, and weird dudes tried to pick us up. Other people would slow down, look at us, and drive on really fast. I looked fairly normal, but my friend had a Misfits-style haircut and she was wearing a dog collar with these big nail spikes on it. I was like, "Maybe you should take your collar off."

There was something so weird out of this whole thing. This is totally true. I swear to God on my life. We were almost out of beer and I was going to go back to the store. I stood up and turned around and looked out to the desert. You know how the desert shimmers? I saw this dude or something walking towards us out of the fucking desert. As he got closer, I could tell he had long hair. He didn't have a shirt on. He had a shirt tied around his waist. I turned to my friend and said, "Dude! I think we're fucking dead, because there's Jesus." She turned around and she was like, "Oh, fuck. I think we are. Hit me, punch me, pinch me." So I pinched her and she said, "No, we're not dead."

So, this dude comes walking towards us and he's like, "Hey, sisters. What are you doing?" We're like, "We're hitchhiking. What the fuck does it look like?" We're punkers, right? And he goes, "Far out. Do you like peyote?" We said, "Yeah." He goes, "Hold out your hand." He gave us peyote buttons. I took them right then. Like the bitch I am, I ate his peyote and said, "Dude! You can't stand next to us. Nobody will ever pick us up with a guy here." He said, "No problem, my sisters." He went down to the end of the off-ramp.

Fucking shit! I am not lying to you. In five minutes, a car stopped and picked him up. He was nice enough to get us a ride.

He sat in the back of the seat between me and Anita. All these people in the car were deadheads coming back from that Ventura show that goes on every year. They were heading to the next show in Albuquerque. I thought, "These deadheads got it going on." It didn't freak me out until we got halfway to Tucson and I start coming on to the peyote. They were smoking weed. I had quit smoking weed, but I took a hit. I don't know why. And boy! Mistake! Now I was tripping balls on peyote and I was high from this weed. So the first off-ramp we got to in Tucson, I said, "This is it! Right here. Cool!" Because I was picturing them taking us into the desert and hacking us up like *The Hills Have Eyes*. I was just freaking out. We were about ten miles out from our house, so we spent the night in a graveyard. We were tripping balls. Again, we panhandled enough to get some beer. We just sat in the graveyard and tripped balls all night until daylight. Then we called a friend of ours to pick us up.

I lost my job from going on this little Phoenix excursion, so at this point I was doing side work, day jobs. In June of 1983, Black Flag did a show at the Santa Monica Civic. I flew into L.A. to see that show. I was put on the guest list. It was fifty bucks to fly from Tucson to Los Angeles. I had just enough money to spend at the show. Back then, people didn't have cell phones. They were lucky if they had home phones. The next day after the show, my sister and her old man just dropped me off at LAX and left me at the curb. I got up to the ticket counter and the lady said, "That will be $115." I didn't have that, so I started crying. This dude came out. He had been at that Black Flag show and he was like, "Let's see what we can do for you." He asked, "Did you like the show?" I said, "It was fucking awesome." He goes, "It was, wasn't it?" He flew me back to Tucson for just the tax of the ticket. It was just like the Grateful Dead. I was thinking that in my head. People look out for each other.

I ended up leaving Tucson, because I had no reason to stay
there. I went back to L.A. I stayed with my sister, who is crazy. She
threw me out. I was wandering the streets of Hollywood. I was
living in a place called Hotel Hell, and I was lonely. One night I
was at the Cathay de Grande, and there was Dez Cadena and Jim
Gardner. They took me in. That was in 1984. I was working at
Wherehouse Records. My boss was very awesome. He gave me the
position of being the buyer for independent imports like the Dead
Kennedys. Carducci and Mugger came in a couple of times. They
were keeping in touch with me. I helped do mailings and stuff for
SST. Then the Summer Olympics came and I left town, as did
everyone else. When I came back that time around, I was staying
with another family member who got evicted when I was staying
there. Again, I was homeless on the streets of Hollywood.

I had been homeless for a few weeks. I was looking at the *L.A.
Weekly* and I saw this show at Club Lingerie. I got down there and
asked for Davo, but Mugger came to the door. It was a Minutemen
show. Mugger seemed sexist, but he really wasn't. When I told
him what was going on, he got the keys to the van and took me in
the van. So we went back that night and spent the night in Global
Network Booking in Black Flag's practice room.

The next day, D. Boon and Jeanine [Garfias] showed up and
Mugger said, "Jeanine, can she come live with you? She's a cool
chick." D. Boon said, "No doubt, come live with us." So D. Boon
took me in off the street. I did a lot of roadie work when I lived with
D. Boon in '85. I also started hanging out with bands in San Pedro,
and I would roadie with them or do mini-tours with them. Pedro is
a weird little town. It's kind of off by itself. It's like living in a small
town. So in the scene, no matter what music or genre, everybody
supported each other. That was a cool little scene down there.

I was supposed to have been in the van that rolled over [the
accident in which D. Boon died], but I couldn't get off work. I was

back at Wherehouse Records, and I was a buyer. When that wreck happened, Jeanine broke her back. She told Mugger, "Call Kara. Tell her what happened." A few days later, Mugger called me and said, "I've been talking to Jeanine and she says the only person she wants in mail order is you. So I'm going to offer you this job." We buried D. Boon on that Saturday, and I started working at SST on January 6, 1986. That was how I got the job at SST. I remember that funeral. Me and Mugger and Linda, the secretary at SST, sat together. It was a horrible funeral.

At the time, SST Records was located in Hawthorne on Hawthorne Boulevard. Later on they moved over to Long Beach, and that's when Greg Ginn came back to work. I started out in mail order and Mugger was really quickly impressed with me, so he handed me the reins to the warehouse and shipping and receiving and, right behind that, distribution and sales. I grew it. Me and Mugger working together were a team and a half. He's one of my mentors. I worked there January of '86 until I was fired by Greg Ginn in May or June of 1990.

Out of all the distributors I worked with, I can only recall one woman out of twenty-two distributors. Even the buyers were mostly all men. I don't recall any women buyers at records stores, unless it was a mom and pop shop. Very strange. That's when I realized how lucky I was that they had given me that job. It didn't dawn on me that women didn't do that. That they didn't do a lot of what I was doing.

I went on tour with the Meat Puppets, Minutemen, and Black Flag. I would go to the shows early. These were mostly one-offs down to San Diego, and I did some one-offs out to Tucson. I actually had a full-time job, so I couldn't go on a long tour, so I did one-offs. When I roadied, I helped carry gear. Black Flag had a lot of gear. I just remember their stuff was really heavy. The speakers and cases. They had their own sound system. By 1986, they were touring with a giant truck along with their regular van.

I toured more with the Meat Puppets. With them, I did a lot of the drums. I carried the drums and helped set up the drums. I did some stuff with the Minutemen. It was hard, but when I was in Texas I was a brick laborer, so I've always been like, "I'll take it." This is where being a chick comes into my mind. I will not complain in front of men. I want to do the same job as men. Even if it's killing me, I'm not going to let them know.

One time I had been loading gear in all day for the Meat Puppets, when I went and changed clothes and was coming in the back door. Some back door dude made a comment and asked me if I was on the list. I didn't have a laminate on. I had one on earlier and took it off. I was like, "Dude. I've been loading gear all day. Are you fucking kidding me?" He said something like, "Groupies can go through the front." I chested up on him. "Who the fuck are you calling a groupie?" He picked me up in a bear hug, which was his first mistake. I latched on to the bottom part of his ear. I bit his ear off. He probably never picked up a chick in that direction again. He had me with my arms down by my side. In my mind, all I saw was a man grabbing me and I freaked out, so I bit him. Yeah [laughs]. He went home. He got fired, because I worked for SST. I was mean. I was really a little skinny thing, but I could fight like a dude and would.

I never thought of myself as a woman. I'm kind of a tomboy. They call me the female Bukowski, because of the way I talk or whatever. I love Charles, so it's a compliment. My foster mother never really wanted me around, so I hung out with my foster dad in the saw mill. I just always wanted to do guy stuff. I never ever let anything be a roadblock. Even though I know they're there. I consider myself a feminist in the sense that, if I want something,

I'll just go do it. I'm not going to wait for the government to pass a fucking law that tells people they have to hire me. As a matter of fact, I'd rather be hired because of my talent, my skills, and my know-how than some law.

My foster dad has a lot to do with it. He told me I could do anything I wanted to do and be. I grew up in the '60s and watched the bra burnings and that kind of stuff. I was very much into that. I would ask questions like, "Why don't women already have rights?" I just didn't get it. I would say, "I want to be a biker when I grow up." My dad would be like, "Well, I don't know if there's a lot of money being made in riding a motorcycle around, but whatever." I'd say, "When I grow up, I want to be a logger." When the Sex Pistols toured, I was watching it. I was fascinated. I turned around and told my foster dad, "When I grow up, I'm going to be a punk rocker." My daddy said, "Well, I reckon it's probably got a bit more money than being a biker. Whatever you want." When I got hired at SST, I actually called my foster parents to tell them, "I'm making a living as a punk rocker." My dad said, "I knew you'd do it. I knew it."

There was one person at SST that made me feel discriminated against, but that was more because I was a high school dropout. Mugger put me in charge of something. If someone wanted to get master tapes, they had to sign them out with me. This really upset this dude. I can remember him and Mugger going into the warehouse and I could hear everything because we were still in a small space, and he was flipping out. "Fucking bitch! Little bitch! This little high school dropout bitch." Mugger said, "I was a fucking high school dropout." At the time, though, he was going to college. Mugger said, "She's doing her job. She's really smart. Leave her alone." I could hear him yelling, but I also heard Mugger sticking up for me.

When Greg fired me, I was really the last one there except this one dude who hated me. When he fired me, I walked out and there were police outside. Yeah, I guess they were afraid. He had people watching me. He had a couple guys watch me box up my desk and get my stuff together. I was tripping. "Do you think I'm going to fucking steal from you?" I think that was what we had a fight about, about him stealing from people. It wasn't like just being fired from a company. It was my family, my surrogate family. In my mind, it was like I was put out by family. I didn't listen to music or really do anything in music until I started booking with Springwater in Nashville.

When I came back to Nashville in 1995, I was working at a place called Jamaica's and I asked if anyone knew where Cantrell's was. When I lived with D. Boon, he told me about a place called Cantrell's in Nashville that had a dirt floor. It was his favorite place to play. I wanted to go see this place and pay a little respect. They all started laughing and were like, "You're standing in the lobby of what used to be the entrance of Cantrell's." Talk about the world coming full circle. The guy who used to own Cantrell's now owns this other dive bar called Springwater. No one would play there. I started working at Springwater off and on in '96 and '97. In March 1999, I started working there full-time.

Springwater was really a rough place, but I went in there. One of my favorite sayings was, "Fuck you, motherfuckers. I fucking worked with Black Flag. I roadied with Black Flag. This ain't shit." At first I didn't tell people I had worked at SST. I was embarrassed by it. I thought everybody knew. It was really devastating to me, that job and that company and what happened. But that is the one thing I have to say about working for SST. I didn't realize what SST really was until I got to Tennessee and started booking for Springwater. I realized exactly what that label meant to people. I started booking bigger and bigger names. Someone came through and knew who I was. They recognized my name and said, "You used to work at SST." That kind of got out and it became easier to book. Then I was like, "Fuck it! I might as well use it. Because, goddamn, it ain't like Greg Ginn didn't use me there at the end."

One of my things has always been to just be yourself and be nice to people. When you do good for people, it will come back. The way my work ethic is, the way I was when I got in the van with Black Flag, and how I acted and behaved and carried myself, that stuck with them. It's how I was raised. People see that. I've done right. I did the right things. It has all come full circle somehow, in some weird randomness.

KATHY RODGERS

Born in 1967 in Oxnard, California. Lived in Oxnard, Los Angeles, California, and London, England, and attended shows at various venues throughout Los Angeles County and Ventura County in the '80s. Worked as a photographer, contributed to *60 Miles North* fanzine, and created *Mute on the Floor* magazine (1990s). Currently lives in Ventura, California, and works as a photographer, filmmaker, publisher, and journalist.

MY PARENTS HAD CHILDREN LATE IN LIFE, so unlike other children born in the '60s that maybe had hippie parents, my parents were more from the '50s. I grew up hearing Frank Sinatra, '50s big bands, and Nat King Cole.

I had two introductions to punk rock. A neighbor girl, Debbie, was into everything and was very progressive. She was six years older and her sister was the same age as me. This would have been about '76 or '77. She was buying the B-52's, the English Beat, Van Halen, and Led Zeppelin—literally everything. She was really immersed in music. When I would go over to get her sister to play, we would end up in Debbie's room listening to records. There were no categories. I didn't know that the English Beat was ska. It was just music to me and it was cool. She had the Sex Pistols, but I didn't know that was punk. I was just nine years old. A nine-year-old ear is different than a thirteen-year-old ear. I think the cool thing about her is that she didn't really define anything, so I liked that she was almost more punk than punk.

Then, when my sister was in high school and I was in seventh or eighth grade, I distinctly remember she came home from school and she was pissed off. In science class you had to have a partner, but she didn't discuss this with any of her friends in advance. She got to class late and got stuck with a punk. She was not happy about it, because she felt that he was going to just take advantage and have her do all the work. Little did she know, he was really smart and pulled his weight. He started telling her about his band and this radio station that played punk rock and that she should listen to it. It was KROQ and the show was *Rodney on the ROQ*. We could barely pick it up. My brother ran a wire out my window to the TV antennae to get better reception.

I would make tapes of the show. Some of the tapes are amazing and I still have them. It was like the best of punk rock. I was fixated on listening. I got really into the Germs. I was really into X. One of my favorite bands is the Clash. My background was such a mix of influences, and Joe Strummer loved reggae and loved ska and brought all of that to his music. They weren't just punk rock songs. I can remember hearing the Clash, and they just sounded so different than the bands that were really trying to be punk rock.

I was considered too young to go to shows when I really started getting into it. I used to cut the listing of the shows I wanted to go to out of the *L.A. Weekly*. This same time period, my mom had gotten sick and was being treated at UCLA. We would drive there for her checkups. She had breast cancer, and had major surgery. She didn't get chemo or radiation, but I think she got checked on quite a bit. She would drop me off at Melrose, so I would go and spend the day on Melrose while she was at UCLA. I didn't get to go to shows. I would just daydream about going to a show and meeting more punks. I was twelve or thirteen. I would buy records and just obsess about it. My sister started dating a guy that would go to punk shows. I think I ended up going to a show with them. Then we got tickets to the second concert I ever went to. It was the English Beat opening up for the Clash.

I think maybe the third show I went to, I took my camera. I believe I was fourteen and already in high school. It was a Misfits show and the film didn't come out, because I didn't know what I was doing. I kicked myself on that one. I got it figured out and stopped shooting color, because that was a little bit harder to get it to come out right. There's a wider range of error in black and white. That girl, Debbie, was going to summer school at the junior college, so I would hitch a ride with her and take photo classes there to process the film and make prints.

I took photos at some shows, but mostly just local shows with Oxnard bands. For a while, we had really great bands coming through Oxnard, so I got to shoot the Adicts, Peter and the Test Tube Babies, and Suicidal Tendencies in our little club that was a quonset hut. The club held maybe 200 people, but they were able to get these bands that would play at the Olympic Auditorium in literally the next day.

This guy put out a little fanzine called *60 Miles North* and he started processing my film for me. He would use the photos in the fanzine. I never wrote any articles for them, but he would do band interviews and use my photos. Then the band Ill Repute used four of my photos. I was pretty excited to have my photos published on their album. I ended up shooting for their second album, too.

I had a gallery show years later when I moved to San Francisco, and I had to come up with an artist statement. I found a cool questionnaire that made me think about how I got from point A to point B. I figured out my shooting style came from having a lack of film and actually premeditating my shots, which I really wasn't aware of before. This is because I was given a roll of film and maybe there were five or six bands to shoot. I would sit there and wait. I didn't really realize I was doing that consciously.

The other thing was considering the medium that I'm using. I would say it backfired on me. I started bringing my camera to shows to keep people away. I thought if I was there to take pictures, I didn't have to socialize and I didn't have to have that pressure, because that made me very uncomfortable. I had a few friends and I was happy with that. But it didn't work, because bands would ask, "Oh, did you just take pictures of us? Did you just shoot our show?" It actually did the opposite. I thought it was my barrier between me and society or at least the people at the show. It ended up not being that way. I did end up socializing with these bands, because a lot of them wanted pictures.

■   ■   ■   ■   ■

With punk rock, after I got into it, I realized that it was pretty much the same as any other group of people, but I had an idealistic thought about what it would be like. You thought you weren't going to be judged by how you looked, but it ended up being that way. The music was different and the uniform was different, but it was still the same as the geeky group of people and the hip group of people. There was still a hierarchy. There were still the people that were popular. There were still the girls that were considered the good-looking ones.

Before I got into it, I felt that it wasn't going to be that way, because of the lyrics and what people were singing about. I felt like it was a place that would be more comfortable for me. It ended up not being that, and that could also have been my own issues of being insecure, which I now know about. I didn't know then it was social anxiety.

In the '90s, I started a magazine and I got really involved with more indie stuff. The magazine was called *Mute on the Floor*. Once my magazine got published, I would distribute it in L.A. I didn't really know anything about PR people and things like that. Record labels started sending me stuff. They would pick the magazine up and I started getting all this stuff in the mail. I got pre-released cassettes of new bands.

I did the magazine for about three years. At first I had all these pen names, because I didn't want people to know that there was one person doing everything. I had five or six different pen names. They were all different personalities. People would follow one of them for their record reviews. There was one character called the Neophyte. I had people that would literally say that they would buy everything the Neophyte approved of. That was funny. I never told them otherwise that it was the same person.

Mute on the Floor enabled me to interview some awesome and unheard-of bands, like Rage Against the Machine. I got the cassette and it didn't sound like anything I'd ever heard. I was very, very impressed that they were able to mix rap and rock and roll. Even if you took the vocals out of it, Tom Morello is super talented. I was like, "Wow!" I can remember putting that tape in and just thinking, "What the hell is this?" I got a phone call from a really cool PR guy. I found out later why he was so awesome and why he was so supportive of my magazine. He had originally worked at Slash Records. He was an old punk, but now had a wife and kids and needed to pay the bills, but still had that ethic. He asked me, "Do you want to interview these guys?" I said, "Yeah, this is like nothing I've ever heard." He said, "There have been some mainstream magazines clamoring to interview them and Zack only wants to do independent publications." This was around '91 or '92.

I think I went down to Warner Brothers. I don't know if they were on Warner, but Warner owned a lot of other labels, so it was just literally one big building of floors of different labels. It was just an interview with Zack. No one else was in it. We sat on the floor in a conference room. I started asking him questions. He started telling me about growing up in a bad neighborhood and that his father was schizophrenic. At one point, he started talking down to me like I was a little rich white girl and that I didn't understand. Something interrupted us, so I turned the tape recorder off and he left the room. Someone knocked on the door and needed him for something. He walked out. Then he apologized and came back in. I didn't turn the tape recorder back on. I basically said, "You're talking down to me and I really don't appreciate that. You're speaking to me like I grew up with everything handed to me with a silver spoon in my mouth and I just want to correct you on that." I told him where I grew up and that my dad was often unemployed and we would eat government cheese and government peanut butter. The rest of the interview definitely changed when I straightened him out. After the interview ended, we just started randomly talking like two people.

The second interview I ever did was pretty amazing and it totally freaked me out. It was Screamin' Jay Hawkins. I interviewed him at his house in the Valley. When I went to interview him, oddly enough, he had put out a new record. He hadn't released a record in twenty years. It was really the punk community that was there in support of him. It wasn't the blues community.

Some people I interviewed stand out. One of the things I didn't like about meeting bands is that your attitude could change one way or the other towards the music after you met them and you discovered that they were assholes. Or, the opposite would happen. I would walk away going, "Wow! That's actually really good."

The Stahl Brothers stand out. They're from the band Scream, which was Dave Grohl's punk rock band. I interviewed them and they were really, really cool.

Another person that stands out that I have high regard for is John Doe. I put him as one of the nicest musicians I've ever met. I've learned a lot about the music industry from him. He's really humble and appreciative. I think he's grateful he's been able to do what he likes to do, regardless of making a lot of money at it.

The other band that stands out as one of the nicest bands I ever met was the Deftones. I had a great conversation with them before they were famous and got huge. I interviewed them and we went to a two-dollar show in Berkeley. We had conversations about what would it be like if they got rich.

Mute on the Floor interviewed Nirvana when they were just a little punk rock band. We interviewed Kurt on the phone and he was going through withdrawals. He wasn't very talkative, and it was really boring. I found out through the assistant to the PR person, who was an old friend of mine working at Geffen, that the call was from Montana. He couldn't find drugs in Montana. He was going through withdrawals against his own wishes.

■　　■　　■　　■　　■

I think punk maybe reinforced that it's okay to not fit in. Maybe, if I had been part of a different group, it would be different. Even as a teenager, I knew that I didn't want children. I knew that was not the path that was going to be right for me. I have pretty strong thoughts on marriage and relationships and what that meant to me and what that was about.

Punk rock influenced me. It's in the decision I made, probably against my parents' wishes, to go off to art school and pursue things that probably weren't going to make me a lot of money. The same with photography. I think it influenced me to do a lot of things. I lived in London when I was seventeen. I don't think I would have done that if it wasn't for punk rock. I think it influenced me to do whatever I wanted to do. I was already thinking on my own. It was definitely the beginning of a change in my personality to go from a very, very quiet kid. After listening to punk rock, I started to understand about the bite and bark thing. I understood that I needed to start speaking up for myself and defending myself.

My junior high was known as the worst junior high in the area. It was more violent than the high school, so I really needed to buck up or I was going to get eaten alive. I started learning the process of basically telling someone to fuck off and get the fuck away from me. It always worked.

I still feel a connection to the scene. A lot of the bands are playing again, which is cool. I could probably go more in-depth on a whole bunch of stuff. It's kind of sad on some levels that I get to become a statistic of all those songs that I listened to back then. I've gotten more involved with the way our government runs. It's gotten worse and worse and worse and I'm a byproduct of our bad healthcare. I had to fly to India for surgery. My government refuses to help me and I don't qualify for any care, because they claim I made too much money the year before. I do feel outspoken. It's interesting that a lot has been very troubling in my life over the last six years, and that the last three years I've been getting back into punk more.

There are good aspects to it and bad aspects to my involvement in the scene. I would say there's more good than bad, due to the fact that I still have some of the friends that I made, even though I moved away for fifteen years and lived in San Francisco, Tahoe, L.A., and Seattle. After I moved back, they're still my friends.

I suppose that's possible in any other culture, but I think one of the things that makes people gravitate towards punk rock is coming from a very dysfunctional family. You try to get rid of that. You find a different family in this community.

KIRA

Born in 1961 in New Haven, Connecticut. Lived in New Haven and
Los Angeles, California, in the 1970s and '80s and played bass
for Waxx (1977), SAUPG (1977–present), the Visitors (1978),
the Monsters (1979), Twisted Roots (1980–1983), Sexsick (circa
1981), DC3 (1983), Black Flag (1983–1985), and Dos (1986–
present). Currently lives in Los Angeles, where she works as a
freelance sound editor and plays in the bands SAUPG, Dos, and
Awkward.

I WAS SIXTEEN when I first got involved with punk rock. Paul,
my older brother who is three years older than me, introduced it to
me. He went to school with Paul Beahm, who became Darby Crash
in the Germs. We were friends with those guys, him especially,
right into them starting the Germs. My first gig was a Germs
gig at the Whisky. My involvement at the beginning was as a fan,
although I was already playing the bass guitar. Later I started to
play with friends and played in numerous bands in Los Angeles.

I was going to high school every day. I was hungover a lot from

the night before. I was practicing
with bands almost every day.
Schlepping my bass. The scene was
full of people who weren't maybe
pushing that hard. They weren't
working all the time or weren't
working at all, but that wasn't me.

My first band was called
Waxx, with my brother on drums.
Although he was a keyboard player,
he didn't think that punk rock had
keyboards, so he played drums and

one of his good friends, Glenn, played guitar. We had another friend who sang. We got a gig through *Rodney on the ROQ*—a Sunday show at the Whisky. We played with Crime and the Dils in 1977.

I was called Candy Cane. That was my punk rock name at the time, because I thought we had to have one. I don't know how I came up with that. I'd gone to the thrift store and gotten this candy striper's outfit, so maybe it was that. I thought I had to have a name, as if my name isn't cool enough, which I now think it is.

My first band played a few shows. We didn't play very many because Paul joined the Screamers, who were much bigger and kind of known around town. The Screamers were a keyboard band, so it was a much better fit for him. Glenn, the guitar player, and I went on and had two more bands. One was called the Visitors with a guy named Spazz Attack who had been in a Devo video. That was his big claim to fame. He wasn't a great singer, but visually he was a really cool performer and dancer, so he was our singer. We had Dave Drive on drums, who later on was in several bands, including the Gears, who played around town for a long time. After that band, Spazz left and we were in a band called the Monsters. We got Nickey Beat from the Weirdos to join our band. The Weirdos had been one of my favorite bands, so that seemed like a real coup at the time. We had this other guy, Leroy, singing. The only problem was that Nickey was fixated on the fact that we couldn't play live until we could headline the Whisky, because, of course, he had headlined the Whisky with the Weirdos. So we never played live. He just couldn't start at the bottom, which is sort of understandable intellectually, but we were stuck. So we practiced a lot. All the bands practiced a lot. I can't tell you how much time I've spent in garages and practice pads playing in bands endlessly, with no gigs or very few.

In the early days at the Masque, they had practice rooms. I had this deal with the guy who ran it. I would cover in the afternoons, letting bands in and out and renting equipment. In return, he would give me free practice time. So, I would earn free practice for my bands. After school, after twelfth grade, I would come and get my band practice time. Those were my early band experiences.

I also played in a band with my brother called Twisted Roots. It was basically Paul's band and his songs. He was the ruler of that band. He threw me out three different times for various reasons that I don't think were related to my bass playing. I think I've been thrown out of every band I've been in that wasn't my band, and not for bass-playing reasons. Twisted Roots did record a set of things that is now out. There's a single that is out and there is an LP that is out under Paul Roessler and Twisted Roots or something.

I had my own band, Sexsick, that was supposed to be an all-girl band. My friend, Michelle Bell—Gerber, as she was known to some—and this girl named Elissa Bello, a drummer who had been thrown out of the Go-Go's because she wasn't cute enough or something. I can't say that for sure. I've heard such rumors. She was adorable by the way, so it doesn't really wash. We practiced a lot, but didn't play a lot of shows. By the time we did, Elissa quit or something, because we ended up with a guy drummer who had been in Twisted Roots as well. We sort of asked him to play with us.

My experience with all-girl bands is to not do it. My experience, specifically with playing in a band with other women, is that they don't treat it the way guys treat it. To guys, it's like work. The emotions are kind of taken out of it. It's like, you show up, you practice—there's no drama. With the girls it's like, "I'm tired." There was always something. It was somehow a big put upon to go to practice. I had been going to practice for years. I was buying practice time and stuff, and these girls were too tired or didn't feel like it. It was really a bit disheartening, but we did do that for a while and we did play a few shows, but we never recorded anything.

I had just joined DC3 with Dez Cadena and a drummer. We were going to have a three-piece power trio. We were all excited about that. They practiced at the same place as Black Flag. Two weeks into that, I got a call from Henry Rollins saying, "Do you want to be in Black Flag? Why don't you just stay after practice with DC3 and play with Bill and Greg." So I did, and it was weird. After practice with Dez, I hung around and they acted like they knew nothing about it, but they were up for it. So we jammed, and they asked me to join the same night. I got an opportunity and I took it. I have no regrets about any of it.

I was still going to UCLA the whole time. I said, "If I do this, I need to finish." I was three years into UCLA by then. This was 1983. I said, "I'll take quarters off, but we need to work around my schedules." I studied economic systems science, which is basically half economics and half computing and programming. My idea was that if I wasn't in music, I could do computers, and there would always be jobs in computers. Of course, nothing I used in college really was that useful in the end. You just finish, because you do.

I was in Black Flag from fall of '83 to fall of '85. I did a bunch of touring and made a bunch of records and then I started in Dos with my husband-to-be and now ex-husband Mike Watt. It's a two-bass band, and we have had this band now for twenty-seven

years. He plays bass. I play bass and I sing. At times it is largely
instrumental, but there is some significant amount of singing. I
have another band that is more of a project that I do some singing
in called Awkward, with a stand-up bass player, which is also a two-
bass band.

I've also had a virtual band with roots going back to 1977.
Glenn (the guitar player from Waxx, Visitors, and Monsters),
my brother, and I have recorded material over the years, which is,
as yet, unreleased. In the old days this was on cassette, including
bouncing cassette to cassette in order to multi-track. These days it
is done over the Internet, as Glenn lives in Ohio. In the early days,
I was a much more minor participant. We are actually working
towards some possible releases.

■　　■　　■　　■　　■

Billie Holiday has been very important to me from a young age. I
cover her in Dos. She is, in some way, perfect. It does not matter
what the style is in music. What matters is if it makes me feel,
and she makes me feel. There have been others that make me feel,
but she was sort of the first. I was so connected to her and her
unrequited love songs. You could just wallow in your misery with
her so perfectly. So she was big.

I had a very short Elton John phase. I saw him at Dodger
Stadium. I think it was my first gig, when I was thirteen or
fourteen. My brother got into prog rock stuff. I couldn't really get
into that. I sort of jumped over, more into Stones and Bowie. I had
huge Bowie and Rolling Stones phases. This was before I got into
punk rock. I was a hippie for about six months. It all happened
really, really fast. It accelerated because I was young, and then I was
into punk rock.

The Germs, obviously, they were friends of ours. I really
loved them. I loved the Weirdos. I loved the Avengers from San

Francisco. I think that might have started because I thought the
bass player was really cute, but it did grow. The Avengers grew on
me in other ways. They had a female singer [Penelope Houston]
who had spiky, short hair, and she was a little bit tough. I was a
tomboy from birth. When I was little, my school made me wear
skirts, but my mom got me these cool skirts that had shorts
underneath them, so at recess I could literally take the skirts off. I
am a hardcore tomboy. I identified with Penelope—with guys in
general, but with her.

I think it's weird when I'm asked questions about being a
woman, because guys don't think about being guys. It's kind of
weird that women think about being women, but we kind of
do and guys think about women being women, so I do get it. I
understand why I'm asked the question, but my first thought is
that it was never something I was really sort of conscious of. I was
so much less of a girlie girl than all the girlie girls that I didn't fit
in with them. I would hang out with the guys. To get into gigs, my
big thing was to hang out and move equipment at sound check so I
could maybe get in free, because I was broke. I didn't identify really
with the girls in the scene.

The cool thing, though, in the early days of punk rock was that
it was very heavily women. There were women who were powerful
women who were on the covers of the fanzines, because they were
setting the fashion trends. These girls weren't even in bands. They
just looked wild. I was sort of in awe of that. They were celebrities
and they weren't even doing anything, but looking incredibly
punk. That was really cool and in that way, it was welcoming.
Even onstage, you had a lot of women, especially bass players. The
Eyes had a girl bass player. The Alley Cats had a girl bass player.
The Bags had a singer and bass player. Practically every night at
the Masque, there were women onstage. The truth is that it was
happening before that. We had Patti Smith out there rocking it.

People forget the
Runaways. I tried to
get into the Runaways
at the Starwood when
I was thirteen. They
kind of laughed at me
and told me to go away.

I was never
intimidated. I never
felt that way. When
I picked up the bass
guitar, my brother was

in this prog rock band. They didn't have a bass player. I was like, I'm
going to practice really hard and get good enough. If I want to be
able to be a good bass player, I can. I never felt like I couldn't, and I
never felt like it had anything to do with being a woman or not.

When the scene got a little bigger, you had this sort of influx
of the South Bay influence. It did get a little less woman-heavy.
You had a lot of guys with short hair who wanted to slam. It got
a little less friendly. Pogoing was a lot easier and girl-friendly than
slamming. So there was a sort of shift. You could call it violent. I
don't think that was the intention of it. They were just guys being
guys. They were getting their rocks off banging into each other.
They didn't really care about the music. They could have done
it anywhere. It just happened to be that that was where it was
happening. I was there more to listen to the bands. I would never
go to the Fleetwood, because it was just one of those clubs where
you couldn't watch the band. Basically, there was this huge pit and
you could be plastered up against the wall. That's no fun. So, it did
get a little less friendly to women a bit later.

When I was in Black Flag, there were some difficult situations
at times, but there were also a lot of people who thought it was
really cool, so there were balancing factors. I had numerous
different political conflicts as a result of the fact of me being the
girl. It causes more friction than it should, because we're human.
I didn't behave perfectly professionally and others didn't behave
perfectly professionally, so, sure, there were issues. But it's almost
like anything. You're talking about a marriage of six to ten people.
We've got road crew; we've got other bands. You've got this sort of
microcosm happening. It's complicated. You're together all the time,
and there's no privacy. You're exhausted and emotional and you're
away from home. You're away from your emotional support. All of
that stuff.

Black Flag certainly forced me out. That is just a statement
of fact. As to why—they didn't want to play with me anymore, I
certainly played a part in that and they certainly had a part in that.
I think, truthfully, Henry is in touch with how hard it was for him.
Therefore, he's more able to see that, of course, it was physically so
demanding for me. It was trying to train for the Olympics. To Greg,
it was never that way. It was never that hard for him. I get that, and
I got it then. We'd practice until me and Bill would be dropping on
the floor, and then Greg would go jam with someone else. Guitar
is just easy, and Greg is just an animal. But physically, for me, I
was just absolutely against the wall all the time. I think Henry
understood that a lot, and Bill always was compassionate about
that. Drums being by far the most physical, he went through a lot
of that. We were always operating at full capacity. Pain. Exhaustion.
Endurance. Max. I think Henry acknowledges what it is and was
for me more sometimes than the others.

When it actually came down to it, Bill had been kicked out
first, before the 1985 tour. He had been a strong supporter of
mine. My behavior during the 1985 tour rubbed some people the

wrong way. By the end of the tour, they had decided to throw me out. What the exact reasoning was could be anything, or just how I behaved on the tour. It could be they had a sense that they wanted to do that before, but they needed to do the tour. Or it could just simply be that me being a woman did create some difficulties in and of itself. They would never admit that, because they chose to have a woman to begin with. Although they may appear to be misogynists, I would say that's not really who they were.

■　　■　　■　　■　　■

Of course the scene influenced me, because everything we experience influences us. In some ways it may have skewed my ego, because I was given some attention and level of importance that a lot of young people aren't. That often comes with a backlash of realizing you're just not important in the world. That's part of just growing up and maturing, but it may have been a little harder adjustment.

It's always interesting that today Black Flag is sort of a household name, so it will come out in a weird context. You see the look on someone's face and it totally changes their view of you right there. Bam! It is usually positive. They're like, "Whoa! You were in Black Flag." And you're like, "Yeah, and I'm the same person I was two minutes ago and that was thirty years ago." But no, to them it's like "Whoa!" It's usually cool, but it also makes me feel old. I've done so much since. It's like, "Really? That's it? That's who I am to you now?" It can be cool. It can give you some street cred with someone who's got some walls up, who maybe drops his walls down. You earn a little bit of respect in some way, but it was a long time ago. When people make too big of a deal of it, then I think they're minimizing everything that's happened since. They look at you. Clearly, you're not a punk rocker. It's like, "Dude, do you have any idea of how much of a nonconformist I still am to this day?"

I'm a total punker, but they don't know what it is.

What it is to me is that I don't conform to the rules, which means if you've got some rules about what punk rock is, I don't fit it. I don't want to fit it, 'cause that's gross, because punk rock isn't that. It's not fast and hard and loud. Yeah, Dos isn't fast and hard and loud, but it's really punk, because how many two-bass bands do you hear? I'm constantly pushing the envelope, still. It's frustrating in that way. You were this, but you're not cool anymore. You're a traitor, because you have a job or whatever. You know what I mean? It becomes a little bit frustrating if it gets turned into "You were only cool then."

In a way I'm thankful that I was involved in it so long and so far from, in a way, the beginning. I'm not trying to make myself bigger than I am, but I was there and I feel like I've seen it evolve from such small roots to this resurgence that's happening today. I'm able to sort of say I think I kind of know what is and isn't punk. When someone tries to tell me the rules, I resist that. Being a tomboy at my core, I don't fit in. I don't fit with girls. I don't fit with boys. I don't fit with your idea of what punk rock is. I don't fit with the intellectual crowd. I don't fit in with the creative crowd that does movies. I'm a total weirdo to them, too. I don't fit in anywhere. I worked in the corporate world for eleven years. Total weirdo there, too. Me and my dogs. We can relate to each other, but most people, I don't relate well to. I think that's absolutely part of this whole punk rock thing we're talking about, because you don't necessarily conform into it and go, "Well, if I just do xyz, then I will be more accepted." It's never been about being accepted.

I got into punk rock and I got to be, in a sense, validated. There are other people who sort of feel that way, too. Fighting the society. Fighting the disco at the time. And the hippies. Being anti-everything, it seemed. Because at the time, it seemed like that was okay. Sort of hating things was okay and that was kind of what I

needed, 'cause that's kind of who I was. I felt validated enough that I got to take of it what made sense to me. That was then, and I've moved past it. Not that I've moved past it [to the point] that I'm not a punker anymore, but I've incorporated that into who I am today. I still play. I still write music. I still do all sorts of things, and it manifests itself in this whole other way. That growth and maturity and change is normal and a part of being human.

I see a lot of people who are sort of hung up on those being the glory days. None of the music since then is any good, or whatever. And I say, no. Even if I have no idea about the new music, it's me that hasn't gone out and found the good new music. It's out there. I'm convinced it is. It wasn't better then. It may be what I knew then. I might have gone to more shows then, so I saw more bands live, and seeing bands live, you get that tactile experience of it. I'm sure you could get that today. It takes some work to be part of a scene. I'm sure there are scenes. It may be the fact that it was small [that] helped. I don't buy the idea that that was somehow special and unique, because we were there. I'm glad I was there. I got some great validation, but I'm sure someone who's a teenager today could do it. I don't believe it was a unique, special time. And I don't believe that being a woman was necessarily a unique experience that way. I'm merely saying that, from my standpoint, it was equal that way. And in some ways that's the most important thing about being a woman—to feel equal and part of, and not feel put down or separated. We tend to feel ostracized by something that is a little bit male-oriented, and I don't think that was. Sure, I had to get my hands dirty sometimes. There were some badass girls. You had to be willing to fall into some difficult situations, but that's true in life, right? I mean, sometimes you need to stick up for yourself, and I don't mean physically or [to] fight, but I do mean you have to pick those battles which mean a lot to you and stand your ground.

KIRSTEN (BRUCE) MEEKINS

Born in 1969 in Redlands, California. Lived in Redlands in the '80s and attended shows at various venues throughout Los Angeles, Riverside, San Bernardino, and Orange Counties. Currently lives in Virginia City, Nevada, and works as a teacher.

I THINK I WAS AROUND FOURTEEN. I went through the new wave phase in the early '80s, but I think it was around 1984 or '85 that I really started listening to punk.

I came from a musical family. My mom taught guitar from our home when I was growing up, so I always had musical influence in general. My parents took me to both US Festivals in '82 and '83. The first year, I got stuck with their music: Grateful Dead, Jerry Jeff Walker, Jimmy Buffett, etc. I still like some of this music, but the next year they were cool and we went to the new wave day. This was my first live music venue besides some small bluegrass events.

Growing up in SoCal, we had the influence of KROQ, so I had already been listening to bands like the Stray Cats and the Clash, both of whom were on the bill at the '83 US Festival along with Flock of Seagulls and the English Beat. I have to give huge credit to KROQ and Rodney Bingenheimer's show as being a major influence. Also, in Redlands at the time, the university had a radio station and every day after school they had a punk show. I'll never forget the politically charged set by the Clash and their last performance with Mick Jones. The Clash instantly became my favorite band, and I miss the hell out of Joe Strummer to this day.

Aside from the musical influences from my parents, I distinctly remember friending a mostly unpopular boy in middle school named Tom. Tom had his hair bleached white and always wore flannels and boots. I was immediately attracted to the style. I had already cut my long hair short and was experimenting with color. One day in class, I caught a glimpse of his Pee-Chee folder on his desk and it had all kinds of band names written on it. Some I recognized, but one that I did not stuck out in my mind: the Toy Dolls. What a silly name, I thought. I asked him about them, and the next day he brought me a cassette tape full of stuff I had never heard and I was hooked. I think after that, we sought out punk rock at local record shops and started picking up flyers there and going to shows.

We went to shows religiously—every weekend. In the beginning, there weren't any shows in Redlands, so we always had to find someone who drove to get us to the gigs. I think my first show was at the De Anza Theatre in Riverside. It was the Circle Jerks and I can't remember who else, but I do remember someone shot off a gun inside during the show and then people started rioting, tearing seats from the floor and throwing them. Excitement level 100 for a first show! Throughout the years, we traveled all around SoCal for shows—mostly Riverside, San Bernardino, Corona, Pomona, and Los Angeles. I went to shows at Linda's Doll Hut, the Olympic Auditorium, the Grange, Monopolys, the Glass House, the Cathay, the Barn at UC Riverside, Madame Wong's, Spanky's Café, the Whisky, and I'm sure a whole bunch of small places I can't remember the names of.

I do remember that Social Distortion and D.I. seemed to be

"house" bands for a lot of these venues, playing in one of them every weekend. I still have an affinity for SD, and Mike Ness's voice still makes me feel invincible, like a kid. Nothing better than driving my '55 Buick and screaming along to "Telling Them" with Mike Ness.

Once we were at a show at the Olympic in L.A., watching Social Distortion back when we used to joke that the long sleeves Mikey wore were the only thing keeping his arms attached. He had developed a nasty heroin habit by then. After the show, we found him wandering around, so we went up and talked to him and ended up sitting on the floor of the Olympic drinking beer with him as they closed down. The rest of the band had left him there. It's one of my best memories.

Aside from shows, I wrote a few pieces for *Maximum Rocknroll*. That and *Flipside* were huge influences back then.

■   ■   ■   ■   ■

By 1985, I had regrown my hair for a year or so just so I could cut a mohawk that would be twelve inches when up. The summer of my sophomore year, my boyfriend and I cashed in all the money we had, which was around a thousand dollars, and we hopped a Greyhound bus bound for NYC. I had become obsessed with the story of Sid and Nancy, and I was determined to stay in room 100 of the Chelsea Hotel. Long story short, we made it as far as Wisconsin, spent the summer there with his extended family on a farm, and never made it to the Chelsea. I did come home and immediately went on a trip to Hawaii with my family with my freshly cut mohawk and pierced nose.

I started out listening to the standard punk rock: Black Flag, Circle Jerks, Fear, Dead Kennedys. Around 1986, I got involved in the skinhead movement and started listening to more of the Oi bands like the Business, Cock Sparrer, Skrewdriver, the Cro-Mags, etc.

I do have to say that the band that had the biggest impact on my life was Bad Religion. It is still one of my favorites to this day for two reasons. One, I was raised completely without religion, but everyone I knew claimed some sort of affiliation with some kind of church, so I was an outsider there. BR gave a voice to those of us that were raised without it and had never bought into it. It made me do research, and I believe it really sparked my desire to always question and seek out answers on my own. Number two, along those lines, I was always impressed that the guys in the band were educated and were constantly in school. Punk rock was their voice, but they had passions for other things. Same with Milo from the Descendents. I loved the smart things they sang about.

There was sort of a division in punk rock then. A lot of the kids thought punk rock was about being homeless, saying fuck the man, and begging for change and cigarettes down at the mall. I went the other way and became academic and entrepreneurial.

I never really thought about the scene and women until I got into the skinhead scene. I felt that punk rock was welcoming to everyone. Even with the skins, we had black skins in our circle, so I never felt there was prejudice in the beginning. As the skinhead scene grew and gang affiliations got bigger, there was a clear division between punks and skins, whites and other races, and men and women.

Skinhead Confessions by T. J. Leyden is half of my story. We grew up together. His right-hand man in the book was my best friend, and he even mentions my daughter's father. He makes a clear point that women were around but not prominent, at least in that scene. I was on my way out of that scene around '87, '88.

■   ■   ■   ■   ■

I always listened to other kinds of music. Being brought up with music, I appreciated a lot of stuff no one else had ever heard. I

really liked the old folk-type stuff, mainly because it is what my
mom played on her guitar and listened to in the house. This
included Marty Robbins, Hank Williams Sr., Don McClean,
and Jim Croce. I also got into Black Sabbath for a while and
started playing the bass guitar. I never really got into the '80s stuff
everyone loves today like Depeche Mode, but I do love me some
Flock of Seagulls! I like a handful of typical '80s stuff now, like the
Psychedelic Furs, the Cult, etc.

I don't think my musical taste changes; I think it grows. I've
never abandoned my punk rock roots, and if I'm listening to music,
probably eight out of ten times it's punk. For me, music has to
make me feel something. I have to want to sing or cry or dance
or something in order to like it. I love some of almost all forms
of music now. Even stuff I thought I hated, I now appreciate. For
example, I have attended Burning Man for the last three years and
the music out there is predominantly played by DJs and is that
electronic, repetitive, never-ending cacophony of sound. Somehow,
out there in the wide-open desert, it works and I like it. I'm not
rushing out to buy any CDs, but I like to appreciate things in the
moment, in the context in which they are being presented.

Right now I am really liking some of the newer folk-inspired
bands, like Rose's Pawn Shop and the Avett Brothers. Rockabilly
is big in one of my circles, so I listen and frequently go to shows
of that nature. I'm into old cars and antique motorcycles, and this
scene has seemed to adopt a lot of the rockabilly music scene. They
say rockabilly is where old punks go to retire.

■   ■   ■   ■   ■

I know punk rock influenced my life. I think it formed the basis of
my personality. It definitely sparked my creativity and ambition,
and it led me down an academic path and taught me to question
everything and seek out answers to things I don't know, rather than

to hold on to one-sided opinions and beliefs. I still constantly buck the system when I think it is wrong! It has taught me to live life and not to be afraid of trying things, even if the attempt leads to failure.

I have owned and built several businesses in my days. The first was a punk rock record store. After my second business, a multimedia marketing firm, I went back to school and received my undergraduate degree in business and management. After that, I went on to receive both my elementary and secondary teaching credentials, as well as a master's degree in teaching. I spent five years teaching middle and high school graphic and web design classes. I am currently working in a foster home with four teenaged girls. I know it is my background, especially in punk rock beliefs and values, that has instilled a love of teaching and nurturing kids today. School isn't always about test scores, and not all kids go to college. I had no problem telling my students this. It didn't make me popular with teachers, but I really did try and instill the passion to follow your dreams in these kids. College is great and I think everyone should do it, but not always just to gain a career. It teaches responsibility and gets you knowledge you may never seek out on your own and hopefully gets you out of your hometown. I'm all about seeking knowledge and less about SAT scores.

I am very successful with the teenaged girls that I care for. I get them. I wasn't ever in foster care and was the only person I knew growing up whose parents were still married, but if nothing else, I have a great understanding of human nature and I connect with those that are more misfortunate, creative, and sometimes outcast.

I totally still feel connected to the scene. I still go to shows. Most of the best people I have met in my adult life are old punks. I'm still connected to a handful of my friends from high school, the ones who got their shit together, and I have met some outstanding friends just in the last two years or so through the antique motorcycle scene, all of whom seem to have roots in punk rock. I guess we gravitate together. I think it has influenced our adult hobbies, such as cars and bikes. I still have my pair of blue Doc Marten boots I got on my sixteenth birthday, and wear them occasionally on motorcycle rides. And keeping with tradition, when purchasing a new pair of moto boots, I ended up buying another pair of Docs.

I had a daughter in 1986, and she was raised around punk rock. Although she didn't carry on in that specific scene, she has a great appreciation for music and a love of some of my favorite old bands. We have gone to several shows together over the years. She is twenty-seven and has a seven-year-old daughter of her own now. I'm proud to be a punk rock grandma!

I feel very fortunate having grown up where and when I did. I had a rocking childhood. I wouldn't trade my involvement in the scene for all the money in the world.

KRISTINE McKENNA

Born in 1953 in Dayton, Ohio. Lived in Los Angeles, California, in the 1970s and '80s, attended shows at various venues throughout Los Angeles County, and worked as a journalist covering the punk rock scene for the *Los Angeles Times* and other publications. Currently works as a self-employed writer in California.

I WAS BORN IN DAYTON, OHIO, and I lived there until I was three or four. I'm the middle of three children, and I have an older sister and a younger brother. My father was a violent alcoholic who left when I was about four, and my mother raised us by herself. We moved to Los Angeles around 1958. I think my mother wanted to become independent of her family, who were controlling, so she came out here.

I went to art school at Cal State Fullerton and got a degree as a painter. At that point, most of the painters at that school were taught to be photorealist painters, so that's how I was trained. When I got out of school in 1976, I couldn't get a job, and I had a graphic designer friend named Eric Munson who'd moved to Los Angeles. He said, "Why don't you come up and you can be my roommate?" So I moved in with him in this horrible storefront in a frightening neighborhood for seventy-five dollars a month. The day I got to L.A., I looked in the want ads and got a full-time job at Capitol Records filing royalty statements, which was the most boring job on earth.

Through my roommate, I heard about the Masque and started going to all the shows there, and I immediately loved it. The Masque was a filthy subterranean dungeon in a basement off an alley off of Hollywood Boulevard. You'd go down the stairs and you'd be in this basement. There was graffiti everywhere, and there were bathrooms that were completely trashed and disgusting that you'd never want to go to the bathroom in. The whole thing was a little scary. It was a small, crowded place, and in the summer it was hot in there. You were right up on the band, because there wasn't really a stage, so the audience and the band were almost completely intermingled. Everybody was excited, because they knew they had something new.

My favorite band right from the start was X. They were just amazing. The Screamers were very theatrical, like a performance art group, and they were really good, too. I loved the Plugz, and Dred Scott, and the Zeros, and Black Randy and the Metrosquad, because he was completely insane and a great showman. There were other bands that I didn't love, but they were all interesting.

I started writing letters to Robert Hilburn at the *Los Angeles Times*, saying, "You're not writing about this stuff. You should let me write about these shows, because the paper isn't covering them." I also started writing to *Rolling Stone*. I was very motivated and just struck out on my own. I guess you could say I was a feminist in that it never occurred to me that I couldn't do what I wanted to do as a writer, and I wrote to lots of different publications. Robert Hilburn let me start covering punk rock for the *Los Angeles Times*, and it just all grew from there. I think I learned to write from growing up reading *The New Yorker*. I always loved reading magazines, and journalism went through a golden period in the late '60s and '70s. What you could do within the format of a magazine article really exploded then, and it was inspiring. In L.A., we had *Slash* magazine and all these underground magazines, and I started writing for a lot of them.

I felt like I could help serve this stuff up to the public, because very few people knew about it then. I also wrote for *New York Rocker*, which came out in New York. I was the West Coast editor for *New Musical Express*, which was an alternative music publication in London. I wrote for lots of different places, and many of them were underground publications. I realized that if you're determined enough and you're interested in something, you can find a place to write about it.

People in the punk scene found out fairly quickly that I was writing about punk for the *L.A. Times*, because I wrote a piece on the Masque and interviewed Brendan Mullen. I was always treated with respect, and I totally felt part of that community because it was a small community and I was really committed. I was at shows four nights a week and I saw the same people all the time. Anybody who was committed enough to show up all the time was a respected member of the community.

■   ■   ■   ■   ■

I was always interested in alternative culture. All of my friends always took drugs. I didn't, but I was always around people on drugs, and I always stood outside the norm and never had conventional goals. I think this was partly because of the family structure I grew up in, and not having a father. How to build a conventional family wasn't modeled for me, and I never had that plan of, "I'm going to get married and have children" or "I'm going to get a PhD." I was really wandering aimlessly for the first twenty-five years of my life.

I think I've led a feminist life in that I've been really independent and certainly never depended on a man. None of my goals have ever revolved around that. I haven't had children, I've never been married, and I've led an unconventional life. A lot of the people who came out of that scene went on to lead unconventional lives. A lot of them died young, too. I felt conservative in that scene. In the eyes of the people there, I probably seemed that way. I'm really not conservative, but I didn't dress like a punk or try to blend in, and never felt like I had to look like everybody else there.

One of the things that was great about the early punk scene was that it had very peculiar sexual politics. Women were really on an equal footing with men, and gender wasn't an issue. It wasn't like, "Oh, a woman singer." It was just a person, and those issues really weren't on the table. I always found that early punk scene very non-sexual. It was about something else. It was about people being individuals, and I don't think women presented themselves in traditional ways to please men. It was very different in that way. There were really amazing women musicians in the scene that weren't categorized as women musicians. They were just musicians.

When it first started out, punk had a very bad reputation. Shows happened all over town, and it moved around all over the city, and people were always looking for new places where they could do shows. There'd be a punk show at a venue, and everybody would trash the place, and there would never be another punk show there. This happened at the Stardust Ballroom, the Larchmont Hall, the Ukrainian Culture Center—punk tore through lots of places. The clubs that ended up being staples were Club 88 on Pico, the Whisky, and the Hong Kong Café. The Masque was always the most important, though, and it was closed down repeatedly by the fire marshals. There was briefly a place called the Second Masque, at the corner of Santa Monica Boulevard and Vine, and there were a few shows there. Brendan's shows were always huge. There'd be five bands on the bill, and the show would last forever.

For the first six months of my writing life I just covered punk, but I love all kinds of music and I quickly started moving into other kinds. I always specialized in the weird underground stuff, though. I was a champion of Nick Cave, and I wrote about Tom Waits early on in their careers, when people weren't really into them yet. I started doing interviews almost right away, and my first substantial piece in the *Times* was the interview with Brendan Mullen. In 1978, I conducted my first lengthy interview when I spoke with Iggy Pop for *WET Magazine*. I subsequently published two collections of interviews, *Book of Changes* in 2001, and *Talk to Her* in 2004.

I was really shy and withdrawn when I was growing up, so I always identified with the weirdos that didn't fit in, because that's how I felt I was. The early punk rock community was a haven for those kinds of people. I totally felt like it was my tribe, but I was a little shy in that scene, too. In doing interviews, my curiosity superseded my shyness, though, and I was able to do it. I've done thousands of interviews. The ones in my two books are culled from a really long list. They all meant something to me.

A few of the people I interviewed made me nervous, but you never know who's going to. Some really famous people made it very easy and were lovely, while other people made it hard. In the punk scene, Exene and X were just so great. I was impressed with them and I really admired them. Exene is an extraordinary and really unique person, and it was exciting getting to know her. I got to know Craig Lee from the Bags, and we became friends—he was very smart and funny. I interviewed Black Randy once, briefly, and he was scary. I loved interviewing Brendan Mullen because Brendan was a fantastic person. He had so much energy and passion and he really could make things happen.

A couple of people I interviewed I really revere. Leonard Cohen would be first on that list, because talking to him is like medicine. He's very wise and he has a really light touch and he's funny. I've interviewed him a few times, and it meant a lot to me. Interviewing Jacques Derrida was pretty mind-blowing, particularly since I feel like I know very little about philosophy. I crammed for that, of course. The interview I did with Nina Simone isn't particularly good, but it was amazing getting to talk to her.

I interviewed people in different kinds of places: Jacques Derrida in his crummy office at U.C. Irvine; Exene in my tiny

apartment in the Los Altos on Wilshire Boulevard; Iggy Pop
at the Tropicana Motel, which doesn't exist anymore. I did lots
of interviews in hotels, quite a few backstage at concerts, and I
occasionally met with people in their homes. I interviewed Nico
in the apartment of Paul Morrissey, who was part of the Warhol
crowd with Nico. I did lots of interviews at the Chateau Marmont
when it used to be shabby and charming.

■   ■   ■   ■   ■

Making a living as a freelance journalist was possible back then
when I started, but it's barely possible now because of the way
journalism has changed. It took me a while to be able to make a
living at it, though, and for the first seven years that I was writing,
I had to have other jobs, too. I quit the horrible job at Capitol
Records after a year, and after that I was an assistant to an artist,
and I worked in a couple of galleries. Beginning in 1984, and up
through 1998, I made a decent living as a journalist. Then a very
sad thing happened to journalism with the Internet, and papers
started dying. I left the *L.A. Times* in 1998, after twenty-two years,
and at approximately the same time, things started drying up for
freelance journalists. I realized I had to reinvent my career and
started working on books.

When I left the *Times*, I started working on a biography of
the artist Wallace Berman, and I ended up collaborating with art
historian Michael Duncan. We co-curated *Semina Culture: Wallace
Berman and His Circle*, a huge exhibition featuring fifty artists that
traveled to five museums in the country between 2005 and 2007.
We produced a beautiful catalogue for the show. When I was
studying to be a painter, I curated an exhibition at the Los Angeles
Institute of Contemporary Art in 1976. Then I didn't curate
another show until 2005. Since then, I've organized approximately
a dozen shows, including two exhibitions of Exene's collages. I love

her and her work. Organizing an exhibition has to be a labor of
love, because you don't get paid much to do it.

I also worked on a book with photographer Ann Summa
called *The Beautiful and the Damned*. She's a very dear friend who
I met in the punk scene, and she took tons of photos back in the
day. I always wanted to go through her contact sheets and pick out
images I loved, and she let me do that, which was really nice of her,
and we made that book. She very kindly allowed me to include
some pictures she wasn't crazy about, and I really appreciate that.
I think the book we made together is very beautiful. I've also
made ten other books—countercultural histories, photography
monographs, and so forth.

■   ■   ■   ■   ■

I fell away from punk in 1982 when hardcore took over, because
there wasn't a place for women in that scene. There were a lot of
movements in the '80s, like the new romantics and new wave music,
but I didn't care about any of that. I definitely still feel a connection
to punk, though, and I still love the music. Punk is clearly what
galvanized me as a writer, because I wasn't writing before I
encountered that music. I've never taken a writing class, and I
don't know what made me think I could write about this stuff, but
I could. It came easily, maybe because I wanted to share it, and I
wanted the bands to get credit for how wonderful they were. I feel
really lucky and grateful that I got to be part of that world and that
moment in time, because it had genuine meaning.

LAURA BETH BACHMAN

Born in 1965 in Milwaukee, Wisconsin. Lived in Palos Verdes, California, in the '80s and attended shows at various venues in Los Angeles County and Orange County. Currently lives in Lomita, California, where she works in healthcare for underserved populations and plays drums for the Neptunas.

I THINK I WAS ABOUT FOURTEEN. I was in high school. My best girlfriend had a boyfriend who was a little bit older than us. He exposed us to a lot of music, like local punk rock stuff that was happening. We started going to shows with him. He would take groups of people, and that also introduced me to more people who were going to see live music and who were listening to punk rock.

The first show is significant to me. It is a very strong memory. It was at Godzilla's. In my memory, the bands that were playing were Channel 3 and the Adolescents, though there is nobody to corroborate that show actually happened. It is probably a hybrid of bands that I saw, but I definitely remember it being at Godzilla's. It was very overwhelming to me.

It was probably '82 or '83, which would put me at about fourteen or fifteen. All of these dates are give or take a year or two. I'm not totally clear. We got to this place, and my memory of it is that there were hundreds of people. I was cultivating a look to the best of my ability, with some limitations. I didn't have a lot of cash flow. I was a teenager. I had

very conservative parents who kind of forbade a lot of the clothes I wanted to wear. I also didn't know where to buy them. I didn't know how to make my hair look a certain way, but I saw pictures of boys and girls that looked a certain way and I was trying to be that way.

When I went to this show, I thought, "What? Where do these people live?" I was seeing mohawks and leather jackets with studs. This was not something I saw regularly where I grew up. I remember looking for any sign of punk rock in people I would see in the streets in my neighborhood and where I went to high school. There were just a handful of them.

This first show was overwhelming, because the thing that I remember most was that there were so many people that were like what I wanted to be and what I wanted. I felt connected to them somehow. I still felt like an outsider a bit, because I hadn't really figured it out, but that was my introduction to this whole counterculture.

At the time, we saw whoever played. We jumped in a guy's pickup truck and we all just went. Because of where I lived, in the southwest portion of Los Angeles, there was a really great punk rock scene and I got to see many bands. We are talking about the stretch between the L.A. airport and the harbor. At that time, in the '80s, we had Black Flag, Circle Jerks, the Descendents, the Minutemen, and tons of other bands. We had a label: SST.

There was a place called Mi Casita, which was just this Mexican restaurant that for some reason allowed these shows to happen. I saw the Suburban Lawns there. I saw Black Flag there. There were so many great shows in that little place. It's a McDonald's now.

There was another place that still exists called Alpine Village. It's a big stretch of land just off the Harbor Freeway in Torrance. They had a good-sized auditorium in there and were having punk rock shows in the '80s. I saw lots of shows there. I remember seeing the Dead Kennedys there.

There were a couple of different things that were happening at the shows. There was what would be interpreted as violence that wasn't violence. That was interpreted by maybe non-punk rock people somewhere like on the news. They would show a video snip of people dancing, which looked like violence, but wasn't. The intention wasn't violent. However, it became violent sometimes when people pushed each other around. There was violence. Punk rock evolved, and unfortunately things developed that were very territorial. There were definitely factions and there eventually were gangs, which I don't really want to talk too much about, because it wasn't part of my story. It is like an unsavory and really terrible and sad part of what happened to punk rock. I think that is more boy punk rock. I know there are girls that were in some of these gangs that developed, but it wasn't people that I knew or that I was close to. There was violence between punk rockers. There was also violence outward.

I have never been in a fight. I'm six feet tall. Maybe girls don't want to pick a fight with me, but I wasn't a violent person. I was inherently opposed to violence, because that was the thing I didn't like about my life that I couldn't control in my upbringing. I didn't want to beat anyone up. It is not magical thinking, but I think, because I wasn't interested in being violent, it didn't come to me. Violence didn't come to me.

■   ■   ■   ■   ■

There is an infinite number of ways to be a teenager in this world. My personal experience with being a teenager was I really didn't believe that I fit in with the majority of people that I encountered in high school. There was something about punk rock. I discovered the music through a handful of people, and then discovered the whole culture subsequent to the music. I think the music spoke to me, and it spoke to me because I was troubled. I was lost. I didn't feel connected to anything or anybody. There were lots of things I could have connected to, but none of that fit.

I think there was also an aesthetic in punk rock that was very separated from the mainstream. Honestly, there was a violence to it that I connected to, because I grew up in a violent situation. There was something about the violence that felt familiar that I didn't see anywhere else. There was something about an expression of anger that I didn't see with the surf culture. At the time, there was a preppy culture that I didn't connect to. With punk rock, I felt like it was us against the world. I didn't feel that way with other kids.

It was definitely a sense of belonging that I didn't feel somewhere else. I think it was because those other kids had struggles, too. The connection was born of a special brand of teenage angst and confusion. Everybody finds where they belong. The reason that spoke to me was because I was struggling, and so were the others. In retrospect as a fifty-year-old, I think every single teenager struggles. It is a coming of age. I had exposure to other types of groups of kids, and that's the one that fit.

My primary connection to punk rock for many, many years was as an audience member that connected with the social part of the scene and the music. There was a community and a camaraderie that I felt. Then, much later, when I was thirty years old, I started playing music. It was a punk rock band at the very beginning of the 1990s. It was post-'80s punk, and my sister and I started a band of our own called Ball Gagger with a friend named Johanna Hackett. That ended up being the beginning of a lifetime of playing drums in different types of music. It took me so long to do it, because I didn't know that I could.

We made up everything. It was really important to me. Music was extremely important to me. I wanted to do it. Instead of worrying about how, we just decided, "Okay, anyone can buy instruments." My sister bought a Fender guitar and then an amp. I got a drum kit. We had friends in a band. It was the same guy who introduced me to punk rock. We shared a studio space with his band called the Smut Peddlers. This was in Hermosa Beach.

We just brought our equipment and got in a room with Johanna Hackett playing bass. We just made it up. We had no idea really how to do it. Later, my sister took guitar lessons and learned how to craft a song and became a legitimate songwriter and singer and guitar player, but we didn't know what we were doing. I still pretty much don't until this day. We were inspired by the spirit of punk rock. We manifested it by making it up.

It was probably 1994 when we started playing shows. Early on, we got to put out a record by a local independent record label called Theologian Records, owned by Marc Theodore. He supported us and was really great to us. That record label supported a tour. We did a month-long tour of the United States. The band itself lasted several years. We put out a full-length record called *Ache*.

I was able to join another band immediately after. I think it actually overlapped with Ball Gagger. I joined a surf band called the Neptunas, which I am still in today. It was a big deal to me, because I love surf music. I loved surf music simultaneous to punk rock. The Neptunas existed prior to me. I joined probably in 1996 or 1997. We sort of went into a hiatus for about ten years. Then, about a year and a half ago, the Breeders asked us to tour with them, so we resurrected the band. Now we have fallen back in love with each other and with our music. We are continuing to play now.

■   ■   ■   ■   ■

I didn't ever feel that I was not welcome in the scene because I was a girl. I think the boys wanted girls there for boy reasons. I was invited in the pickup truck just like everybody else. It was as important for girls to be there as boys. I think that was just the nature of the experience.

I am not a traditional woman. There was something empowering to me about doing things that boys do. Sadly, that comes from boys having more power. However, you can also, as a girl, maybe extract some of that power by doing boy things. I like surfing. I like playing drums. I did longshoring for a while. A lot of my attraction to those things was because they were things that women traditionally didn't do, so it felt empowering to do them.

I was raised by a very traditional woman who is a Sicilian immigrant. She worked, but she was a nurse, so she did a very traditional women's job. She was married very young and is still to this day married to my father. I didn't decide to be different than her out of disdain for her. I think I just wanted to feel empowered, because I didn't feel empowered as a kid or as a teenager. I wanted to do things. I never consciously said I'm going to be different than the tradition. I was attracted to doing things that made me feel empowered. Men are inherently considered more powerful, and the things that they do are considered maybe more powerful. It is irrelevant whether it is fair or not, because we live with that. So do what you want to do. If it makes you feel more powerful to do things that are boy things, why not?

I've never been married. I am attracted to men, I just haven't married one. I don't have children. I really am outside of the tradition of what a heterosexual woman my age does. I love men and I love having relationships with them. I love working alongside of them. I just didn't do things the way that everybody else does them.

Punk rock was definitely an empowering experience. Because I never felt unwelcomed by men, it also allowed me to step into an arena with men. Whether it was going to shows, playing music, contributing in some way, through art or whatever, or literature, you had kind of an equal footing. When you have that, you are not as likely to just make a default choice because of tradition.

Being a teenager, it doesn't matter really what you are involved in at that time. I got really lucky that it was punk rock. It was something that was new to the world. It taught me so much. Most of my coming-of-age experiences happened in that framework. I learned how to assert myself, especially a little later when I was making music. My band being heard mattered more than me being shy. I learned how to assert myself because I learned that if I didn't, I wouldn't enjoy my life as much. I think I could have learned it from other things, but this is where I was and it was the time I was in.

I learned that sometimes things matter more than what you are afraid of. It doesn't matter what has happened to you. It doesn't matter how afraid you are. You can still do something, because something else matters more than whatever you are afraid of. I learned that in punk rock. I learned that because of the songs I listened to. I learned it because there was a communal spirit. I found that the spirit of contributing to something bigger has helped me in being a person in a working world and being able to contribute as a team member in a job and caring and working towards a better thing. Still, the scene wasn't always all-inclusive. If people tell you that everyone was accepted, that wasn't my experience. I watched people be mean to each other, and that was part of what happened. I learned a lot about life.

I earn my living doing something that I feel matters. No matter how I feel about the people I work with, we all want to keep the ship afloat, because the ship being afloat can help more people. I learned that in the community spirit of punk rock. It is that "us against the world" kind of thing, but in a good way. It is us against the world, because we want to contribute to the world. Whatever injustice you think is going on, find the other people who feel the same, and you can work together. I learned a lot of that from punk rock.

There is a phantom of the 1980s punk rock scene. Its ghost lives. If you talk about a specific time frame, it's over. Those of us who survived our life have continued. That time frame and those things that happened, they aren't here now, but the memory of it is. It also lives because that particular time frame influenced a lot of things. It influenced politics. It influenced art. It influenced music. There is something very special about punk rock, and it will live on forever.

There were probably more men than women in the scene. The women continue to be the women who inspire me the most in this world. I don't want to begrudge all the amazing women in this world who have lived and who live now and who will live that do other things besides play punk rock music. Even though they make new, inspiring women every day, those women, those early punk rock women, they kind of forged a way for us. There's a certain grit to a punk rock woman. I think all women have it, but we don't all show it. The truth of the world is it takes grit to survive as a woman.

LINDA ZIGGY DANIELS

Born in 1966 in San Diego, California. Lived in England and Los Angeles, Hollywood, and San Francisco, California, in the '80s and attended shows at various venues throughout England, Los Angeles, San Francisco, and Orange Counties. Currently lives in Mendocino County, California, and works as a caretaker, horse caretaker, organic gardener, and community activist.

I CAN GIVE YOU MY ROAD TO PUNK ROCK. When I was really young, in the early '70s, I was listening to Shaun Cassidy and the Partridge Family. I admit it. Then I got into Kiss. I totally got into Kiss in a big way. I saw them, I think, in 1978. Then I got to see Devo in 1979. That was the time I started listening to the new wave, ska, and punk stuff.

I consciously and actively became punk rock in 1979 and started going to shows in 1980, '81, when I was thirteen or fourteen. When I first got involved in the punk scene, I was living in the San Fernando Valley. I was part of the SFV Punks, San Fernando Valley Punks, in the west end. I went to Columbus Jr. High School. I was the only girl punk at my school. We were the very first punk rockers in my junior high. One of my teachers was the legendary rockabilly musician Ray Campi. I went to El Camino High School with people from Bad Religion and Fishbone.

Some of my first shows were the Dickies at the Starwood,

the Ramones and Black Flag at the Palladium and the Stardust Ballroom. I hung out at Oki Dogs a lot and went to shows at the Starwood. There was also a place called Phases in Canoga Park— that I hung out at before I was old enough or able to go to shows— which was a disco that a lot of punks hung out at and used to go dance to new wave, which was pretty fun. That was 1980.

A lot of the time, I couldn't get into shows because I was underage. It was also very difficult to get the buses out to Hollywood at that time, before they built the subway/Red Line. I would just hang out with my friends outside, and that was just as important as actually going in. Physically hearing the bands playing inside, knowing I couldn't get in because I was so young, but still hanging out and hearing the bands was totally as important as going in.

There was one show—I think it was a Black Flag show. It was such a horrifically violent show. It was another show that got shut down by the police and by the owners of the Stardust Ballroom. The cool thing about that was when everybody was going in, they were making us take all of our chains off, all of our studded belts, our jackets, everything. They filled about four trash cans full of all this punk rock shit. Halfway through, when it got shut down, everything got smashed up. All the glass got smashed up. Me and my boyfriend broke into the ticket office at the front, and we dragged the trash cans out and we were throwing all this stuff at people. We were literally running down the street, either Sunset or Santa Monica, with our arms in front of us with all of these chains and belts and spikes and shit. We were giving that stuff out to our friends for weeks. It was awesome. It is now a Home Depot store. That was one of my favorite crazy punk rock show stories.

I think the Black Flag shows were so violent because of the lyrics. It was because of the anger in the lyrics and because of the testosterone and the male violence, and Black Flag encouraged people to be violent. Not all punk shows were like that. That was basically it in a nutshell. People wanted to go to a show and let out all of their stuff, which I understand. We were letting all that anger and all that aggression out on each other, which is what ruined it for me. That's one of the reasons I went up to San Francisco and got involved in the punk scene up there in '81, because I could go to shows without fear of being pummeled to death or punched. It was far less violent, the scene was even smaller than in L.A., and there were no punk gangs.

Because there were so few punks back then, you'd be walking down the street and someone would be like, "Hey, punk rocker, I'm going to kick your ass." That kind of crap. I had people try to run me over with their cars. Consciously try to kill me. I was walking down the street in the Valley, and I had a hunk of concrete thrown at me from out the back of a truck. I had people actually attacking me. Someone tried to kill me with a machete. My parents hated that I was punk rock. I was kicked out for that. I was beaten up by my parents for being punk.

Most of this time, I was living on the streets and I was homeless. I was homeless from the time I was fourteen. I was going back and forth between the Valley and Hollywood. I was homeless in L.A. and SF. As I said, I also moved to San Francisco in '81 and became a part of the scene up there. The L.A. scene was so violent. People don't even know unless they were involved. Obviously a Dickies show wasn't violent; it was fun. That was awesome. It was completely the opposite of a Black Flag show, but there were many shows I went to in L.A. where the police physically came into a small space and had everybody huddled in a big circle, like in the floor, and they came and they were beating on us individually, like at Mendiola's Ballroom. Also, as the scene got bigger, you got a lot of kids who were into the punk stuff, but not because it was something they believed in or something that was vital to them.

They wanted to go and have a fight. That's where a lot of the violence came from. Some of the bands really encouraged that violence. It's a shame. You're like, "Smash the system." Then you go to a show and everybody is smashing each other. We were doing the police's job for them.

So back then I was just going to shows, hanging out with my friends, making clothes, trying to survive being a punk rocker, going and seeing the bands, reading *Flipside*, writing letters to *Flipside*, and getting made fun of for writing letters to *Flipside*. I would listen to *Rodney on the ROQ*. KROQ was the only radio station that would even play any punk. I don't care what anybody says, I loved Rodney's show, because he played punk rock and nobody else would. I would go to record stores like Vinyl Fetish. It was such an important part of my life, and it still is.

When I got into punk rock, you could say that was when I started to understand oppression and things like that. I became politicized through being involved in the punk scene. In the '80s, nuclear destruction of the planet was such a big terror. I was becoming more and more aware about things. I consciously called myself an anarchist from about 1984, and got involved in the anarcho punk scene in L.A. I'm still an activist. I still call myself an anarchist. I still call myself an old school feminist. I do a lot of community work.

I'm into lots of different things now, which is good. My heart is punk and absolutely will always be. It inspires everything that I do.

Back in the day, there were a lot of girls involved in the punk scene, and that was mostly as fans. There were also a lot of girls singing for bands or playing instruments, but it was still totally male-dominated. We were strong, and we were fierce. We weren't standing in the back holding our boyfriends' jackets or whatever kind of thing, as it seems to be now. There was a lot of involvement. As a girl, it was so empowering for me. I go to punk shows now and it seems to be all-male bands mostly. It is depressing.

I was a total tomboy when I was growing up. I was always doing stuff that girls weren't supposed to do. Punk rock really helped free that up. I didn't have to be feminine. It was really liberating. There were really nice punk guys back then, but there were some really horrific, bad people involved in the scene, too. I'm not going to cover that up. It's half-empowering and half-bittersweet. Sometimes it was totally cool and it felt really equal, and sometimes it felt like a struggle.

I am not heterosexual/straight. I'm bisexual. I don't identify with what is now called "gender queer," because I'm such a strong feminist. Anybody who understands that at all will understand what I've just said. I see myself as a woman. I'm a very strong female. I love being a woman. I love being female. I reject femininity and I reject masculinity, because I see how horrifically crippling that is for women, as well as men. I love being a woman. I don't want to be a man. I'm not transsexual.

The punk scene has so fully gotten sucked into porn culture and commercialism with things like Suicide Girls, etc. It is pretty upsetting. It is just mirroring the "system" it claims to be so against, in the same way that punk has just become a lifestyle choice and half the time I can't even afford to go to punk shows now because they are twenty-five dollars. Those bands should be ashamed of themselves. It is the same bullshit as Punk Rock Bowling in Las Vegas. So I would say I am a DIY old school punk, and support smaller underground shows and bands. It is depressing that so many old punks and old bands I know are now all about the money, and have forgotten their do-it-yourself backgrounds.

Even though I'm in a relationship with a man right now, I still have to deal with homophobia. I have to deal with shit all the time, because I'm not totally feminine. There's all these contradictions. Feminists hated me because I was a punk rocker, but the punk rockers hated me because I was a feminist. I was like, "Hold on a minute. I'm a feminist and I'm a punk rocker." I see all these old punk guys I know and they all have these non-punk trophy wives. I'm like, "What are you doing? Your middle-age crisis is getting out of control."

■   ■   ■   ■   ■

I listen to a lot of different music now. When I was in England, before I came back to this country, I was leading a Brazilian samba band. I was the band leader, and I was also playing. I drummed. Apart from punk rock, the samba drumming is one of the reasons why I'm going deaf. Samba is Brazilian, marching, carnival music. I was making costumes and doing it all free in the community, which was awesome. I can't read music. When I was in the samba band, you would listen and you would play. It leads back to punk rock, because back in the day it was one chord. It was about music being accessible. Anybody could pick up the guitar. Anybody could pick up a drum. Anybody could sing. That's why I got so into samba, because it's such a big part of the community in Brazil. Everybody learns how to play it. You don't have to read music. You can be totally crippled and blind and still play samba. It's so similar to punk rock in that way. So accessible.

I also started appreciating jazz. I have a favorite jazz radio program that I listen to on Sunday nights. I always have this morphing stuff going on in my brain, which I think is really cool. It's a creative way to think about music.

Punk rock influences everything that I do. It influences my creativity. It influences my relationships. Everything. My activism. It's so exciting to think about it. Before I came back to this country, I was doing a lot of community arts work with the samba and carnival work. I was starting to do some creative work with kids. Then I came back here and I was traveling around as a volunteer organic farm hand.

My activism now in the beautiful Emerald Triangle, which is the Mendocino County region of Northern California, is peer-led mental health support. I do a lot of one-on-one, walking down the street, talking to people who are sleeping on the street. I've had a lot of homelessness in my life and want to give back now that I am able. I do a lot of direct questioning: "Do you need support? Do you know this is where you can get some food? This is a place you can stay." I do it totally grass roots, and not necessarily with an organization. I don't get paid.

I'm also a caretaker on a horse ranch. I've been doing that since 2010 with my partner, Boris, the drummer for Whorehouse of Representatives and No Class. We take care of the horses. I maintain about a quarter-acre organic vegetable garden. That's a mix of organics and permaculture. I've been getting into food justice, and I've been vegetarian or vegan since 1984. I'm mostly vegan now. I prefer to be vegan. I've really gotten into fermenting and making my own food. When I first became a vegetarian it was for the animals, and it still is, but I've made all those connections of understanding where the food is coming from and understanding about the corporations and human rights. You have to have animal and human rights. You can't have one or the other. It really helped when I made those connections as a vegetarian and vegan about human rights. Even though I totally believe there's way too many of us, we've got to figure out a way to not totally destroy the planet.

Being punk rock, it's helpful for when I'm involved in community work and I'm working with people who are not alternative in any shape, form, or fashion. They see somebody like me, who looks the way that I look and behaves how I am. They see that I'm a human being like them and have a lot of the same experiences as them. I just look different and I'm into different things. I think that's really important, because even now the media depiction of punk rock is so bad.

I'm so glad I was able to discover punk rock and, especially being a girl back then, to step out of the whole feminine, long hair thing, and to do something which was so against those things. It was majorly revolutionary. I'm definitely one of those people who can say, "Punk rock saved my life." Absolutely.

LIZ SABA RAYON

Born in 1965 in Orange County, California. Lived in Mission Viejo and San Diego, California, in the '80s and attended shows at various venues throughout Orange, Los Angeles, and San Diego Counties, and in Tijuana, Mexico. Currently lives in San Diego and is the owner of Presley Fine Jewelers.

I WAS FIFTEEN. My uncle, Mike, lived in South America. He wrote me a letter and asked me to go to a record store and pick up a couple of records for him that he couldn't get in Peru. One of the records was *Never Mind the Bollocks . . . Here Comes the Sex Pistols*. I always thought he was a cool uncle, so I thought, I'm going to buy myself a copy. If he wants that all the way in Peru because he can't get it, it's gotta be something cool.

The minute I listened to it, that was it for me. That was the first punk record I ever bought. It changed my life right there. It was my way to rebel. I came from a really strict Catholic family. I'm the oldest of five children. I wasn't allowed to do anything. I wasn't allowed to go to school dances. I wasn't allowed to get my driver's license. That record started it all for me. All the rebellion. Taking all my aggression out.

At my school in Mission Viejo, it was so new. There were maybe ten of us that liked punk rock. We were pretty much outcasts. The jocks made fun of the way we dressed. I was on the soccer team, so I had the punk rock life and then I had the soccer life. I started going to shows when I could sneak out. I would pretend I was going to a movie, and I'd go to a show. The first two years I was into punk rock, I didn't go to as many shows. It was really hard to get out of my house. I wasn't allowed to spend the night anywhere.

I used to change my clothes after I left home. I had a change of clothes in my purse, so that I could change to go to the show. It was the same with school. I would change my clothes at the bus stop. I paid my brothers money so they wouldn't tell my mom and dad what I was actually wearing.

Once I turned eighteen, I started going to a lot more shows at the Olympic Auditorium and Fender's Ballroom. You name it. All over the place. Places in San Juan. There was a pizza parlor there, and the Couch House even had punk rock shows at the time. We would drive wherever there was a show.

It was crazy at Fender's. I remember being at one show there. I think it was Valentine's Day. There was a Hispanic wedding going on at the same time. In the other ballroom was the punk rock show. I just remember the fights that ensued afterwards and trying to get out of there, hoping you weren't going to get stabbed.

Once I moved away to go to college, when I turned twenty in 1985, that was when I hit every single show I possibly could, because there was no one to keep an eye on me. I would say I saw the majority of the punk rock bands from 1985 to the present. I saw everyone you could think of or would ever want to see.

There was a bar in San Diego. It was a little dive bar called the Pink Panther. It was just a beer and wine place. After shows, a lot of punks would show up and hang out. I got to meet a lot of people after their shows. I also worked at a bar called the Casbah in San Diego back in the day. That's one way I got to meet the guys in the bands, because I served beer to them while they played.

I have a lot of crazy stories. One time, my best friend Joni and I had no money, but we decided we wanted to see the Ramones on their entire West Coast California tour. Basically, we took her Mobil card and we went from Mexico to San Francisco and did everything with the Mobil card. We ate at Mobil stations and pumped gas at Mobil stations and slept in her jeep and went to shows for a week. We bought our beer at the gas station. It was pretty cool.

One time, there was a Social Distortion show at San Diego State at the Back Door—a really small show. I was with Joni. It was sold out and we had no way in. We sat at the bar, and Mike Ness was sitting there next to us. He asked us if we were going to the show and we told him, "No, dude, it's sold out." He had a guest list of two women. Apparently, they were porn stars and they didn't show up. He told us to go to the door and say this is who you are and you'll get in. I was Linda Lovelace and I can't remember which porn star Joni was. That was how we got into the show. There was always a story when we went out.

One time, Johnny Rotten came into the Pink Panther. All I used to do at the Pink Panther was shoot pool and drink Jolt Cola. I was on the pool table, and he wanted to shoot pool. He had to play whoever won the game. I beat the guy I was playing, so Johnny came up to the table and I said to him, "Can we bet on this game?" And he said, "What do you want to bet?" I said, "If you win, I'll buy you all the beers you want all night. If I win, you have to sign one of my records." He said, "You have a record here?" I said, "No, that's the catch. I'm going to go home. I live ten minutes away. I'm going to bring my record back and you're going to wait for me and not leave and you're going to sign it."

I beat him at the pool game. I said, "You're going to wait?" He said, "Yep." I went all the way home and grabbed my record. For some reason, I couldn't find *Never Mind the Bollocks*, so I grabbed *Rock 'n' Roll Swindle* and a Public Image Limited postcard. I raced like a bat out of hell and sure enough, he was waiting at the bar when I got back. When I got there, he looked at me and said, "You brought the wrong record. I will not sign the *Rock 'n' Roll Swindle*. We all got screwed on that record. We made no money." But he

signed the postcard.
Everybody was
laughing.

I met Joey Ramone
after a show, at a place
called Bacchanal. He
was standing there
after the show. I met
him and chatted with
him. When I went to
New York years later, I
was invited to hang out

while they were auditioning a new bass player.

One time, Johnny Thunders played at the Bacchanal and he
was so high on heroin that he was falling asleep while he was
playing. Then he showed up at the Pink Panther, the dive bar, after
the show, and I asked him to sign a cocktail napkin. As he was
signing it, he just puked all over me. That was 1987.

One time, nobody wanted to see Iggy Pop, so I went down to
Mexico by myself and I drove across the border. I parked my car in
front of Iguana's. That was probably one of the scariest things I ever
did, because I was surrounded by some sketchy people. Luckily,
some other people came by and helped me and I was able to drive
away safely. That was probably the dumbest thing I ever did, but it
was totally worth it.

At that time, it was cheaper for bands and they got paid more
to play in Tijuana, because the promoters didn't have to pay the
insurance that they would have to pay in San Diego. There were
shows all over Tijuana, from little clubs like the Long Bar to
Iguana's, a big place where there were a lot of punk bands. When
you went to Mexico, that was when you were really scared, because
that was just crazy. Any time you went into the Long Bar, fights

ensued. You were watching yourself, your back, and your friends. That is probably where I saw the most violence, was at the shows in Tijuana. It wasn't just California bands playing there. Everyone played there. The Ramones played Tijuana.

■   ■   ■   ■   ■

I think there was violence, but I think there was always respect towards women. The guys were always there to watch out and protect women, whether they knew them or not. I never felt unsafe at a show from the punks that were there. It was the outside influence. At Fender's, for example, people coming in and trying to start fights with punks. But I always felt completely safe surrounded by punks. They always watched out for the girls. They were happy to have women in the scene.

Guys wanted women in the scene. They wanted women to date in the scene, because you had stuff in common with them and they thought it was cool. I'm definitely different from mainstream women. Punk rock taught me how to be a leader and not a follower and not to be afraid of anything. That you don't have to worry about what people think of you. We were looked down upon by women all the time. And still, the values that most women have, I don't share. I never wanted to marry rich. I wanted to be a self-made person, and I'm able to do that. Punk rock really did get me through it all. It taught me how to be myself.

The punk rock scene influenced every aspect of my life, except for sexually. I had my own values. Politically, it opened up my eyes to what the government is doing and what they've done and how I vote. It's influenced me on how I raise my daughter. The one thing I want to instill in her is independence, and to not ever care about what people think of her. Socially, I surrounded myself with strong women who were like me and in the punk rock scene. My two closest friends were both in the punk rock scene, and we're still friends to this day. Most of my other friends are friends from the scene.

I still go to punk rock shows. I saw Fear a couple of months ago. Before that, it was X. Whenever there is a good show, I'm there. I still play my records. I have a really good record collection. I take my daughter to shows. She is ten years old.

Punk rock was the best thing that ever happened to me. Besides molding me into the person I've become, I have lifelong friendships that I will have until the day I die. At the time, punk rock wasn't acceptable. You couldn't go to Hot Topic and buy your punk rock clothes. It taught you how to be strong. I am strong. I've survived two marriages that didn't end well. I'm a single mom and a home owner. Without punk rock giving me a source to look at the establishment, my family, and everything in a different way, I don't think I'd be the person that I am right now. It taught me to stand up for myself and not bow down. Punk rock made me question authority.

LORI WESTOVER

Born in 1963 in Houston, Texas. Lived in Bryan, Texas; Laughlin, Nevada; and Fountain Valley, Shadow Hills, Grass Valley, and Needles, California, in the '80s and attended shows at various venues throughout Orange County and Los Angeles County. Currently lives in Needles and works as a social services professional, teaching parenting classes and running domestic violence groups.

MUSIC IS A BIG PART of who I am. The first band I can remember when I was little was the Beatles. I have a memory of my dad and I singing along with "I Wanna Hold Your Hand" as we walked down the street holding hands.

My parents divorced when I was young. They were both into music. My mom was a big Elvis fan. She also had a collection of albums including Tom Jones, Engelbert Humperdinck, and Neil Diamond—all the guys with hairy chests and low-cut shirts. At my dad's house, it was the Eagles, the Allman Brothers, and Crosby, Stills, Nash, and Young. That was where I first heard Jethro Tull, Alice Cooper, and the Doors. In fact, I still have a lot of the albums from his house.

In middle school, I found Elton John and fell in love. I begged my mom to take me to the see the movie *Tommy*, because Elton John was in it. I didn't know about the Who until I saw that movie. My mom took me, because she liked Ann-Margret. It was pretty wild. That sparked my curiosity into other things. After seeing that, I started getting into Zeppelin and fell in love with Jimmy Page. I liked the Runaways, Black Sabbath, Judas Priest, Queen, David Bowie, and the Rolling Stones. My first concert was Pink Floyd at Anaheim Stadium when I was in the eighth grade.

When I started high school, I was a rock chick. I was a

Zeppelin girl. I wanted to be Stevie Nicks. I met a girl who became my best friend. She loved Zeppelin and she played guitar. We would go home after school. She would play and I would sing. We got really pissed when we heard Heart, because we thought they stole our idea.

How I first got involved with punk rock is a little blurry. I'm sure I was between fifteen and seventeen. Most likely we got flyers about bands playing. We just started going to garage parties.

I went to Fountain Valley High School. There were different cliques of people. We had the surfers, skaters, stoners, and jocks. Then, all of a sudden, there were people showing up with spiked hair and leather jackets. I think it just evolved from there. You were delving into something different. It was just a party scene at first. It was fun. There were some people who were really serious and angry, but for the most part, I just liked going out and having fun.

You could go to the thrift store and make up your own fashion design. It was like the weirder you did it, the better it was. It was you and you weren't trying to look like someone else. The other girls I knew in the other scenes had a certain style of clothing and if you couldn't afford to keep it up, then you weren't as cool. This wasn't like that at all. I really liked it. I loved thrift store shopping.

After a while, it went beyond garages and houses. I started going to the Cuckoo's Nest to see a lot of the shows, because it was close by. I have memories of places like Dancing Waters, a club in San Pedro, Madame Wong's, Cathay de Grande, the Whisky, the Roxy, and the Hollywood Palladium. I remember going to a place in Santa Monica. I think it was a boxing arena. There was a place in Garden Grove called the Rendezvous. It was, I guess, a dance club. My senior year of high school, I saw the Ramones there on a Tuesday night. That would have been '80 or '81.

I didn't have a lot of cash. That was one thing that was cool about punk, too. It didn't seem like anyone had a lot of cash. I would make friends with the bands and bouncers to get into the shows for free. I didn't like the bigger clubs, because you couldn't do that so much.

At the Cuckoo's Nest, there was always a crowd. It was fun. It would get really packed inside and loud. A lot of the time I would hang out in the parking lot with friends. There was a lot going on there. The pit could get violent. There were fights. With some of those clubs like that, I don't even remember the songs or the bands that were playing. I don't want to say too much about it, but there was a lot of drinking and drugs. My memory is vague [laughs].

One night, we were walking back to the Cuckoo's Nest from a liquor store that was down the street and we heard gunfire. The guy I was with pulled me down to the ground. That was a very intense night. There was a lot of controversy about the club with the neighboring businesses.

There were some bands I saw over and over again: TSOL, Black Flag, China White, the Vandals, Middle Class, the Crowd, the Adolescents, the Germs, Social Distortion, Agent Orange, Red Kross, and 45 Grave. A band called the Detours. I didn't see the Sex Pistols or Generation X, but I listened to them all the time.

A lot of the bands practiced in storage units. My friend was dating a guy in the Detours. They had a storage unit for practicing and put up egg crates and carpets on the wall to help with the acoustics and also so they could have parties in there and the cops wouldn't know.

Once, I had a lost weekend. Chemicals were involved. I went with some friends in a pickup truck to follow TSOL up to San Francisco. They were doing a concert at Berkeley Square. It was a two-day concert. We went with a group of people. We stayed in a house occupied by three men. They were friends of someone in our party. The guy I was dating was a nice guy, but there was no spark. The first night there, we were sleeping in this room with all of these other people, and he chose that to be the first time he tried to have sex with me. I was refusing him, and he got really pissed off. The next day was the first day of the concert. He paid my way in, but pretty much took off and ignored me.

Another guy I loved to death found me. Then he found these people who were so crazy-looking. They looked like the maid and the butler from *The Rocky Horror Picture Show*. We got in a van with them and they took us back to their place, and from there we went to different parties where there were a variety of scenes going on. One was a very vampire scene. I remember feeling uncomfortable because of the chemicals but assuring myself they were just pretending, and then having the thought of, "Well, what if they believe they are real vampires and that they need real blood." I can laugh at that now. We went to a bar for a while before we made it back to where we were staying. It was above a leather-and-chains gay bar. We watched out the window at the goings-on at the bar. I got through the next day. The guy that brought me to San Francisco drove us home, but this time I had to ride the whole way in the back of his pickup.

I have another memory of being in a Xerox shop with my dad. He was getting some copies made. A guy came in who looked like one of the Ramones. I kept looking at him. He was getting flyers made of the Ramones logo. He came over and said, "Do you want one of these?" Then he said, "Do you want it signed?" And I said, "Sure." He signed everyone else's name and put an X by the name Marky. I guess he just forged everyone else's signature and put an X by his own name.

■   ■   ■   ■   ■

The scene was kind of rough, and wasn't welcoming to women. You had to have a thick skin. One thing I did like about it is that you didn't need to be a Barbie in spandex to fit in. Any girl was welcome, no matter what. When I was eighteen, I got my first tattoo. Back then, I didn't know any other girls who had a tattoo. I felt like it was a punk rock, feisty thing to do. For me, punk rock was liberating and my view of many things changed. Girls got more sexually aggressive. They could act like a dude, point to someone, and say, "Come here" or "Get lost."

I've never been a tough girl. I'm not hard, but I can be hard if necessary. I never had to be in a fight, but there were threats and standoff situations where I had to hold my ground and act like I knew how to fight. Luckily, I never had to find out whether I would have been good at it or not. I did admire many of the hard or tough girls that I knew back then. I love Debbie Harry. She is a great mix of sweet and tough.

My dad and I were very close. We shared a love for music. His mother was a singer, and at one time she played the drums. She was awesome. When I was young, my dad taught himself to play the guitar, and I cannot remember a time with him when music wasn't playing. He would drive me home on Sunday nights from weekend visitations at his place. It took about an hour from L.A. to Fountain Valley. That was good conversation and music sharing time. We would often listen to the Dr. Demento radio show on that drive. He loved to sing along with the Ramones to "Beat on the Brat," among others.

My dad also liked to drink his scotch. The more he drank, the sillier he would get. I remember he used to like to try to shock me. One night we were talking about suggestive songs and he got out an album and watched for my reaction as Jimmy Buffett belted out "why don't we get drunk and screw." I laughed and then I put on the Dead Kennedys "Too Drunk to Fuck." My dad almost fell out of his chair laughing. Good times.

My involvement in the punk rock scene was a great experience. I moved away from SoCal and have had many adventures. The greatest of those has been raising my kids. I have had many ups and downs, as all of us do throughout life. I feel like the punk girl in me kept me going. I am grateful for the circumstances that brought me to live in that place during that time. God Save the Queen.

MELANIE B.

Born in 1970 in Ft. Gordon, Georgia. Lived in Huntington Beach, California, in the '80s and attended shows at various venues throughout Orange County and Los Angeles County. Currently lives in Huntington Beach and works as a hairstylist.

I WAS FIFTEEN YEARS OLD and I had a best friend in middle school who I hung out with quite a bit. She had an older brother who was two years older than us. He was into punk. I was very intrigued by him and his friends and the way they dressed and the music he would play from his bedroom. I was into Duran Duran and stuff at that time, but when I heard the music and saw the way he dressed, it was so intriguing that I crossed over. Luckily, I switched schools, too, so no one thought I was a poseur because you can't go from Duran Duran to punk rock the next year. I was able to start a clean slate as a punk rocker at age fifteen. That's how it all came about, from my best friend's brother.

At the time, I was only able to go to all-ages shows, so I mostly went to Fender's in Long Beach. Inside Fender's it was very dark and kind of scary. I never went to the bar area that was kind of in the back and on the side. I was always at the stage and in the slam pit area. There was a lot of smoking. It was all ages, so people would bring their babies. I tripped out about seeing these punk moms, 'cause I was only fifteen. It was kind of disturbing for me, seeing those young babies there and how loud the music was and the slam pit going on. I remember a lot of people sitting on the floor and smoking. It was intimidating to me, because they were a lot older than me. I just focused on the pit and had a great time. I didn't pay attention to people who were getting drunk or high.

I enjoyed going to shows, because it was a great way for me to relieve stress from my parents. I had the time of my life. I remember when I was in the pit, how people would pick you up when you fell down. I liked that. Sometimes I would fall down on purpose to just get picked up by one of the big guys. It showed there was some compassion out there. It was like a bond with people.

I had some trouble with some heavy metal people back then. Because there was nothing else to do once on New Year's Eve, I went to the Ozzie Osborne show at the Long Beach Arena, maybe in '89 or '90. They were throwing cigarettes into my mohawk and crap at me. I thought I was going to get beat up by these guys, but another Hessian guy helped me and protected me. I'll never forget that day, so I never went to another metal show.

At age sixteen, I took college courses at Golden West College during the summertime. I took a public speaking class. I focused all my speeches on punk and educating the class and the professor to not stereotype punk rockers as being stupid, violent, gangbanging criminals, or drunks and drug addicts. I wanted to show them that punks can be intelligent and make something of themselves, but still not conform with the way they look and the way they think. That was a big thing for me, because my parents were so against me looking punk. I was determined to prove them and everybody else wrong about the stereotypes. My parents fought me the entire time and put me in private schools that had dress codes. The biggest thing was they didn't want me looking like that. They found it shameful and embarrassing for them. They didn't worry about things that most parents worry about like good grades, because I had all that. I just wanted to express myself through punk and dress that way and listen to the music, but otherwise I was a good kid.

I was making a statement with the way I dressed. I wanted to make a statement. At the same time, I didn't like being stereotyped. I know that's just the way it is. People stereotype all the time, no matter what. Appearance is the first thing they see, and they automatically stereotype you. It's unfortunate. That used to bother me a lot when I was kid.

I liked being an individual and not being scared to express myself and not caring what other people thought about the way my appearance was. I remember having older people sometimes making comments about the way I looked, and I didn't care. I remember one time I was in line at a grocery store, and this woman turned around and said, "Are you one of those skinheads?" and I said, "No, I'm a punk rocker." She said, "Well, I wouldn't be too proud of that." I said, "Actually, I am proud of that." That was my statement: that I was proud of myself and I wanted to express myself no matter what people thought, but I didn't want people to think I was a drug addict and violent.

■　　■　　■　　■　　■

Despite that there were more punk guys than girls, I did feel that it was pretty welcoming to women. The only thing is when I would

210 WE WERE GOING

go in the pit with the guys. They would grab at me in my private areas, and that was always a bummer. So there was a little bit of disrespect that way. When I see the girls get in the pit today, I don't see that happening to them anymore. At Fender's they would often grab me. I would push them away and they would stop. Otherwise, I felt it was welcoming and did not have any problems.

If I was with punk or death rock girls, I felt like I fit in. I felt comfortable. I felt part of the crowd. If I was with cheerleaders and typical all-American girls, I had nothing in common with them. I didn't want to talk with them. They didn't want to talk with me. I think they looked down on us. We didn't have the curled hair and makeup and all that stuff. We weren't like that. We didn't have the same interests.

I am the person I am today because of my involvement in the scene. It saved me from what I went through with my dysfunctional family. I was able to be me without being judged or being told I was embarrassed or ashamed to be seen with. I felt understood when I was at shows and among my peers. I felt I was accepted, and there was no judging. I didn't have to pretend I was something that I'm not. If I didn't have the punk scene as an escape, I'm not sure I would have made it through my childhood. My mother and stepfather were so against the scene. Because they pulled me out of public school where there was no dress code and put me in private school, I went to four different high schools all four years. I think, because of that, it made me want to do it even worse. If they had just been cool, I may not have been so crazy about it. They threw out all my records. They threw out all my clothes. When I first cut my hair into a mohawk, I ran away that weekend. When I came home, my parents shaved it off. I was bald, and they bought me a wig and made me wear a wig until my hair was an acceptable length. That's when I went into my first private school.

I have not spoken to my mother or stepfather for about

MELANIE B.

seventeen years. That is the best thing I've done in my life. They were very abusive. It was horrible. Thank goodness I had the punk scene and something to accept me—something I could rely on and feel good about myself. My involvement in the scene was absolutely good. It helped me so much.

Punk still affects me. I'm vegan now, thanks to the band MDC. I've always eaten mostly a plant-based diet, but since listening to MDC and the lyrics and doing more research about veganism, I've switched over. It is actually so simple. I wish I would have done it a long time ago. I don't wear leather now. I will never buy leather again.

Being vegan has always been for ethical reasons. Health was the second reason. I already ate a healthy diet before. I watched the band Propagandhi's video "Purina Hall of Fame." I watched that and it sealed the deal for me—to never have meat, fish, dairy, or egg again. After seeing Propagandhi's video, I cried myself to sleep and woke up crying. It was that bad. I'm just ashamed I didn't do it long ago. I thought that they just raised the animals and they humanely slaughtered them and that was it.

I think I still have in my head that I'm different. I'm still able to be different and be proud of it and be independent and express myself. I think there's punk rock in every little thing I do. I still go to shows and I see kids in the slam pit. I live vicariously through them when I watch. I have always been, and always will be a punk at heart.

MONICA CARAPELLO

Born in 1961 in Downtown Los Angeles, California. Lived in Long Beach, California, in the '80s and attended shows at various venues throughout Los Angeles County. Currently lives in Huntington Beach, California, and works in human resources.

IN 1980, I WAS NINETEEN. I was working at my aunt's beauty salon in Seal Beach, because I had gotten a manicuring license. Outside of her salon, I saw this guy walking on the sidewalk. He had bright orange hair and was wearing a long green trench coat and combat boots. I had just been hearing about this punk rock/ new wave stuff. My cousin Denise told me about some new wave party she went to. It sounded interesting. Then I saw that guy. There was something in the way he looked. I never saw anyone like him. I was very intrigued.

I was also working at Marie Callender's in Long Beach, as a waitress. There was a maintenance guy who worked there. His name was Mike, but he went by Waldo. I think he's dead now. When I would go to work, I would see him painting the curbs. I thought he was cute. He had spiky, white bleached hair. It seemed like he had new bruises every time I saw him. Somehow, we just started talking. We became good friends. He said he was going to these punk shows in Los Angeles, and I should go. I think that was the first time I heard the word "punk." That's when I learned about the Hollywood scene.

I went to tons of shows with my girlfriends, Linnet, Kim, and my cousin Jennie. Fender's in Long Beach and all the places out in L.A.: the Whisky, Madame Wong's, Cathay De Grande, Perkins Palace. It was cool to change your name if you were into punk. Some guy started calling me "molecule" at work, so I became

Moly Cule—not punk unless I spelled it Maul E. Cule [*laughs*]. Linnet was Ella Trick. Kim was Jenny Ration. We went to shows probably four nights a week. Anything that we heard about. I'd get an *L.A. Weekly* every week, and I would circle what shows we'd want to see. I was a waitress at the time, so I could get a shift off if a good show was coming up.

I'm not an artist, but I love art. I'm an art appreciator. That was another thing about the scene back then. There was a lot of artistic expression. I also went to a lot of performance art shows, like Johanna Went. Once there was this tall, gaunt guy up onstage at the Anti-Club. He was wearing women stockings and nothing else. He was putting chicken heads up his butt and shooting them out. Just weird shit like that. I loved anything that was weird.

We went to Cathay de Grande a lot. Once Hervé Villechaize from *Fantasy Island* was in there smoking a cigar and having a drink. Another time at the Whisky, this guy was standing next to me with these beautiful dreadlocks and said, "Look in the back of the club. Grace Jones is in our presence." I turned around and saw Grace Jones in full fatigues . . . camouflage hat and combat boots. She was beautiful.

Another cool memory. In 1981, I was standing in line to get into the Whisky. I remember exactly what I was wearing: 1950s white pedal pushers that I bought at a thrift shop and my dad's blue-and-white-striped shirt. I had blue lipstick on. Somehow I found blue lipstick. This one super tall guy was standing near me. He had a camera. I remember he said something to me like, "You are a work of art." It was a great introduction, so we started hanging out. He would bring over this massive big photo album with all these amazing photographs of bands like Black Flag, Circle Jerks, Christian Death, and 45 Grave. It was Edward Colver. Many of those same photographs are now totally famous. I'm so happy Edward took so many photos back then. He really memorialized the whole scene.

The bad parts of the scene were the drugs, drinking, and violence. Drinking was my own problem, but it was a major part of the whole scene. So many people drank a lot. My girlfriends and I would go to shows in one car, get drunk, then end up getting home separately, not even sure how. I would black out a lot and find myself in really bad situations. I ended up getting raped by four guys I thought were my friends from the Target of Demand crew we were hanging out with. A lot of people I knew back then are dead. I think some of the guys that raped me are dead now. A lot of people were into heroin, too. I think that was another real negative part of the punk scene.

Before punk, I felt suppressed, insecure, and had so much anger in me. I think that's why the scene appealed to me. I was verbally abused by my father from thirteen to seventeen, until I moved out. The punk scene happened and I realized I could say, "I'm not going to take any more bullshit from anybody." I loved the music and the energy and being able to not give a shit about how I looked. People were like, "Fuck this and fuck that." It was fun and empowering.

I always loved music, and felt it was a sanctuary for me. Even now, it changes me. If I'm in a bad mood, I'll come home and put on some music. I still have my little pink album player here in my living room and listen to my albums a lot. Music is still my sanctuary.

■   ■   ■   ■   ■

I didn't really associate with a lot of women in the scene. It was male-dominated. I think, because of the violence and the energy

and the angst, more males were attracted to it. There were girls around, but I really only felt comfortable around my close girlfriends.

I love being a woman, though. We can do so much on our own. It's probably why I've never gotten married. I just feel like I can do things on my own, and I didn't have the greatest male role models in my life. I love men, too. I just think roles have changed so much. A woman can have her own career and raise her children on her own. I raised my son on my own. I have a degree, and I support myself. I feel like I'm a pretty empowered woman.

My greatest role model was my grandma. She loved me unconditionally. Even when I was into punk, she treated me with love and respect. She would even ride with me in my blue Ford Pinto that was spray-painted with punk graffiti. She helped raise me, since my biological mom gave me up when I was three months old. She was very traditional, so I would always see her cooking and cleaning. She also worked as a seamstress. I learned from her how strong women could be and how much they could do on their own, because she did.

I've always been very independent. I put myself through school and paid for it myself. Probably when I was very young I thought I should get married and be a housewife with kids, but that just never ended up being my thing. I remember at twenty-five I was living in Belmont Shores, still waitressing, and said, "I'm bored of this. I'm going to go to school. I don't care how long it takes, but

I'm going to stick with it until I finish." I started at Long Beach City
College as an accounting major. By the time I got into my upper
division at Long Beach State, I started hating accounting. I loved
my psychology and human resources classes, so I switched majors
and graduated with my degree in human resources. I only took off
one semester to have my son.

■   ■   ■   ■   ■

Punk rock definitely influenced me for the rest of my life. I got
into animal rights and vegetarianism at that time. The scene made
it okay to think about things, social injustices, and animal rights.
It made it okay to be and look different. It didn't matter if I had
a little run in my stockings. There was always this competition in
my family over who was going to look the best. When I got into
the punk scene, my cousin Jennie and I purposely ripped up our
stockings. There weren't stores yet where you could buy punk
clothes, so I got stuff from thrift shops and made my own clothes. I
would cut my skirts in the front and keep them long in the back. I
wanted a pair of combat boots like the guys were wearing. I went to
an army surplus store and everything was too big. I found this really
old pair of ice skates that laced up at a thrift shop. I had the blade
removed and I painted them black. Those were my combat boots.

The scene started out really fun . . . the music, energy, and
anarchy of it all. Through the scene, I developed confidence. It
brought me out of my shell. It's not so much that I was a real shy
person. It just allowed me to not be as scared of things and not care
what others thought of me. It allowed me to say what's on my mind
and be more carefree in my thoughts and actions. Unfortunately,
the scene got progressively violent. Violence, drugs, and alcohol
became the focus, so I stopped going to shows after a few years.

PHRANC

Born in 1957 in Santa Monica, California. Lived in Venice, Hollywood, Pasadena, and San Francisco, California, in the 1970s and '80s and worked both as a soloist and a musician in the bands Nervous Gender, Catholic Discipline, and Castration Squad. Currently lives in Santa Monica, where she is a teaching artist for the Los Angeles County Museum of Art and is known as "The Cardboard Cobbler" for her work as a paper sculptor.

I WAS BORN IN SANTA MONICA. I was adopted at birth and grew up in Mar Vista. My father was a salesman, and my mother was a dental hygienist. I went to the local Mar Vista Elementary School, which was right across the street from my house. My grandmother was a painter on my mom's side. She introduced me to art at an early age. I took my first guitar lessons when I was probably nine. I hated the lessons, but I'm still a guitar player today.

My best friend lived across the street. She always encouraged my music. When I was a teenager, her parents had a fancy cassette deck in their bedroom. I would go over to her house and we would have these concerts. I would pretend that I was performing, and she would introduce me. She still has some of these cassettes of my early concerts and my very primitive songwriting.

All the time growing up, I felt very different and I probably knew I was a lesbian from kindergarten on. When I was seventeen, I came out. I left my parents' house at that time. I was looking for people like me. One night, I was at a magazine stand across from Canter's in town and I saw this magazine called the *Lesbian Tide*. In the back of the magazine, there was an ad for this lesbian, feminist drop-in rap group. I thought, "I'm going to check this out." I told my mom I was going to the library. I lied and I rode my bike to this woman's center on Hill Street in Santa Monica. I walked in, and there were these women sitting in a circle, talking. They welcomed me, and they were all at least ten years older than I was.

I remember my strongest impression from that first meeting. They asked me to introduce myself and I said, "Well, I really like chicks." They all started going "Peep, peep, peep, peep." I thought, "What is this?" Every time I said the word chick, they would start peeping. One finally said, "Women are not chicks." I was like, "Oh." It was my first lesson in consciousness-raising. I liked the group a lot.

Not too long after that, I got myself out of the house. My parents did not like that I was a lesbian. I played my guitar on the boardwalk in Venice. I stayed with friends. There was a feminist newspaper called *Sister Magazine*. It was on newsprint. It came out in Venice. I got involved in that and with the *Lesbian Tide*. I helped do the graphics. I had very political and strong smart women all around me. It was very, very inspiring. It was the start of the women's movement. It was '74, '75. It was super exciting.

■　　　■　　　■　　　■　　　■

I was born with this name that I really don't care for at all. It's Susan. I'd get all the jokes, like that I was a boy named Sue. I was a tomboy. When I was coming out, I went to the Lesbian History Exploration, which was a weekend conference in the Malibu Mountains. There were all these amazing women artists and lesbian artists. It was Alix Dobkin, a lesbian folk singer; Liza

Cowan, who was a lesbian artist and documentarian; and Elsa Gidlow, a lesbian poet. At that time, I think Elsa was late in her seventies. I was really young. Betty Dodson was there. She had this amazing slide show of vaginas orgasming. I was taking this all in. It was just amazing.

Liza Cowan showed this slide show called "What the Well-Dressed Dyke Will Wear." It was all of these women in these beautiful suits. Her friend was a tailor, and she made all these three-piece suits. It was this lesbian fashion show that was just spectacular. Liza's hair was cut off. Totally buzzed. I came home and went right to the barbershop and cut all my hair. My hair was really long down my back, and I cut it to my shoulders right before I went on this retreat. I came home, went right to the barbershop, and buzzed it all off. It was very empowering. It was very much an empowerment ritual to cut your hair back then. I think it still is. It's a real statement of identity, and it's very personal.

I also changed my name to Franc then. I went to see my friend who lived across the street from the women's center and I said, "I'm Franc." She said, "Just wait right here." She went in the other room and got a blue baseball cap. She came back and she put it on my head, and it had a "P" on it and she said, "Phranc, P-H-R-A-N-C." That's how I got the "PH." That's how I became Phranc.

It was a natural progression from the Westside lesbian feminist community to becoming involved with the Woman's Building. I went to a women's dance down at the Woman's Building. This was the original location on Grandview, right across from MacArthur Park, in the old Chouinard Art building. It was a two-story building, and there was this big room that the dance was in. There were galleries and the Sisterhood Bookstore on the bottom level. There was a coffeehouse. Talk about your mind being blown. I thought, "Wow, this is incredible." I already identified as an artist and there was this coffeehouse, Dorothy Baker's Coffeehouse, where I could come and play my guitar. I realized there was also this whole art program there called the Feminist Studio Workshop, which was started by Judy Chicago, Sheila de Bretteville, Arlene Raven, and Suzanne Lacy. It started at CalArts and came to the Woman's Building. This was an opportunity for me, who was a high school dropout from Venice High. I applied for the Feminist Studio Workshop.

I spent two years at the Woman's Building, in the Feminist Studio Workshop. It moved from the location on Grandview to Spring Street. That was the start of an incredible experience. It was a small community of women. There were consciousness-raising groups and ways to follow whatever your artistic passion was. There was a lot of discussion and a lot of processing. It was a special world that was completely devoted to women in the arts. I apprenticed with Cynthia Marsh in the Women's Graphics Center, which was an amazing place. In her offset press and darkroom, I silkscreened. I learned how to do all of that there.

I was completely involved in this community, and it was a real education. After two years at the Feminist Studio Workshop, I wanted to find a new women's community. I went to San Francisco. It was supposed to be gay Mecca. I didn't know anyone up there. My friend had given me two names. I went up there, and I met them. They were artists and they said, "Come across the street. We want you to meet these people." I walked into this place on Howard Street at Howard and 8th. They were all punk rockers. It was this flat, and four people lived there. They were all so different. They were all so interesting and so cool. I was like, "Oh, wow."

I think I saw the Avengers play up there. All of a sudden, there was this whole punk rock world. When I found punk rock, it wasn't just politics and passion. These were people who were my peers. They were my age. They were angry. They were creative. They were making some noise. They were my people. I didn't know anybody,

but I went down to L.A., got my stuff, and I moved up to San Francisco. I lived there until right about when Elvis died.

There was the Deaf Club and the Mabuhay Gardens. I didn't play music up there. I tried to get work as an offset printer, because that's how I was trained, but I couldn't get work anywhere. Like the rest of my gang that lived in my house, I became a nude model for the art institute. That's how I met most of my friends. They were either going to school as art students or they were modeling. That was the only work I could get up there. Elvis died, and the Sex Pistols came to San Francisco. Those two things happened almost simultaneously.

I came back to L.A. The only people I knew were lesbians. I thought, "How am I going to meet punk rockers? What am I going to do?" I got dressed. I put on my little suit and my tie. My hair was short. I got my nerve up and I walked into a hall that was like a dance hall or something on Vermont, near Hollywood Boulevard. I just stood there up against the wall and tried to look cool. This guy came up to me and said, "Want to be in a band?" I'm like, "Yeah."

It was Edward from Nervous Gender. He said, "Great. The band's Nervous Gender. You're in." At the beginning it was Edward, Gerardo Valazquez, Michael Ochoa, and Edward Stapleton. It was great. It was an electronica band. It was all synthesizers. I never played a synthesizer in my life. I'm a folk singer. I played acoustic guitar and wrote songs, playing a little in the women's community. Punk rock, though, is just folk music that's louder and faster. The content is very much the same. The content in folk music, it's

oftentimes political, but what it does is tell a story. It expresses the
way people or a group of people are feeling or it's an individual
expression of an opinion. That's what punk rock is.

In Nervous Gender, I played the synthesizer and I sang. I did a
very poor job of playing the synthesizer. It was really fun. We were
all onstage and we were impassioned. It was a very avant-garde
band, even for that time. It was very, very outside. Nervous Gender
still exists today. Gerardo's gone, but Edward and Michael play and
they have other band members that have rotated through the years.
They are very dedicated and very unusual and fantastic.

I think I was still in Nervous Gender when I got involved in
Catholic Discipline. Craig Lee, who also was in the Bags, played

drums, and
he was also
a journalist
for the *L.A.*
Weekly. Claude
Bessy—Kickboy
Face—from *Slash*
magazine was
the lead singer.
Robert Lopez,
[who] left to be in

the Zeros, was the keyboard player. Rick Brodey played bass. It was
a lot of fun, and that band is documented in *The Decline of Western
Civilization.* I was the guitarist. Castration Squad was another band
that I was involved in. Alice Bag, Shannon Wilhelm, Mary from 45
Grave, and Tiffany Kennedy were all in that band.

Around 1980, I wrote a song: "Take Off Your Swastika,"
which was my personal reaction to the idiotic fashion of wearing
swastikas just to piss off people. The L.A. scene evolved from
being kind of a friendly local scene to being a more aggressive,

male-dominated scene. It just pissed me off. I wrote the song and
I decided to play it on acoustic guitar, so that you could hear the
words. I wasn't trying to be a folk singer at that time, but that is
how I started coming out onstage. When I stepped onto the stage,
I introduced myself as your basic, average, all-American Jewish
lesbian folk singer. People usually cracked up. It's a great icebreaker,
but it's also a political statement. It's fantastic. I only came to doing
that because I wanted to make myself heard. I wanted to address
the issue.

I started performing solo, and I really wasn't in any bands
anymore. I'd be on the same bill as Nervous Gender or Monitor
or Johanna Went. I would play all the same clubs that I played
in when I was in the punk bands, but it was just me and my
acoustic guitar. The audience already knew me from these other
bands. Sometimes people threw stuff at me, but if somebody did,
somebody else would punch him. I've got this great picture of me
onstage at the Whisky, and it's just all these heads and then this one
guy just giving me the finger. I remember I played "Take Off Your
Swastika" and people were taking off their swastikas and they were
getting into fights in the crowd about it. It was really a time. That
was my community.

When I made my first record in 1985, I had been playing solo
probably from '80, '81. I had written all of these songs and I really
wanted to make a record. I took $1,200 that I had saved from
teaching swimming and I went into Radio Tokyo Studios, which
was a little tiny house on Abbot Kinney Boulevard. I knew what
kind of record I wanted to make. I wanted to make a full record,
like the first Bob Dylan record. I wanted it to be just acoustic
guitar. I wanted to sing all the songs that I had written. I made that
record with my own money. Gary Stewart from Rhino Records,
who had been coming to the Whisky and seeing me play all these
years, said, "I want to put the record out." So Rhino put my first

record out. My life took off after that. I toured all over. I went overseas. I toured with the Pogues. Here, I toured with the Violent Femmes and Hüsker Dü. Eventually I toured with the Smiths, and then I toured with Morrissey. I got to travel and perform solo. In '91, I was performing and had made three records by that time. I was getting ready to play at Madison Square Garden and I got a call that my brother had been murdered.

I came home. Everything just stopped, and I didn't want to perform. I couldn't perform. I didn't. At the same time, a friend offered me the studio over at 18th Street that's in a wonderful artist complex. It's 18th Street Arts Center in Santa Monica. I went back to making my visual art. It was a way to continue being creative without having to be onstage. I just shifted right back into my visual art. That was almost twenty-five years ago now.

■　　■　　■　　■　　■

I made art from when I was very young, because my grandmother, a painter, made sure I got to go to art class. Something happened that changed my perception of art when I was nine. I was in this class seeing an exhibition of pop art, and the Claes Oldenburg billiard balls were brought to the museum. They took the kids from these classes to see the installations before they were open to the public. I remember seeing this installation and for the first time realizing that art didn't have to be a painting. It could be anything. I fell in love with these billiard balls, which at that time were almost as big as I was. They filled the room, and it was spectacular.

The art that I made during that time was all made from found cardboard. In my punk rock days, I didn't have a lot of food, but I would make food out of cardboard. I would paint food. I painted on cardboard, because cardboard was free and you could find it in the trash. My medium was always free. My paint was expensive, because I loved using this gouache, which was so expensive, but the cardboard was always free. I just went to the trash to get my cardboard. That's the art that I still make today. It's a complete thread in my art from when I was nine years old to now.

The cardboard representations are related to the pop art world. It's very much about making the personal political, which comes from my lesbian feminist training and making the everyday object exceptional. There is also a lot of humor in the work, in the same way that there's humor in my music. Humor is the greatest form of communication. It's such a window into anyone's heart, if you can make them laugh and you can open their heart and mind. I use very much the same approach as I do walking down the street as I do in my music, and in my visual work.

I started by making two-dimensional art that I made back in the punk rock days. I would just draw or paint on a piece of cardboard box. Something really interesting is that I failed sewing a million times in junior high. I hated it. Who would ever need to know how to sew? I thought it was such a stupid girly thing. Now my cardboard art has gone from being flat to being 3D. Somebody gave me a glue gun, so I start making three-dimensional pieces. I thought it would be so cool if I could sew them. I asked a mom at my daughter's preschool to teach me how to sew. She showed me, and I'm off and running. I have my grandmother's old machine. Now

almost all of my pieces are sewn.

For a while there, when I was making my art, I was a Tupperware lady, because I couldn't really go back on tour. By then, my family had started and I didn't want to go back the same way. I became the all-American Jewish lesbian folksinging surfing Tupperware lady. I was very successful doing that, and I did that for a long time while doing my art. Slowly, things started to happen. I had a show at my little studio and I had little tiny openings of my own.

About five years ago, I was bagging groceries at Ralphs. I went to work there, because I wanted to become a cake decorator, but they made me the bag person. It was brutal. I was wearing my "Phranc" name tag. It was very humbling. One day, this guy came through my line and he said, "You're Phranc," and I said, "Yeah." He says, "Oh, I love your work." It was my artwork. He'd been following my artwork. This is how I have a gallery space now. I've been with his gallery, the Craig Krull Gallery in Santa Monica, for almost five years. It's about being in the right place at the right time. What misery it was bagging those groceries at Ralphs. Who would've ever thought what would happen from it?

I'm now teaching art classes at LACMA, too. It's like a dream come true. It's incredible. This thread has gone through my whole life. I feel very, very fortunate because I had all these incredible opportunities.

■　　■　　■　　■　　■

If you think about all the things that you've done in your life, you go, "How did I do that? How did I ever get out of my parents' house? How did I say fuck you, and just leave?" I don't know, but I knew I had to. It was a life or death situation. I needed to be who I was, and that's all there was to it. It's not that I didn't struggle with wanting to die or feeling completely overwhelmed. I don't know what it is, but there's that spark that keeps us alive. Somehow I had that spark, and it got me where I needed to go.

Community is what has saved me. Community is still what

saves me. Community is so important, and that's what's so scary about the world today—the powers that be, whoever they are, are trying to destroy any place we have together as a community. When we gather as community, we have strength in sharing. When you don't share and you're isolated; when you don't go to a store and buy things from real people; when you don't talk to real people on a real telephone; when you don't sit on a couch and talk to people or have coffee in a coffeehouse; when you only do things electronically and you have no human contact, well, that's the beginning of the erosion of community.

I have been very fortunate. The community of women in the feminist world were very strong, independent, and generous souls that took care of me and supported me. I was young, and they kept me alive. They fed me when I didn't have money. They made sure I got jobs. In the punk rock world, we took care of each other. We were all on the outside. A lot of us didn't have homes that we could go back to. Some of us lived at home and some of us didn't, but everybody was just struggling to not only be who they were, but to survive. We had that survival instinct. It's that passion that is part of you.

PLEASANT GEHMAN

Born in 1959 in New York City, New York. Lived in New York
City and Los Angeles, California, in the 1970s and '80s, created
Lobotomy fanzine, and played in the Screaming Sirens (1983–
1991). Currently lives in Los Angeles and works as a writer,
dancer, actor, tarot reader, and painter.

I WAS BORN IN NEW YORK CITY, but when I was a small baby,
we moved to upstate New York. We were living in the middle of
nowhere, in a farmhouse that had been built in the 1700s. It was
really beautiful. We had acres of woods behind us and a big old
rock quarry. Me and my brother used to run around naked. We
had a pond. My parents were like New York acting and literary
bohemians. My father was a really well-known writer. He lived
in New York City, and his work took him all over the world. He
was a novelist and he wrote biographies for celebrities that were
mostly his friends. He wrote for tons of magazines and newspapers,
including *Cosmopolitan* when it was a men's magazine, *Playboy*, and
all sorts of entertainment stuff. So did my uncle. My uncle was Nat
Hentoff, the jazz columnist.

My mom had been a dancer and a singer. She was on Broadway.
She toured with big bands. We'd be watching something like *Lost
in Space* and she would know the people on it. I didn't think it was
abnormal for your parents to know people on TV. It took me a
while to realize that that wasn't usual. Even though we were living
sort of a rural life, all kinds of jazz musicians and visual artists and
actors and dancers were coming through my house constantly.

Then, when my parents split up when I was really young,
my mom moved me and my siblings to Connecticut, because she
went to work teaching musical comedy at Wesleyan University.

PLEASANT GEHMAN

So, again, we were in a huge
center of art and learning. It
was all about literature and
theater and musical comedy
and visual arts. It was the mid-
to-late '60s, so I also witnessed
things like the Grateful Dead
playing on a football field with
the Merry Pranksters bus
there. Someone was doing an
upside-down lotus position

headstand, and there were around 300 people dressed in crazy
hippie rags playing ring-around-the-rosy. My babysitter painted
my face and took me to that. I drank wine for the first time there.
I think I smoked pot. Nowadays, anyone would get arrested for
child endangerment, but it was all normal to me and it was kind of
normal in those days.

I wound up being sent to a boarding school that was a really
kind of upper-crust, awesome boarding school. They were actively
looking for scholarship students and I was really smart. Apparently
my IQ was off the charts. I was also doing stuff like having sex
and taking drugs with my mom's students. I was about thirteen
or fourteen when this was happening, so I wound up going to
this boarding school where everyone was like preppies before the
word preppy became a thing. This was around 1973 and 1974. I
remember introducing all these people in L.L.Bean turtlenecks to
the New York Dolls, David Bowie, and Iggy and the Stooges.

On the pay phone in the hallway at the boarding school, my
mom told me we were moving, but she wouldn't tell me where. I
hung up the phone and I was crying, because I didn't want to move
and leave the school. I finally felt at home. I was really depressed
all week long, and then the next week she called me to tell me it

was for sure that we were moving. She said it was to Los Angeles. I hung up the phone and I was like, "Whoa!" I always wanted to live in L.A., because of what I read in rock and roll magazines, which I had been addicted to since I was eleven or twelve. I felt my life is now beginning. That was in 1975.

Within the first two weeks of being in L.A., I was at a Queen concert at the Santa Monica Civic and this older man in front of me handed me a joint. I took it and then I realized I was smoking pot with Tony Curtis. Then, two seconds later, I got distracted from the fact that I was smoking pot with a movie star that I had adored for ages. I saw these two guys coming down the aisle, and one was dressed all in white with a red Bowie cut with a lightning bolt down his face. The other one was shirtless and wearing black satin bell bottoms and a black cape. I didn't know who they were, but I wrote my phone number on a matchbook and threw it at them. They called me the next day. It was Georg and Paul from the Germs, who turned into Pat Smear and Bobby Pyn, later Darby Crash. We started talking on the phone every day.

This was during the little transitional gray area between glitter rock and punk rock. It was a big scene of pre-punk stuff here in L.A., including the Runaways and the Quick, and even the Motels and Van Halen. They would all play with each other. The scene here was morphing from glitter into punk and was very inclusive of everything. Nothing was put into hard boxes. The big divide was kind of between rock and roll and disco. Most of the people that were

into glitter rock or glam rock, whatever you want to call it, wound up being punk. There were also people that had come in from other places. There were some older people that either came from out of the warehouse scene in New York, or maybe the very end of Haight-Ashbury and the Beats in San Francisco, or people that had been involved with underground movies or were artists. I say they're older. They were probably twenty-two to thirty. I remember thinking they were really old. God love me.

It was a scene that was full of not just crazy teenagers and disenfranchised teenagers and suburban teenagers, but in those days, most of the kids that were involved in it were very smart and kind of on the outside. It wasn't just bored, suburban kids. There were also a lot of older people that had already clearly, at least in my eyes, been living what would have later been called an alternative lifestyle for years. They didn't seem to think it was weird to be friends with a fifteen-year-old, because it was like everyone was really into something. They liked the same kind of music. They had read the same books. We'd seen the same films. In those days, also because there was no Internet, if you saw someone that looked a little bit different or odd, you just immediately knew in a tribal kind of way that they would have your frame of reference.

I knew that punk rock was a really important movement that was going to be later seen like Paris in the '20s or like Greenwich Village or North Beach in the '50s. I knew it was going to be a very big cultural moment when other people thought it was just like crazy teenager rock and roll.

■   ■   ■   ■   ■

During the early part of punk rock, from I would say '76 to like '80, I wrote tons of songs. I wrote poetry. I hadn't really thought of singing, and I think it was because I was doing my fanzine *Lobotomy* and I was putting on shows and I was just hanging out, but my mom was a singer and I always liked singing. I did musical comedy when I was younger, and I was always writing.

I kept diaries nonstop. In the diaries, I wrote songs. One of my first friends here in L.A. was Joan Jett. I met her through Randy Kaye, who I started *Lobotomy* with. They had known each other for years. Randy and I used to cut school to go and watch the Runaways rehearse at SIR. One of my roommates at the punk house was Belinda Carlisle, but I actually met Jane Wiedlin first and I was really good friends with all the Go-Go's.

A lot of people that I was friends with during punk were in bands. I just never did it. I don't know why. My band didn't happen until around '81 or '82. Finally, the Screaming Sirens came to be in '83. My concept for it was that I wanted it to sound like a cross between Kitty Wells and the Andrews Sisters and the Ramones. I wanted us to look like Hells Angels meets a saloon girl. I had this whole vision. It was called the Screaming Sirens because of the Greek mythological sirens. We were together until 1991 and toured all over the place. We had records and singles.

No one was locally chronicling punk rock at the time. Robert Hilburn from the *L.A. Times* interviewed me. I don't know why, but he picked me out of a line at the Whisky. He wrote these pieces about new wave and the explosion of punk rock. I was featured in a few of the stories in the *L.A. Times*. I saw what he was writing about and I didn't know that writing for a newspaper was formulaic. I would read *Cream*, and that was just crazy stream of consciousness and really creative writing. Nothing against Robert Hilburn, but I didn't think he understood it. I thought I could write better than that, because I knew what it was about. I also realized that I could get free records and get in free to shows. Randy and I started *Lobotomy* because we thought there needed to be something on the scene.

Unfortunately, I had cut typing class to get high in high school, because I thought typing was stupid. I wrote reviews of some shows and albums for samples and it would take me like six hours to type them on a manual typewriter, so half of my fanzine was typewritten and half of it was written long hand because it was quicker. We would put it together on the floor when we were shit-faced drunk. Sometimes we would shove pieces of paper and pens or hold a tape recorder to someone's face that had never written before and say, "Write a review," because we wanted it to look like we had a big staff. I didn't take photos, but Theresa Kereakes did. We worked together. Her apartment was called the Lobotomy

Apartment, and so was mine. It ran for almost three years.

I felt like it was my own magazine and I could just write whatever I wanted. There was no one there to edit it. In the first issue I was writing something about the Runaways, and then I wrote something really sarcastic and derogatory about Kim Fowley. I can't remember exactly what it was. He called up my mom's house, threatening to sue me. At first I was like, "You can't sue me." I was seventeen. I didn't even own anything except a typewriter. He said, "Well, I'll take your typewriter." I was like, go ahead, try it. When he started talking about lawyers, I got a little bit scared. He said I had to print a retraction. It cost about twenty-two dollars to print all the copies. I couldn't afford that. I don't even know how we scraped it together. What did I do? I took a bus and hitchhiked to the various record stores that I had brought it to and I fucking cut out the stuff on the page with scissors. So that was my version of a retraction.

Very quickly after *Lobotomy* started in 1978, I wound up at the *L.A. Weekly*, because they saw it somehow. Their publisher, Jay Levin, asked me if I wanted to start a gossip column, and it was like a rock and roll scene club gossip column called *LA Dee-Dah*. It ran for years. I wound up writing features for them. I ended up writing for *Variety* and every magazine you can think of. I worked at the

Hollywood Reporter.

We would take *Lobotomy* to the Masque and sell it. It was like seventy-five cents, but that was worth it for a publication that had everything in it all the time, with pictures of local things. The Masque was heavenly. It was like a really dank, awesome graffiti-covered basement of little rooms that were all spray-painted, and that's not even counting the little rehearsal rooms. It had weird tunnelways and bathrooms with no doors that weren't really working. I went down there a couple of years ago when it was open. I can't even remember why it was open. Alice Bag was there, too. It was like that cave in France with the prehistoric drawings. It was all preserved. All of our graffiti was there, and we would remember where we wrote stuff and go there and it was still there. It was pretty amazing.

It was an awesome place. I don't know how anyone never died, because the steps were so steep with concrete and no railings. Everyone was so wasted all the time. You had to enter through the alley.

From '78 to '88, I lived in a big punk house called Disgraceland. It was within walking distance of the Masque and Cathay de Grande and Club Lingerie and all the rock and roll clubs. It was at 1553 Cassil Place in Hollywood, between Selma and Sunset, behind Frederick's of Hollywood. Any band you can think of stayed there and partied there. Guns N' Roses, the Germs, X, Screaming Jay Hawkins, David Lee Roth. Belinda Carlisle lived there. We owed back rent every goddamn month. We had such noisy parties. It was a total slum.

■   ■   ■   ■   ■

Ever since I was really little, I wanted to be a dancer. I was always putting on shows in the living room or the garage. I was in the audience dancing at a Fishbone show at Club Lingerie when I went in the bathroom and saw this girl. She looked at me and said, "Hi, are you a belly dancer?" She said I moved like one. I had always been seriously obsessed with belly dancing, because my father had written a story in *National Geographic* and there was this article in the issue about Istanbul. I cut out the picture of the belly dancer in the article, because it looked so amazing. The girl in the bathroom was a belly dancer. We exchanged numbers. Then she started showing me dance moves. We'd be locked in a closet or a bedroom at some party at three in the morning, and people would think we were doing drugs.

I started taking actual classes. Then someone gave me a ticket to Greece. I said yes, and I immediately quit my job at *The Hollywood Reporter*. I changed the ticket to Cairo. I wound up staying at this place for weeks and weeks. I saw belly dancers and started learning from them. I got a little cheap costume. When I came back, I was taking classes, but also performing. It just went on from there. The way that I correlate that to punk rock is I saw the opportunity and just said, "Yes. I am following this." I go all

over the world teaching and performing. Some people can't see the
connection between that and punk rock, but I see it immediately. I
saw the openings and I just went for it. Who fucking starts a dance
career at the age of thirty with no training?

Society would probably look on me a little bit like I'm non-
traditional or a lot like that, but, in some ways, I feel like I'm
really traditional. Sometimes I feel like I'm the village witch, or
sometimes I feel very motherly. I've always had an open house, and
I'd take strays—people or animals. I think those things are kind
of traditional. I also think that I never really conformed to societal
standards in ways of dress. I always liked looking like a slut or a
tramp or like a femme fatale or like a scary kind of butch person
or a real glamour girl. I always liked those archetypes and I didn't
think it was anything different switching from one to the other,
depending on what I felt like. I never wanted to dress for success or
really follow fashion.

I never took no for an answer. My mom was very involved in
the feminist movement in the late '60s and early '70s, so that was
kind of indoctrinated into me early. It just seemed normal to me.
I think that if I would've had a child or children, I would've been
very traditional in that sense. I've always felt very protective of
children. I would've probably ceased my crazy punk rock lifestyle
much earlier. I wouldn't have been one of those people dragging
kids to gigs.

I'm a very happy crazy auntie to a lot of kids. I never mourned
the fact that I didn't have children. Sometimes I think I missed out
on it maybe as a life experience and it would've been amazing to
have a kid, but I have plenty of kids in my life.

The main way that I think punk rock influenced my life was
that it showed me that you didn't have to entirely conform to
societal rules. You didn't necessarily have to go against them, but
you could find your way around them and that you could do really

whatever you wanted. I made my own opportunities. I would just send my writing to anywhere, and I think a lot of people don't do that. I think a lot of people sort of live in fear or doubt. I'm not saying I'm special, but punk rock showed me that you don't need to have fear or doubt. You do it and if it doesn't work out, at least you did it. You tried, you know?

RENIE

Born in 1969 in Fullerton, California. Lived in Placentia, California, in the '80s, was a contributor/distributor of *Anti-Establishment* fanzine, and attended shows at various venues throughout Orange County and Los Angeles County. Currently lives in Placentia and works as an office assistant while she pursues a bachelor of science degree in psychology.

HIS NAME WAS STEVE, and he is the one who introduced me to punk rock. It was around 1984. I was sitting on my porch and I saw this guy walk by. He was wearing red plaid bondage pants, a navy-blue Levi jacket with a patch on the back, and black worn out boots. I was intrigued. One day we started to talk, because he knew my brother. He was talking about the punk scene and he told me I could pass for a punker, which was funny, because I grew up kind of poor. I was wearing my brother's blue flannel with a white t-shirt underneath, and my hair was short and messy. I didn't know if it was a good thing at the time! I really didn't make sense of it all. I was just interested in hearing about the music he described as punk rock.

The very first band I heard, because of Steve, was Social Distortion. He gave me a cassette tape of the album *Mommy's Little Monster*. He also gave me other music tapes, but that is the one I listened to the most. I loved it! The energy and the sound were amazing. It became even more exciting getting lyrics.

In high school, I started to meet more people who were creatively expressing themselves. A friend by the name of Cher gave me my first flyer. It was PiL that I hung up in my locker. Sadly, I do not have the flyer anymore, but I managed to save a few, plus all my ticket stubs.

I was always at Fender's International Grand Ballroom in Long Beach, every single weekend. I loved that place. I always got a kick out of the name and have so many fun memories. I've been to other venues, such as the Celebrity Theatre in Anaheim. That place was nice. I really liked the whole layout of it, and just local spots. I really liked a place called Club 369 in Fullerton. But Fender's was the place I went to most often.

The reason I was able to go to shows all the time was because I worked, but I had to give my mom my checks. She would give me an allowance from that, lunch money for school, and weekend money, but I would save it all. That money would buy me a ticket and beer!

I remember there were no chairs or anything at Fender's. People just sat on the floor. In between band sets, you couldn't even walk anywhere, because everybody was just laying or sitting all over the place. It was like a game, trying to walk around. You just had to hop over people and stuff like that.

It was also very hot and sweaty, and the music was loud. We always used to stand next to the speakers and when we left, our ears would be ringing for days [*laughs*]. But after a show, we were just drunk with excitement and booze and sweat and cigarette smell. You would go home and crash out and the next day, you had that scent. You know what I mean? It was exciting! From what I can remember, Fender's was just really hot and sticky and sweaty and smelly, and it was just fun. I don't remember how we got home in all cases. We got home though.

I saw some great bands, like the Exploited, Agnostic Front, Cro-Mags, Bad Religion, Social Distortion, Adolescents, M.I.A., MDC, D.I., the Adicts, GBH, and many other bands. I also supported local bands like Doggy Style and HVY DRT from my hometown. Shows back then were like ten dollars, from what I can recall. When older friends went to shows, they would buy the beer. We always put our money together to buy what we could. If we didn't have anyone to buy the beer, we'd stand around a store and ask people. We called it "pimping." I remember one time we gave this guy money to buy a few forties, and that ass bailed out the back door! Here we were, waiting around, the show is about to start, and we're wondering what was taking this guy so long. We walked in the store and the cashier was like, "Yeah, he took off [out] the back door!" I think it was the first time going to a show sober! [*Laughs.*] That's pretty bad. There were a few times we drank cheap stuff, like Thunderbird and Night Train. That's all we could afford at the time.

I remember going back to school on Monday, nursing a hangover. Back then it didn't faze me; that was the reason for feeling sick all the time. But by the end of the week, I was good to go and it started all over again! That's what it was all about. I always looked forward to shows. They made my week. The excitement of it all would get me through the school week and home life.

The shows were full of fun, excitement, and pure energy. I would always hear about the fights and cops around, but I guess I was pretty much oblivious to it all. I remember a few fights at shows, but I just dismissed them. I guess that tells you where my focus was: the music. I mean it was like, a fight breaks out—okay, so I walked to another area. Not only for my safety, but I couldn't see the band!

When I was sixteen years old, I posted an ad in *Flipside* for pen pals, and this guy Jae Lee wrote me. We became good friends and with a group of other friends, we helped with his fanzine called *Anti-Establishment*. It was great fun to express views on everything. It wasn't all about bands or interviews. It was political and about awareness. Very interesting for a bunch of teens! We had a lot to say! My friends were animal & human rights activists, so it was all about strong messages of awareness—powerful stuff for adolescents to convey. I am proud to have been part of that movement.

We used to collaborate on issues that were hot topics for that time, and write commentaries on anything social or political. We even had poetry, and I think we did band interviews with bands that were activists. The zine was DIY. I remember working on the last few issues that were half pages, a mini zine, and I'd give my sister the original. She'd take it to work and make copies for us. We'd sit around, drinking beer and folding the zine together.

We used to take it to different music stores. We used to go to a place in downtown Orange. They loved us. We used to go there and give them a certain amount, and every time we'd go in there, they would tell us, "Oh! We sold out. We need more. We need more." And they even gave us money to run more copies, and our zine was free! They liked it so much.

■　　■　　■　　■　　■

Growing up, I liked a lot of bands, but there were three bands that left an impact on me: Social Distortion, the Subhumans, and the Adicts. I really like Social Distortion's "Telling Them." The part of the song I like is: "They wake me up, tell me to get to work / I slam the door, say, 'Shut up you jerk' / I can't wait till the show tonight / When I'm with my friends, everything's all right."

The reason I like this part is because it was true to what I was dealing with as a teen. I came from a large, strict, Catholic family, and my parents were stagnant in their ethics, meaning they raised my siblings and I the same, despite the generation gaps. They did not see beyond their own scope of the world. I never spoke up against my parents or I'd get it: a belt or slap. This part of the song made me release that anger, especially when I was going to shows and hanging out. I felt free and accepted. I loved the part that says "When I'm with my friends, everything's all right." And it was.

Another band which I could relate to was the Subhumans. I love the song "Religious Wars." The part I like is: "The ultimate excuse is here / Die for a cause / Religion is fear / Fear of the threat of something unreal / Abdicate the way you really feel." Having strict, religious parents, I could not speak against their views, ask questions, or start a debate. These words from the song had a profound impact on what I felt.

I believe words are interpreted on the basis of one's own knowledge or form of reasoning. This was why I loved to read band lyrics or interviews, because I wanted to know what people had to say that I could relate to.

I also love "Too Young" by the Adicts. I don't think I'll quote the lyrics, because I was the total opposite! I took the lyrics as sarcasm—the shock value of looking innocent, but really living.

        ■   ■   ■   ■   ■

There were a lot of women involved with fanzines and other stuff. Everyone pretty much did their own thing, but we all were there for the same purpose: to convey a message, and for the music. I felt men were very encouraging and accepting, and were really enthusiastic about whatever activity you were taking part in. Everybody was just so supportive of each other and whatever everybody did. It's cool, because back then, you could hold a conversation. You started getting into a dialogue and it was exciting, because it was a collaboration of creativity. I loved it.

Everybody would just hang out and get along with each other. Everybody was accepting, from what I can remember. Any fights that broke out were at shows. I don't remember how they started or what they were about, but I knew it had to do with alcohol. I never really paid attention to that stuff. I never experienced anything pertaining to somebody's culture or ethnicity or anything like that, or gender.

To be honest, all the negativity that I experienced was coming from my own family, because of the way that I looked. It was sad that they couldn't accept me for my individuality. My siblings used to make fun of me—the way I dressed, my hair, and the music I listened to. My mom once told me I should dress like a young lady! I shaved the sides of my head to rebel!

Anyway, I do remember that I did encounter one form of sexism. I went to a show in L.A. with a friend, Lisa. This place we went to was a scary part of L.A. I remember it was behind a store. I think it might have been D.I. who we went to see. I'm not sure, though. As we were leaving, these three guys were standing by the door. I heard one say, "Bye," and I felt a hand brush against my boobs. I turned and socked one in the chest. I was really pissed. I was like, "What the hell?" I think I socked the wrong guy. He was like, "It wasn't me," and then all of them started laughing. I don't know who did it. I just got felt up. I turned and socked whoever was in that path. Poor guy was stunned. He just went back a little. I remember my friend and I laughed all the way to her car.

■　　■　　■　　■　　■

The scene had a profound impact that influenced who I am, because I know who I am now. I learned this from the punk rock scene. I learned a lot because I wasn't allowed or given the opportunity to be myself growing up. I was raised by the idea that children should be seen and not heard. I had to behave a certain way. My opinion didn't matter. I was supposed to do as I was told. Do you know how frustrating it is to not have a voice? This is how I was raised. I wasn't allowed or given the opportunity to express myself. The punk rock scene gave me an outlet to project my thoughts, emotions, and ideas freely.

It's funny, because the topic of discussion these days is about trying to define punk rock. I enjoy reading what people have to say. If you ask me to define punk rock, I would have to say that people came from different backgrounds which had their own form of dysfunction, but we all had the same thing in common, which was an outlet for self-expression. We were not bound by rules that restrained us from being our true selves. We all had something to say that we all could relate to, which made us all accepting of each other.

It isn't about a uniform or about a particular attitude. To me, punk rock was a form of expression and finding yourself—knowing there was an outlet for creativity and becoming independent in thought and opinion. It was also becoming keenly observant of the world and the environment.

I was molded by this scene by becoming enlightened culturally and gaining appreciation, compassion, passion, and respect. The whole punk rock experience was good because of the fun, happy memories that I will always cherish, and the best time I ever had in my life.

SHAREEEEEEK
AKA SHAREE M. MOORE

Born in 1970 in San Bernardino, California. Lived in Dana Point, San Juan Capistrano, San Clemente, and Mission Viejo, California, in the '80s and attended shows at various venues throughout Orange County and Los Angeles County. Currently lives in Anaheim, California, where she sells vintage collectibles and is a culinary arts/catering student.

I WAS PROBABLY ABOUT ELEVEN or twelve. My friend, Heather, and her whole family were punk rockers over in San Juan. We started dressing like it and listening to the music. I went to shows. I drank at shows. I drank at the parties. I drank after the parties. I was a roadie. I went to Fender's, the Olympic, and little bars where I wasn't supposed to be. I got into the bar at Fender's. I don't know how I managed that at fifteen years old. If there is a drink, I'll be there.

At the Olympic, we would make fun of people. Who were we to make fun of them? We looked like a bunch of freaks. I liked it there. It was a lot of fun. I remember going there with no money and walking outside and getting change to get into a show. There

was a lot of unity with people from a bunch of different walks of life. There were teenage kids and adults all together for one common purpose: to listen to music and tell the rest of the world to fuck off. It was kind of cool that we could all be together like that. Punk rockers are pretty spread out, so for everyone to get together, that used to be cool.

At Fender's, the sweat used to drip off the ceiling. That was insane. That place was really wild. Every time I went there, I got into a fight with a group of girls. I remember violence at Fender's. I don't remember it at the Olympic. Everyone got along, but at Fender's, there was always a fight.

I got to interview a couple of bands at Fender's for one of the kids at high school who had a little fanzine. The fanzine was titled *Bought the Farm*. The guy's name was Jimmy. I got to interview Conflict. My only question for them was if they had ever seen Rudimentary Peni. That's all I wanted to know, and that's all I remember. I was probably drinking. I saved those fanzines for a long time, but they are now gone.

The Ha Ha Hotel was in San Clemente, on Del Mar. It was all punk rockers living there, and a lot of aspiring musicians. It was right above a drugstore or something. You would walk up the stairs. It was somewhat ghetto, with little rooms. Everybody shared one kitchen. Our buddy's room overlooked the alley. They would send me and my girlfriend out to panhandle beer money. We came up with a lot of money sometimes. We used to play golf in the hallways. Me and my friend were always running away from home, so we would go sleep in the hallways or find an empty room and get in there and sleep. It was crazy there. Sometimes there would be fifteen people all out on the floor, sleeping and drunk. It was a lot of fun.

The first time I ran away, I lived on the beach in San Clemente. I just couldn't stand my mother. Then I ran away and went to Sunset and Vine in Hollywood. I met a pen pal from *Flipside* there. I lasted two or three days, and then some guy down there got me on the phone and told me to get home. He was somebody that I liked, so I came home. Thank God for that. Who knows what could have happened. I'd probably be a porn star or dead or something.

I had so many pen pals. I found them in *Flipside*. That was one
of my most favorite things: to find out, from state to state, what
the scene was like. I remember thinking that was what I wanted to
do—to go from here to there to see how all the punk rockers lived.
I used to have all of their pictures. I still have one pen pal, and that
is the one I ran away to when I was fourteen. She's doing really well.
I used to love getting my pen pal mail.

■   ■   ■   ■   ■

As far as punk rock, I'm more into the political bands and animal
rights. I mean, big time. I was a vegetarian back then. I went
to a march with Greenpeace. I'm a member of PETA. I liked
everything, but my belief system is about living your own life and
thinking for yourself. You don't have to conform to society. It just
makes sense to me.

I think the more my mother said, "You can't do this. You can't
do this," I said, "Fuck you. I'm going to do it." I would jump off the
roof, sneak out of the house, and run away for months at a time.

I have two children. My daughter just turned eighteen. My son
is going to be twelve. I always told my kids that if they're good kids
and they're doing good in school, they can do whatever the fuck they
want to do, as long as they think about it. If my mom would have
accepted me, I probably would have been a little more successful.

I remember when I ran away to Hollywood, the people I was
with were all doing drugs. I was totally against it. Then, three
months later, I was a full-blown drug addict. I used to take a lot of
acid. I then started doing cocaine. It's kind of sad, but that's what
happened. I wish the cocaine never came. It's bad. All bad. Before
that, I was totally against it. I wanted to go somewhere in life, and
I knew I wasn't going to with that. Where I let that guard down, I
don't know.

I still drink on a daily basis 'cause I'm an alcoholic, but I don't get drunk. My mom died of alcoholism so I probably shouldn't, but I want to live my life happy. I'd rather live a short, happy life than a long, miserable life. If you're going to live your life and go to a job day in and day out that you absolutely can't stand, you're just living this long, miserable life. The other person is happy every day, might be crazy, might be drinking, might be ruining their health, might be teaching their kid the same thing, but they are happy.

■   ■   ■   ■   ■

I found the scene welcoming to women. I'm a different kind of woman. I'm told that every day. What you see is what you get. As far as back then, how I saw myself, I don't know if I even really liked myself, because I was so confused with my mom not accepting me. That does a lot to a kid. I think that being in the punk rock scene is embedded in me. You're either a little rebel or you're not.

I don't think being in the punk scene was good or bad. It just is what it is. I still feel a connection to it. When I see the kids with their cones and leather jackets with the studs and paint, I always have to yell out the window, "Punk rock!" I don't know why. I feel disconnected, too, because they are all young and I'm forty-three. I don't care about shows. The Olympic, there will be nothing like that ever again—a bunch of freaks under one roof, getting along.

As confused and messed up as my head was, I had so much fun. Nothing can ever compare to it, and I can never be that crazy again. I would probably be scared to be that crazy—jumping off roofs and taking that much acid and drinking. Not a care in the world. It was so carefree. I liked it. It was fun.

I think our whole walk through life, no matter how big or small the steps are, is carried with us the whole way through, whether we know it or not. I'm not afraid to speak my mind. I'm still really strong in animal rights. Punk rock made me strong.

STELLA

Born in 1959 in Cleveland, Ohio. Lived in Gardena and Los Angeles, California, in the 1970s and '80s and worked as a radio DJ for KXLU's *Stray Pop* show. Currently continuing her work as a radio DJ for her long-running *Stray Pop* show on KXLU.

I WAS BORN in the rock and roll city of Cleveland, Ohio. My dad was a barber and my mother was a homemaker. My family moved from there when I was six months old to Gardena, here in Southern California. We lived on Spinning Avenue, which is funny. I ended up becoming a DJ, and I grew up on Spinning Avenue. It's kind of interesting, like predestination or something, because my name means "star voice," even though I don't use my last name publicly.

Since I was six months old, I don't remember anything about the move. I'm basically a naturalized Southern Californian. I come from an Italian family. Both sides of my family are southern Italian. My mother was actually half Sicilian. Growing up in Southern California, it seemed different, because I had more of an ethnic or a European upbringing. We didn't eat what the Brady Bunch ate. I always felt weird and different. Actually, we ate really well. We ate Italian food cooked from scratch. We didn't eat Hamburger Helper or anything like that. I always felt a little bit alienated. Growing up in the South Bay, it was a lot of blondes who go to the beach all the time.

When I was a teenager, I started gravitating towards music. We were all waiting for punk rock to happen, so what did we listen to? We listened to glitter rock. We listened to Aerosmith. We listened to Deep Purple. I started at Loyola Marymount the fall of 1977. I ditched my orientation group for school and wandered into the radio station. It was probably the summer of 1977. It's funny. I have a distinct memory of when I walked in there. There was a particular smell. It's a smell of electrical wires. It's so funny what will stick in your memory. God, that'd be cool if I smelled that smell again. It was so new and different to me then.

The university had a 3,000-watt radio station in Los Angeles, KXLU, which was no mean feat. I started to get involved, and eventually I started doing a radio show there. It's a slow process. Back then, it was called a carrier current station. It's an online stream now, but they had a carrier current back then, and that's where you started. I volunteered. I was helping do different things, like writing public service announcements.

You go through the ropes. I started doing a show on the AM station, and eventually got a show on the FM side. I first had to engineer classical programming. Usually the host is on a reel-to-reel tape, and you would have a little stack of records. You would start the reel-to-reel when the announcer would come in and do the opening. Then you would play the segment that he talked about. Then during the next break, you're pressing play. You slowly learned how to engineer everything and how to go to the FCC and get a third-class broadcast license. You had to go down to the FCC in Long Beach and take a test. Everyone would flunk, but you needed to have that to run the board. You just had to go and re-take it.

At first I did shows in the morning. You would have to go in way earlier to turn on the transmitter, which was a process of hitting banks of buttons and waiting twenty minutes while the tubes warmed up before you hit the next bank, because the transmitter was on-site and the antenna was on the roof. Eventually I started doing radio shows in the afternoon, after I went through my trial period of showing up and turning on the transmitter and doing a show very early in the morning.

I ended up doing the *Stray Pop* show, because I was getting in trouble for playing new wave music and punk rock music. I would get suspended. Then the program director just said, "Here, play this shit on a specialty show. I'm giving you a slot on Tuesday nights." I think it was 11 PM to 2 AM. That's how I started doing *Stray Pop*. It was February 5, 1980. Then I had a real place where bands could come in and be interviewed, as opposed to getting in trouble when they showed up in the afternoon.

The station used to be a real dinosaur rock station. This particular program director would even play Journey. The first Germs album, the first Psychedelic Furs album, the first Gun Club album—none of that was added to the station. It expanded more in the mid-'80s. On the show, I would have X and the Gears up. I had a venue where they could come up and be on the air.

Crazy things used to happen all the time. The free-form format gives people more of an opportunity to really reveal themselves. Sometimes you find out more about people from what music they bring up to play than any question I can ask. I got a lot of expertise and crowd control dealing with drunks. Now that I have a kid, I see that dealing with a toddler was a lot easier than dealing with those guys. I don't know which show it was where I had five blenders making drinks versus the one show where there were three Lady Kenmore blenders. Boy, that made a mess in the hallway. It's been a lot of fun.

■　　■　　■　　■　　■

My work as a DJ is such a creative outlet. I'm at the end of my life in sweatpants, as I call it as an adult. Even back when I worked as a magazine editor, being a DJ was so nice. It was a relief to come up at the end of the week and just play music. Sometimes you just let the music do the talking. I don't do a lot of prep time. I have very vague, rough ideas. I really work off of being spontaneous. When I say free-form radio, I really mean it. Sometimes I have no idea what I'm going to play.

I do haul a lot of stuff with me up to the station. I carry ten lunch bags. They're rectangular. They're the perfect shape for CDs. Each fits about twenty to twenty-two CDs. I carry ten of those. They have straps on them. I grip them with each arm, and then I have a backpack that's made for LPs strapped on my back. It has LPs and more CDs crammed in it, and a lot of playlists. I have so much stored in my punk rock geezer memory that I can tap into it.

It is also therapeutic for me. I've done the show for so long at this point, it's really a part of my identity. There are so many ways I can express myself. Radio is such a great medium that way. I'll do the show until I drop.

It was a natural progression for me to get into punk rock, since I had already been interested in music. KROQ used to be a really great station. It was free-form. They had an AM station, too, so you could listen to it in your car on your AM radio. From there, I started hearing stuff on the air. I listened to Rodney [Bingenheimer's] show. That was great, because that's how you got exposed to everything. You started meeting people. Back then, there were only two punk rockers on campus: John Linardos and Tom Morris. Through them, I met all sorts of other people. Before you know it, you're going up to shows in Hollywood.

I went to shows at the Whisky, the Starwood, the Polish Hall, at the bowling alley in Culver City. All sorts of different places. Once I was at this interesting party. I met all these people there. It sticks out in my mind because that was the day that someone got ahold of the early edition of the Sunday *Times*. X was on the cover of the calendar section. That was groundbreaking. Oh my God! One of us on the Sunday calendar cover? I remember someone running into the party with that, and everyone was just astonished.

It was such a vibrant scene. It was so unique. I knew it was really special. The roots of it and how it came about was a reaction. It did something to the whole music scene. If it wasn't for the

Eagles, we wouldn't have punk rock today, because it was, especially for us here in L.A., a reaction to that. The Eagles are the California sound? Are you kidding me?

#   #   #   #   #

Being a woman, your experience is what it is. Some of it I don't think about, but other times, it does dawn on me that something is a certain way because I'm a woman. I have noticed in a lot of documentaries that have been done about the scene or particular bands that there aren't a lot of women in them. I don't know. It is what it is. Maybe some people are busy, and I know sometimes people have wanted to interview me for their documentaries and I've been busy with other things. Maybe I should start doing it more often.

I thought the punk clubs were welcoming to women. I just loved it. The energy was so exciting. It wasn't like this whole violence thing. I've always cracked up about the reputation it has, and how it originally was depicted when network TV tried to incorporate it or do a story on it, because I just loved it. I felt like I belonged, as opposed to the alienation of living in a place where we all go to the beach all the time. I was different, because I didn't have blonde hair or whatever it was that I had put in my mind. Punk rock was not as much of an anger reaction for me at that time as it was just sheer joy. When I would walk in with the people I walked in with, I was embraced by everybody else. I felt very welcomed.

Punk rock is such a part of me and a part of a lot of people. It really is. You have the environment you grew up in, your family, and the community you lived with. Then there's punk rock. It's just such a part of my identity, and my soul, and my happiness, and also my sarcasm. I used to say punk rock is thicker than water. You know what? I was right. It wasn't just a catchy saying. It's the people that have stood with you in battle. It's blood of the covenant. It's really true.

There is the expression "you create your family." Sometimes you bump into someone you haven't seen for twenty or thirty years and it's just like no time has gone by. You're happy to see them. Most of them, the ones that are still alive, you're happy to have known them, and you're proud that you know them. Right before I sat down with you to do this, I went and saw the Gears documentary, which is really well done. It's just like, "Man, I'm proud of what we did. We spent our youth well."

Punk rock is an attitude. It's not just a musical style. It's an attitude. It's not fashion. It's not a look. It's very independent. I think sometimes when it comes to the politics of it, I was just too busy enjoying the music. You're more apathetic when you're younger than you are when you're older, because you know stuff.

Now, punk rock fuels what I am disturbed by, and where I'm afraid things might be going, and where we are now. These songs that are thirty-five, forty years old sometimes now ring more true, at least to me, than they did then. It's very uncanny and kind of frightening. Does anything ever change? Does history just constantly repeat itself or get worse? I don't know.

It's such a relief that the punk rock part of my identity did not get wiped away from having a kid, because I was still going to shows and doing the radio show. I brought my son with me to the radio station. I breastfed and broadcast at the same time. It turned out that he needed to nurse every hour and a half. I had this whole thing where I had him in the stroller and brought him up.

I'm non-traditional. I'm not a real subservient kind of person. Sometimes I'm surprised when I get attitude from people. I'm just not very traditional. I probably was, underneath it all, but I think maybe punk rock just helped solidify it more. I gravitated toward it, and it made me so happy. I'm a punk rock geezer and very proud of it.

TAMMY TALBOT

Born in 1965 in Anoka, Minnesota. Lived in Anoka; San Francisco, Riverside, Huntington Beach, and Silver Lake, California; and throughout Europe (England, Italy, Holland, and beyond) in the '80s. Sang in the band Nature Core and attended shows at various venues throughout Los Angeles County, Orange County, and Europe. Currently lives in Burbank, California, where she owns a hair salon and art gallery.

IT WAS BEFORE I WAS THIRTEEN. I was in Minnesota. My mom's youngest sister, my aunt Shirley, and my uncle Steve loved music. I adored them. I looked up to them. They had parties and they used to let me have half of a beer and some malted milk balls. I was looking at their records and I said to my uncle Steve, who was such a great man, "Who is this ugly girl?" He goes, "That's no girl. That's David Bowie." I didn't know who David Bowie was. At that moment, because of how he said it, I thought to myself, "Wow. There's something special here." I heard Bowie, MC5, the Velvet Underground, and early garage-like punk stuff from them.

I came out to California when I was twelve or thirteen. I was watching TV and the news came on, and there was a flash about the Sex Pistols. I was just a little kid. I jumped up and was glued to the screen. I was so excited, but my mom shut the TV off. At night in my bedroom, during my high school years, I would turn on

Rodney on the ROQ and I would record and make cassette tapes. I
still have my tapes. I would listen to the show and think, "Whoa,
this stuff is amazing." It just started evolving.

At first I was very rebellious. I was running away, acting up,
and I was going to shows. I was very young—around thirteen. I
was into punk rock while in school. We stood out by our clothes. I
was actually voted the senior vice president and "most humorous"
and yet, I was a punk rocker. I was troubled, but not anti-social.
It was a statement, the punk rock thing, because it was like, if you
can get past this exterior, then you can get into my interior. I still
hadn't worked on any of my childhood issues at that point, but I
was always trying to be involved in things . . . gigs, zines, selling for
London Exchange. The political side of it came in the '80s. I spoke
about my past and wasn't afraid to tell people about how I grew up,
what I endured, and how I survived as an abused kid.

I saw shows at the Roxy, the Whisky, Cathay de Grande, the
Olympic, Perkins Palace, the Ukrainian Center, Cuckoo's Nest,
T-Bird Rollerdome, and the Galaxy, as well as many other venues.
In Riverside, there was a place called the Ritz. I spent a lot of time
there. There was the Barn in Riverside. Later there was Fender's,
but I wasn't really a Fender's girl. I went there a handful of times
and found it incredibly violent. I saw Black Flag in Santa Ana down
this little hallway venue that opened up in this teeny little room,
and people were hanging from the rafters. These places were just
open-and-shut. There'd be shows for two months, which basically
was four to eight shows, maybe, and then [it would] shut down.
I went all over. Anywhere from San Diego to Santa Barbara. I
even saw shows in San Francisco. If there was a show, we saved up
enough money and got the day off work. We'd stuff six people in a
car that held four and just go. Whatever it took to be part of it all.

I didn't have the best childhood. A lot of us didn't, and I think that's what our draw to punk rock was. I already felt different, so then I found my clan, my tribe of other misfits, and a place where I could fit in. It was a place of belonging, a family of sorts, a chosen family.

I always felt like I was a feminist. I always felt strong and clear and proud, despite all of the things that I had gone through. Once I spoke out about the abuse/neglect in my life, I then became a real advocate for people who had gone through similar things, or people who needed support—people who were fighting for freedom and equal rights. I was always in the corner of those who were downtrodden or less fortunate. I started anarcho-feminism groups with friends in the '80s. I sang in a band called Nature Core in the '80s.

Before and after Nature Core, I had been in a few garage bands that never evolved or played out. I went on a lot of demonstrations. I wrote letters to political prisoners. I raised money and brought attention to different causes for people who were struggling. When I moved to Europe, I was very politically active. I worked at the 1 in 12 Club, booking bands and tending bar, as well as at a used record store. I had a whole DIY anarchist approach to life. During this time, I was able to put my beliefs into practical support for women and children when I worked as a rape crisis counselor, as a childcare worker at a woman's refuge, and with prostitutes offering support, advice, and education. I also worked for the BBC as a referral call-in service and counselor when there were programs on the television about violence against women and children. I left the States in '83 and moved to Europe, and came back home to Los Angeles in '93.

With Nature Core, there were two vegetarians and two vegans in the band. I sang and wrote songs. I did a lot of poetry back then and spoken word. They were a talented group of guys that I sang in the band with. I'm part Native American, so our songs were about the raping of the earth, equality/inequality, and different things that were happening in the world, such as apartheid and animal abuse. I wasn't a great singer; I just had something to say, and they liked that. I always felt like a leader. I wasn't a follower. That was one of my strengths. I believed in myself enough to be righteous in my way.

During my political time I loved Crass, Chumbawamba, and Poison Girls. I also liked Rudimentary Peni, Icons of Filth, Conflict, Liberty, and so many more. Other standouts for me are Beefeater, Bad Brains, Toxic Reasons, Reagan Youth, BGK, Indigesti, Crucifucks, MDC, Social Distortion, TSOL, Black Flag, and, of course, the Clash. I liked and respected bands that were strong lyrically and musically, like a force to be reckoned with. I also liked bands that were creative, bright, and had a sense of humor. A lot of these bands were bands that I admired. They were also friends and comrades.

■   ■   ■   ■   ■

I think that the punk rock scene in the beginning was very welcoming to women, because we were just kids. We were looking for somewhere, someplace to be to express ourselves, whether through our dress, music, through our words, actions. We just wanted to be respected. I thought it was good up until a certain point. When punk started being influenced by metal and more jocks and rednecks got into it, then it became less of a place for women to be and more male-dominated. Now, men have always been far more active, but women have always been active. There are women that stood out in the scene,

like Exene, Penelope Houston, Kim Gordon, Vice Versa, Alice and Lou of Chumbawamba, and even later L7 and 7 Year Bitch were just so great.

There was a time in the mid-to-late '80s when the guys were knocking the shit out of you. They didn't give two shits about you, women, children, or another man. It was just more aggressive. The gigs were bigger and more intense. There were always individuals and gangs fighting, especially in and around the Olympic Auditorium.

I started getting stronger and stronger and wanted to turn it around and stand tall for people who couldn't. I think that was my knee-jerk reaction, to get even more involved with feminism.

The whole peace punk scene was quite small. Ninety percent of the people were awesome. The guys in the band with me were amazing all the time. That was a time when we struggled as women—not just me, but other women that I know. I struggled with my sexuality. I was a sexual being. I was a sensual being, but was I compromising my feminism by sleeping with men and men in bands? There were times when I chose to be celibate for years at a time to build my own strength and feel empowered within that celibacy. But sadly, I was denying that sensual being that I am, that I've always been. I was very conscious about it.

What I was always blown away with, by being a woman, was that men still viewed women, for the most part, as sexual beings only. I remember MDC. I was so stoked about MDC. I loved them. We started hanging out. A couple wanted to talk politics, but really what they wanted to do was fuck you. When I realized that, I said, "Why don't you just say you want to have sex with me? I would respect that more. I'll talk politics with somebody else." Or, "I'll talk politics with you later, but just say what you want." It was disappointing, because it happened on multiple occasions. I just wanted the bullshit to stop.

I wish I could find the right words for it. It could be disheartening, as a woman. You think that you're brothers and sisters in solidarity. They really didn't view you like that. It was an interesting time.

■   ■   ■   ■   ■

Where I am now, I'm still an alternative being with my views and lifestyle. I'm a single mom and own my own business. I have my core beliefs that are rock solid. I still believe in the same things that I believed in as a teenager, in my twenties, in my thirties, in my forties, and now as a woman who has just turned fifty. Things may appear different than they are, but I'm still that person. I'm a working-class kid who just focused and worked really hard. I believe in the simple things, like being nice to people and treating people equally. It's not that hard to do. Treating people respectfully shouldn't be considered alternative, should it?

I want music to make me feel something, anything. When it doesn't make me feel anything, it's just mass-produced and over-produced and made to sell to the sheep, and it kills my spirit when I hear it. It's empty of heart and soul, and is dishonest. What motivates me is love and beauty and goodness. I love authentic people and what they can produce and create. Music's got to have all that, too.

Punk rock has influenced every area of my life—my closest friends, my best memories, my live-out-loud moments, the best fun, the hardest times. Being beaten by cops as a punk rocker is not a good memory, but being a punk enabled me to have the strength to fight back and express myself. It's how I live. It's like getting tattooed. I've always gotten tattooed. It's one of the ways I express myself. It's my "herstory" on my body. Almost ninety percent of every connection that I have, besides my family of origin, is based around punk rock somehow. Art, books, photographs, records, cars, motorcycles. Almost everyone I'm connected with now is connected to punk rock.

I feel like I contributed to the scene. I didn't just come and take. I gave back by being a fan, too. I like to support people's art, music, shows, zines, books, and livelihoods. Without punk rock, I'd be dead. That's a fact. It saved my life. I take it very seriously. I wouldn't have had anywhere else to go. That's the truth. I'm grateful.

TERESA COVARRUBIAS

Born in 1960 in Los Angeles, California. Lived in L.A. in the 1970s, '80s, and '90s and played in the Brat (1978–1985), Breath of Breath (1980s), Las Tres (circa 1990s), and Goddess13 (circa 1990s). Currently works as an elementary school teacher in L.A.

I WAS BORN IN BOYLE HEIGHTS, which is just east of Los Angeles and across the L.A. River. I was born in a predominantly Chicano neighborhood. My family was pretty large, with seven siblings. I went to Catholic school and had a fairly conventional Mexican upbringing. Maybe the only difference was that my parents were second-generation. My dad was born in El Paso and my mom was born in L.A. We were assimilated. We were more like the American side than we were Mexican, so we didn't have a lot of the Mexican culture when I was growing up. We were more influenced by American culture.

We didn't really listen to any cultural music. My parents would listen to big band music. They liked jazz. My older siblings were very '60s children. I kind of grew up with the whole British Invasion. I remember liking the Beatles when I was five years old, which kind of morphed into liking the Stones when I was eight or nine. From there, it kind of went into glam rock and David Bowie, Roxy Music, Brian Eno. I always felt, growing up, that my interests were a little different than the people that I was around.

I was told about how you have to succeed, and this is the way you do it. You get married. You go to college. You have kids. You get a good job. You save your money. I didn't really feel like that type of outlet or way of looking at life was for me. I think a lot of the people I grew up with were very conventional in that way. They

were willing to toe the line and just do what was expected of them. That didn't feel right for me.

Ever since I was really young, I've always been drawn to music and singing. I came across punk music from Rodney Bingenheimer. He used to play a lot of glam rock, but he was also playing stuff from New York, like Blondie and the Ramones. I think that's when I first thought, "Whoa! I kind of dig this." It had a whole different energy about it. It was energized and in your face. It wasn't overly produced like a lot of stuff was at that time.

Then I started hearing about this scene happening in England, which was about '76. I was totally blown away by that scene, and mostly because there were a lot of women. Since I had grown up in this male-dominated rock world, that was an eye-opener for me. I thought, "This is something that maybe I can get into and do."

I started hearing about shows in L.A. I remember going to the Starwood and the Whisky and seeing a lot of the bands that Rodney was playing. Not only was he playing New York bands, but he would play a lot of local music as well. The Whisky would have matinee shows during the afternoon. They'd be for two dollars, and you could see seven bands. It was just really wide open, and the scene was very all-inclusive. There wasn't a sense of you being the audience, and we're the performers. It was this very inviting feeling.

All the punk shows that I would go see were on the Westside. Nothing was really happening on the Eastside, so I kind of felt isolated, like I was here in this community and nobody really was into what I was into. I had one friend that was also into Blondie and liked the punk thing. We would go and see shows.

During this time, maybe '76, '77, '78, I was more like an audience person just going to see the shows. I wasn't really involved, even though I wanted to start a band and be more on the performer side of it. I saw a jam with the Weirdos and the Zeros at the Starwood, which was probably '78, and that's when I met the guitarist that I ended up putting a band together with.

After that Starwood show, I hooked up with the guitarist. He had a brother that had a band, but they were doing covers. His brother was going to get married, and he wasn't going to be involved in music anymore. I auditioned for him, in a way, because I remember we were drinking beer once and the radio was playing and I just started singing right to him. Everybody was laughing at me and I didn't care. I was just singing, and he said, "Oh, you have a good voice," so we started a group.

At first, it was covers. We would do Blondie and some Cheap Trick. We would mostly play at backyard party shows in East L.A., because there were really no venues at that time. I was about seventeen or eighteen. We were not called the Brat, but it was the beginnings of that. Slowly, we started writing our own original material. I'd say by late '78, '79, we were pretty much doing an all-original set, but we really didn't have any places to play. By that time, the whole Hollywood punk scene had already kind of came and went. Things became very cliquish. And then there was an element that started happening in the punk scene that was really kind of negative and violent, especially when we would go to shows. Before that, everybody would pogo, and if you fell down, somebody would pick you up. It was very friendly. After a couple of years, it got very violent and then it was also a little racist, too.

At the time we were doing the backyard parties, slowly we were getting people interested in the group, but people were basically there for the DJs. People would all be dancing to the DJs and then they needed a break, and we'd play. Everybody would kind of clear the dance floor, and we'd be there by ourselves, but it was an interesting experience.

I think the first show that we did that was a real concert was probably at Madame Wong's in '78, '79. Actually, it was kind of important. I think John Doe and Exene were there that night, and they really dug the band. I always say that I think they had a lot to do with helping us break that barrier, because I always felt there was a barrier. Some people say there wasn't, and there's always this big argument that punk was inclusive and everybody was welcome, but that wasn't really our experience. After Exene and John came and they met us afterwards, they really helped us try to break into the whole scene on the Westside. We opened for them many times, because they requested that we did.

That's sort of the same time that the Vex happened. [Chicano muralist] Willie Herron was working with [Catholic nun, fine artist, and Self-Help Graphics founder Sister Karen Boccalero] to use the Self-Help Graphics space as a space to do shows. They heard about us, because there was word going around. Willie came by our rehearsal place and auditioned us to see if we were worthy to play.

After that happened, the whole East L.A. thing started to gel together. We started doing shows with other bands. The Vex became a venue for Chicano bands that were having difficulties playing gigs on the Westside to have a place to play and get some exposure. Self-Help Graphics was always a community art center that was promoting arts and music and that type of thing in the community, so it was really a nice fit, because that's exactly what we were doing. We were creating music. It was music that was happening in that community, and it just became the space for us to perform there.

There was this element of art as well, because Willie Herron

was part of the [East L.A. Chicano artist collective] ASCO group.
The whole East L.A. scene was not just about the music, but it also
had this art component. [Chicano artist and printmaker] Richard
Duardo did our album cover, so it started to gel into this really
nice sort of community that I wouldn't say was exclusive, but was
very geographic. All of these people were east of the L.A. River.
We all grew up in that neighborhood and had the same vibe. We
were representing something to the public that was really against
the stereotypes that most people thought when they thought
of the Eastside. Usually, when people thought of the Eastside,
immediately, they thought of gangs and poverty. So here were these
groups of people that were artists and writers and poets.

As the Vex grew, people came not only for the music, but for
the artists and poets. We used to do a lot of cool shows where
they'd do art openings with the punk bands and then poetry all in
the same night, and all from the Eastside.

In the beginning, our songs were more about angst, like feeling
that nobody understands me and I'm so upset or heartbroken.
Then, as the band started to evolve, it became a little more political.
I think that was partly from me coming in contact with other
Chicanos. I always felt very isolated, even though I lived around
all of these people. I like to tell people that Harry Gamboa, a very
popular Chicano artist, lived two blocks away from me and I didn't
know.

There was this sense of separateness. I guess that's true of a lot
of communities that are marginalized. You don't have respect for
your own community, because it's been shit on so much that you
just want to get away.

You don't see what's in your backyard. When the Vex started
happening, I was meeting these people that were my neighbors. It
was life-changing. It really was. I had grown up in this atmosphere
that was all about assimilating and becoming an American.

Meeting these people and seeing how they had embraced their culture and were not ashamed of it really opened my eyes and got me more political. I viewed my circumstance in a whole different way, and was proud of it and didn't want to run away. I wanted to be an ambassador for a different view of what it means to be an East L.A. resident. It's not just about cholos and violence. It's beautiful and it's good. It's artistic and it's creative.

I lived in Downey for a little while with my mother, but basically I've always been east of the L.A. River. Now I live in Highland Park, but some people would consider Highland Park east. I feel really comfortable here. Whenever I go to the Westside, there's something about it. Maybe it's just my prejudice, but I always felt like I don't belong there, and they don't think I belong there. There's always that feeling of not being accepted or not being in a place where people want you. Whenever I'm here, I just feel like this is my home. I feel comfortable.

■   ■   ■   ■   ■

Being a performer in the scene, I felt like the audience was very responsive to me. Unfortunately, it was my own band mates that were very backward. I hate to say it, but a lot of Latino men are just very backward when it comes to what they think about women. My band mates didn't treat me very well, and I don't think they appreciated the contribution that I made to the band. Sometimes they'd go as far as saying that I wasn't a musician because I didn't play an instrument, but I was writing the songs. I was writing the lyrics. I always felt like we were butting heads, because I was never given respect. I think, because of the way I grew up, I kind of accepted that instead of being more assertive. I look in hindsight and think, "You should have just left them and found people who respected what you were doing and were really going to support you." I always felt like I was the low man on the totem pole. It was ridiculous to accept that position. Not to sound immodest, but without me, that band wouldn't have been what it was. They still don't see that.

When I think about that, it brings back some really bad memories. We would play, and they would play so loud that I couldn't even hear myself singing. The sound man would tell them, "You know guys, you gotta lower it down. You can't hear your vocalist." They didn't care. I would go back and look, and their amps would be at ten. We're supposed to be a band. We're doing this to sound good together, but it was more about playing guitar. I felt more support from the audience.

Once I started working with Alice [Bag] and Angela [Vogel] and other women, I thought, "This is what it could have been." When I was working with women, especially with the band Las Tres, it really felt like we were doing it together. It felt very real and nurturing. You wanted to be there. You wanted to help. You felt nourished. With the guys, it was more like a battle. You were constantly fighting for your identity.

After the music thing had sort of come and gone, I realized that I needed to make a living. I started going back to school. I went back to college when I was twenty-seven. At that time, one of the best jobs you could do when you were going to college was to be a teacher's assistant. It paid pretty well. You could work three hours, and they were very accommodating to your college schedule. I kind of got into doing that, and I dug it. It was nice being around kids. Kids have a great energy.

It took me a long time to graduate. I started in '87 and I think I finally got my B.A. in '96. Actually, I started at Cal State L.A. when I was in the band, around age eighteen. I couldn't do both, so I basically flunked out. In '87, I started at East L.A. College. After a couple of years, I transferred back to Cal State. I got a degree in child development and psychology. At first I thought I was going

to be a psychologist, because I was really into why we are the way
we are, but because of that experience as a teaching assistant, I
just thought that would be a great job. That's basically how I got
into the teaching thing, and I've been doing it since. I'm now an
elementary school teacher. I'm teaching second grade. When I
started, I did some fifth grade and fourth grade. I started working
with Alice Velasquez [aka Alice Bag]. She was a teacher at Hoover,
and she was teaching pre-K. A six-hour position opened at her
school. I put in for that and got it. I worked with her for a long
time with the little, little ones. That's what sold me. It didn't feel
like work. That's the best kind of job you can have, right, where it
doesn't feel like you're working.

■　　■　　■　　■　　■

I've made some choices in life that are really unusual and definitely
not following the norm. I think I feel that even more as I get older.
I'm just getting comfortable with the fact that a lot of what I am
about is generally not what my
mom and dad wanted for me. I
know they still worry about me.
I'm not married. I don't have
any children. For a Chicana,
a Latina, that's very unusual,
because usually it's about family.

    I think the punk experience
helped me to legitimize this
feeling of being opposed or
standing up. Even though
you may be the only person
or you're on the outskirts of
something, I realized that's
not a bad place to be. I think

that experience helped me see that it is not necessarily bad to
be marginalized. There's actually a sort of a power to be able to
look at something from the outside and not blend in or be part of
something mainstream. I think I've always been that person that's
looking at something from the outside, whether it's by choice or
that circumstances pushed me out there. I think I used to feel really
uncomfortable being an outsider, or being on the fringe. Now I
embrace it. I'm actually proud of it.

My punk roots helped nurture a questioning in me. Question
everything! Don't just accept it because they're putting it there, but
say, "Nah, I don't think so. I think there might be another way of
doing something." That punk influence is still here for me today.
Other people don't know what's best for me. I'm going to make up
my own mind.

TEXACALA JONES

Born in Los Angeles, California. Lived in L.A. and San Francisco, California, in the '80s, played guitar for Boris, Horace, Doris, and Dolores (circa 1981), and sang for Tex & the Horseheads (circa 1982–present) and Texorcist (circa 1989). Currently lives in Austin, Texas, and plays in the band Hey!

I WAS ABOUT EIGHTEEN when my boyfriend introduced me to punk rock. I wasn't playing music yet. He was playing the Sex Pistols. I wigged out. I really liked it. I went with some friends of mine down to the Masque by Hollywood Boulevard. I started watching a lot of punk bands. At that time, I was trying to jam saxophone, like these jazz people in back of Los Perritos on Hollywood Boulevard. Way in the back, there was this little room with a little table. I used to jump on there and try to jam jazz. Then punk rock happened.

I got in this band called Boris, Horace, Doris, and Dolores. I was with them for about a year. I got fired from the band because I was such a horrible guitar player. It was disastrous. I was supposed to practice, and I never did. There was another band before that, around '80, but we only played a couple shows. I hooked up with Jeffrey Lee in '81. Then things really started changing.

I was going to play in the Gun Club, but I only played one show and got fired from the Gun Club. Poor Jeffrey Lee. He really worked with me for a month and everything. I played my heart out, but evidently it just really sucked. The band just said, "Look, Jeffrey Lee. It's either her or us." He couldn't fire his whole band. I understood. He felt bad about it, but that's when he thought of us starting another band, and that's what started Tex & the Horseheads. This was around the end of '81. It was Jeffrey Lee and me and the Vodka Brothers, but it was mostly Jeffrey Lee and me, because we were traveling a lot. We were going from here to there, and we would just pick up people. We would pick up a drummer and a bass player. It would be him on guitar and me on vocals. We were just horsing around and having a good time.

It was pretty much Tex & the Horseheads in the '80s. Around '89, I got in Texorcist. I think it was the '90s when I got involved with the Ringling Sisters. That lasted for about a year. A whole slew of bands. I've been in a trillion bands. There's bands I've been in that I don't remember the names of. I used to have kind of a bad rep, because I was jumping from band to band at one time. I was having a hard time. The first bands I was in, I was playing bass and I was playing guitar. Nobody would let me sing, because my voice was so weird. I freaked people out. They would just go, "Oh my gawd!" With Tex & the Horseheads, I never really quit the band. Everybody always quit me. The way I look at it, I'm still with Tex & the Horseheads, but nobody else is. The new band I'm in now is called Hey! I'm in the band with Lisafer from 45 Grave.

■   ■   ■   ■   ■

The fact that I'm a woman is not really an advantage to me. I'm kind of a little schlub. I'm not that great-looking or anything. I pretty much operate on personality and my voice. I mean, I look all right, but it's nothing to scream home about. Sometimes people would be genteel towards me because of my gender, but as a rule, they wouldn't be. In fact, some people would take advantage of that. You know how it is out there. It's a jungle out there. Some people are very kind, and some people are very unkind. As you go through life, you try to figure out how to detect which ones are which. It's not ever easy.

If you know how to make it happen, I don't think it matters what gender you are. Really, it's a matter of business sense. I just don't happen to have that business sense. I don't blame it on me being a woman. I just blame it on my brain. In some cases, being a woman does get in the way if you let it, but it's also in your mind.

I'm definitely part of the outcast club. I'm down with outcast sisters. I also feel like I might be different in the sense of the kind of music that I'm putting out. It's definitely hard to put it in a genre. It's hard to tell people what kind of music I play. That doesn't help the situation, either. I just try to write songs and call them songs, and I can't put them in a genre. That might be what sets me apart. I can't really fit into a slot.

If it wasn't for punk rock, I don't think anybody would have listened to me, because it was punk rockers that totally tolerated my style and let me play solos and everything. Punk rock made it possible for people like me to go out into the daylight with our blackness and crawl out into life. It was totally a good thing. Still, after a while, you have to put on your big girl pants and just say, "Well, it is what it is."

Back then, it was fun and exciting. I was a single lady out there, whooping it up. I was having a pretty good time. Everybody was partying. There were some really bad things that happened, but I usually don't highlight those things. Whatever you do, there's going to be some good and bad stuff going on.

Sometimes I feel like a punk and sometimes I don't, but I still feel a connection. When I'm touring with somebody, the first thing I do is look for the punks. They'll tell you where shit is. Punks will always be the friendliest people.

ZIZI "CARROT WOMAN" HOWELL

Born in 1961 in Los Angeles, California. Lived in L.A. in the '80s, created and distributed *LCD* fanzine, and attended shows at various venues throughout Los Angeles County. Currently works as an accounting secretary for a CPA firm in L.A.

I GOT INTO PUNK IN 1980. Kids nowadays just can't grasp how different things were back then. If you were a punker, you were really different. First of all, everyone had hair back then—lots of it! Feathered hair and Afros, the bigger and longer, the better. No one had shaved heads, not blacks, not Mexicans—only punkers. The exception would have been Marines, but you could tell they were not punkers by their jarheads.

We were so different back then, and really stood out. It was truly shocking. I got fired from my job for having colored hair. We

got chased and beat and hassled constantly. The music at the time was long rock jams and disco. It was unheard of to have a song lasting one minute, and played so fast. We paved the way for the kids now—that is, it's pretty normal and accepted to look like a punker now.

It was 1979 and I just graduated high school—Uni High in West L.A. My friends consisted of the typical surfer/ stoner crowd who listened to

Led Zeppelin, Lynyrd Skynyrd, and Ted Nugent, and went to the big stadium concerts of the day. I was really bored with this scene. I distinctly remember the day I was riding in the car with my mom and I announced, "Mom, I'm going to listen to punk rock!" as I permanently turned the radio knob from KMET to KROQ.

I was instantly attracted to this new music and scene. It was fresh and different from anything that had come before. However, I had abandoned my old scene and friends, and therefore I had no friends to share my interests with. I cut my long hair to a shoulder-length bob à la Deborah Harry and started dressing new wave, and that felt very rebellious to me. I did stuff that I would never imagine doing today.

As a shy teenager and all alone, it took me a long time to get into the scene. I started going to clubs like the Whisky and the Roxy, and seeing bands like the Suburban Lawns, Oingo Boingo, and the Go-Go's. After a Weirdos show, I was talking to some punk boys outside of the Whisky. I was really excited that I was connecting with "my own kind." We talked about shows that we had seen, and when I mentioned that I had seen the Go-Go's, the boys started laughing at me. That's when I realized that there was an even deeper punk movement: hardcore.

I went to a barber the next day and told him to cut all my hair off! I was nervous about getting a total buzz, but told him to cut it VERY short. The barber hesitated, saying, "Men's and women's hair are different, and I'm not sure that I can create the look you want." He then proceeded and I felt so liberated, walking out of there with my new 'do!

Back then, KROQ played Black Flag, Circle Jerks, and other hardcore bands with full expletives in their normal song rotation, along with regular new wave bands. I remember "Amoeba" was a big hit, and they would play it at least hourly. Rodney Bingenheimer also had his show on the weekends, feeding my knowledge of hardcore music. However, I still was alone in my infancy of the scene. I decided that I needed to see the king of all hardcore bands: Black Flag. It was early 1981, and they were playing at the Vex. As I neared the Vex, I could see crowds of punk kids spilling into the street. They were wild and rowdy. I drove around the block a few times, deliberating where I could safely park, but I was petrified with fear and drove all the way home!

I did this again several times over the next few months. I was too scared to go to a hardcore gig alone. I even did that for [*The Decline of Western Civilization*] when it was first released on the opening night. I drove there, and I was so scared. And I drove around and I went home. I decided I would go see it next week, when there were fewer people. The people were violent. I was a punker, but I could imagine to regular people what it felt like seeing these scary kids.

Then one of my old friends had "turned" punk and called, saying that she wanted to go to a gig. Great! Safety in numbers! The next gig was the big show at the Santa Monica Civic in June 1981. Black Flag was playing with the Adolescents, DOA, and the Minutemen. It was the biggest punk show to date, with approximately 3,500 people. The Adolescents were on and I lost my friend, as I pressed forward through the masses. I soon found myself being violently pummeled and knocked around the pit. Then someone ripped my t-shirt off! Boys grabbed at me as I tried to fight them off. Girls pulled at my hair. I tried to protect myself, and pushed my way out. It was scary. I'd never been so scared in my life. I thought I was going to be raped. I faced the comfort of a wall as a merciful boy gave me his bandana and I managed to tie it around my chest. I never saw my friend again that night. She called me a few days later to tell me that she was *never* going to another gig.

I did not think the scene was welcoming to women. It was definitely male-oriented, and it was kind of like a boys' club.

I think a lot of the women were the rejects. They weren't the popular girls at school. A lot of the girls found their niche by being photographers and writers of fanzines. They found their way to be in the scene and be accepted that way. I was a girl in the pit. I liked slam dancing. I liked the physical feeling. I was always kind of a tomboy, so I was always tough. I think, because I was a woman, they were attacking me in an almost rape-like way, but I saw other people at that time being attacked just for the violence. It seems so senseless now.

There was something about the violence and frenzy of a punk mob, a sexual charge to being pressed against a mass of sweaty bodies, that attracted me. I passed my "initiation"—a sort of gang "jump in." I was bruised from head to toe, but I wanted more. I was ready to embark on the hardcore scene.

I wrote the following poem, which encapsulates the moment in time:

CONFESSIONS OF A PUNK ROCK GIRL
(Circa 1981)

Post high school. Feeling alienated. Wanting to
scream from within and lash out from this stupid
life. Searching for purpose.
    L.A. Hardcore Punk Scene
    Aimless. Scary. Intimidating. Boys. Anger.
Hate. Frenzy. Fury. Broken Glass. Broken Bodies.
Damage. Damage. Damage. Riots. LAPD.
    In the "circle." The slam pit. The spit and the
sweat. Bodies pressed against me. I like the feeling.
Heat from the bodies matches the heat from the
rage. The hurt is sudden and frequent, but I like
it. Wanting love. No love. The mass is a temporary
release. The feeling lingers to please.

 Blue and purple from the previous night's rage
to remind me of a soul lacking love or reason.
 I go again the next night.
 I like the pain.

 I started going to every hardcore gig I heard about. And in this age before social media, it wasn't all that easy to find out about gigs back then. At one gig at Bard's Apollo in the Crenshaw area of L.A., the show got shut down and there was a big riot. I got caught up in the melee, breaking windows and smashing everything in sight. There was a great thrill in being part of this mob mentality. It was during this riot that I met my first punk boyfriend, Vince "Gore" Quiroz. He told me to go with him and his friends, and we ended up at Oki Dogs.

 Gore introduced me to some of his friends, who were John Macias and Mike Vallejo of Circle One. The cops then showed up at Oki Dogs, and the word was to go to Errol Flynn's mansion ruins in the Hollywood Hills. There were about a hundred of us hiking up the hill to party, and then the cops converged upon us there. There were helicopters and dogs and sirens. We could hear people screaming and getting roughed up. Gore and I hid in some thick brush for hours until we could no longer hear any trouble. We bushwhacked our way down the hill and ended up in someone's backyard. We were scratched and dirty, but okay. I think we were the only ones that didn't get arrested that night. Now I think about it, I wouldn't go in bushes with snakes and bugs. I wouldn't do that now or even back then, if there wasn't that hazard of police.

  ■ ■ ■ ■ ■

I enjoyed photography and had a darkroom at home. I began taking photos and writing about the scene. To me, that was kind of my way of getting into the scene, since I didn't know too many people.

It was my own way to expose myself and make friends. I soon had enough material and, along with a poet/artist friend named Carrie White, decided to start a fanzine. It was called *Lowest Common Denominator*, or *LCD*. I sold it at local records stores like Rhino Records and Vinyl Fetish. It was a simple, xeroxed publication. It actually cost me to produce it, but it was a way for me to express myself and I had a small, loyal following. It even garnered the attention of the *L.A. Reader*. A then-unknown writer/cartoonist by the name of Matt Groening wrote a positive review on it! I also recently found a two-page analysis of my fanzine in a book [*Power Misses: Essays Across (Un)Popular Culture*] written by a USC professor. So *LCD* did make an impact on whomever it reached, which is quite satisfying.

The zine was not so much interviewing bands or music scene-based. It was more expressing my feelings. It was a good outlet for me. People who read it, I think they fed on that and I received a lot of mail from people telling me they felt the same way. It was very therapeutic and different from other fanzines at that time. I got correspondence from all over the country. They sent us their fanzines or tapes of their bands and wanted to request a subscription. There wasn't such a thing. They thought it was bigger than it really was. I'm glad it made that impression on them.

I began making more friends. My hair was colored orange, and I would bring bags of carrots to gigs. We would eat them and then I would wear the bag on my head! People started calling me "Carrot Woman." It stuck!

Once, we went to this show and saw Circle One in this West Valley club. I was the driver. I was the oldest of my little group. I picked up all my friends in Santa Monica and we drove to this particular gig in December 1981. It was a great gig. I have a lot of pictures from it. We all piled in a station wagon. A cop pulled us over and he said, "Everybody put your arms out." We all stuck our

arms out and they approached the
car with guns and they said, "Does
anyone have a gun in there?" And we
said, "No, we're just kids." He saw
we were punkers and he said, "Do
you guys hate hippies?" And we said,
"Yeah!" And he said, "So do I!" Then
he let us go. He was still the old-
school cop, hating hippies.

Godzilla's was probably my
favorite venue. The building had
either been a supermarket or
bowling alley—something big and
cavernous inside. It was like a giant
clubhouse, where you could literally get away with whatever you
wanted to do! It was located in the industrial area of Sun Valley,
just off of the railroad tracks on San Fernando Road. There were
some great shows there—almost every band at the time played
there. And when we weren't slamming, we were drinking and
fucking and fighting! It was crazy. There were railroad tracks.
It was industrial, so no one cared. You weren't bothering any
neighborhood. There was a liquor store on the other side of the
railroad tracks that sold to minors. It was a giant clubhouse, but
unfortunately it didn't last long. Nothing good does. It opened at
the end of '81. It closed, I think, in mid-'82.

Besides Godzilla's, we had to drive pretty far distances to see
shows, because club owners were getting wise and not letting
bands play due to the destructive nature of the shows. I would
drive anywhere—from Oxnard, where I saw Ill Repute's first show,
to Pomona, where I saw Social Distortion at the Boxing Club, to
backyard Suicidal Tendencies parties in Venice, to the Cuckoo's
Nest in Costa Mesa. There were lots of great shows there.

Nothing good lasts forever. The punk scene was no longer unpredictable. Cops would show up to most gigs and shut a lot of them down. I slowly became disillusioned with the scene that I had once loved so much. I remember John Macias invited us to an empty warehouse in Downtown L.A. to have a meeting with the punk community to announce that he was creating P.U.N.X., a sort of punk advocacy group. I was no longer enjoying what the hardcore scene was about. It was starting to turn political instead of just fun. I wanted to go to shows and thrash and be violent with reckless abandon! I didn't want to have "meetings" about getting along!

My last gig was at the Ukrainian Culture Center in March 1982, for the Bad Brains/Bad Religion gig. I continued to write *LCD* for another year, but with more of an artsy feel. I felt a lot of pressure from my parents to "straighten up." My mother, in particular, hated me being a punk. She would cry when I left the house and would stay up late waiting for me to come home—even some nights when I didn't come home. I always reassured her, "Mom, just let me do this! I'll be okay!" Now that I'm a parent, I understand how hard it must have been for her. My parents were Catholic, old-world WWII survivors, and—especially my mom—nurtured me in a way that I felt a lot of guilt, which expedited my exit from the punk scene. I turned my back on punk and my punk friends, got a full-time job, and just lived a clean, boring life for the next twenty-five years. It's like I went into a time capsule. I think that's why I'm well-preserved. I didn't stay in the party scene.

Luckily, some of my writings and photographs got boxed up and kept in the back of a closet for years. As for the memories, in my new, clean life I almost felt embarrassed acknowledging that I was ever a punker, and suppressed any thoughts thereof.

At the age of forty-five, after years of being in a boring marriage, I had become very unhappy. I got divorced and underwent a sort of midlife crisis and longed for the fun I'd had in my youth. In 2006, I was surprised to see that some of the old bands were still around and playing gigs! I began to attend shows again, make new friends and sometimes run into old friends. Punk was now about just having fun. I go to as many shows as I can, and I still bring carrots!

The difference between punk rock in 1981 and punk rock now is that it's so much more social now—which is great! But back then, it was all about being violent and the music reflected that. Punk has been reborn. There are the new kids. They are so great. They are true punkers. They dress real punk and sometimes they ask me to tell them stories about the old days. They love it. They love my old pictures, but I don't think they realize that we really paved the way. That they just can't walk down the street and not get hassled.

I think punk broadened my musical spectrum. When I first got into punk, I went to Rhino Records, and they had great music for nineteen cents. You could buy a Glen Miller album or something. I started buying a whole genre of music. Zydeco and big bands. Part of being punk was shocking people. I would go in my room and open all my windows and blast the Dead Kennedys, and then I'd put on Glen Miller and blast it, and then put on Tchaikovsky. I just wanted to shock my neighbors, but I truly enjoyed other music.

I've always been a weirdo. Even before punk. I've always been kind of a clown. I always liked to have fun. My friends, lovingly, always called me "weird." And I embraced it. I think when punk came about, I felt, "Hey, I can be weird and be part of this group." I just felt really good jumping into it. I think when I got into punk, it was kind of between the early punk and the hardcore stuff. So it was a weird period of punk. That's why I kind of got into the more new wave bands at first and then realized there's a hardcore scene. I kind of missed out enjoying more of the new wave stuff, so now I enjoy listening to stuff that I pretended I didn't like, because I wanted to be hardcore.

■   ■   ■   ■   ■

I loved and respected my mother. However, she had been so judgmental all my life. I remember how angry she was when I got my first tattoo at age thirty-seven—aren't I a grown-up? When she died in 2004, I almost felt a release and a relief. That's when I thought, "Is this all there is in my life?" I was really unhappy, so I completely transformed my life. I had the license to do so.

Growing up with that Catholic guilt, I was very suppressed about things and didn't want to talk about how I felt. After my mom died, I suddenly had freedom to express myself and found punk again. It felt so natural to get back into the modern punk scene. During this time, I also began to paint and express myself through my art in a way that I would have never done before. I have learned what life is all about now! Now in my fifties, I am also happily remarried to, yes, a punker!

GLOSSARY

JAY ADAMS (1961–2014) was a professional skateboarder and part of the Z-Boys team. He is considered a revolutionary figure in skateboarding. Adams brought a surfing influence to skateboarding and blended the surfing and skateboarding cultures of Southern California.

FRANK AGNEW is a musician and former guitarist for the Adolescents and other bands, including Social Distortion, 45 Grave, and TSOL.

RIKK AGNEW is a musician and former guitarist for the Adolescents and the deathrock band Christian Death.

ROBBIE ALLEN is a musician and former bassist for Tender Fury.

RON ATHEY is a Los Angeles-based performance artist known for his extreme explorations of themes including gender, sexuality, and body modification.

STIV BATORS (1949–1990) was a musician and singer for the Dead Boys and the Lords of the New Church. Bators became an influential figure in the early New York City punk rock scene.

NICKEY BEAT, also known as Nickey Alexander, is a musician and the former drummer for the Weirdos, the Cramps, and the Mau-Mau's.

WALLACE BERMAN (1926–1976) was a visual and assemblage artist who is known for making Verifax collages, which involves the use of photocopied material.

JELLO BIAFRA is a musician, singer, and spoken word artist best known as the former singer and founding member of the San Francisco band the Dead Kennedys. Biafra is also a political activist who once ran for mayor of San Francisco.

RODNEY BINGENHEIMER is a disc jockey who had an influential show on the Los Angeles radio station KROQ. Called *Rodney on the ROQ*, the show was known for promoting and introducing new and alternative music, including punk rock.

CHUCK BISCUITS is a musician and former drummer for several influential bands, including Black Flag, D.O.A., and Circle Jerks.

BLACK RANDY (1952–1988) was a musician and singer for Black Randy and the Metrosquad.

SISTER KAREN BOCCALERO (1933–1997) was a Catholic nun and fine artist who founded Self-Help Graphics with Chicano artists in the Boyle Heights area of Los Angeles in 1971. Self-Help Graphics is both a print studio and community center that held punk rock shows in the 1980s.

JON BOK is a Los Angeles-based designer and modern folk artist. Bok has created most of the interiors for the House of Blues venues.

D. BOON (1958–1985) was a musician and the former guitarist and vocalist for the Minutemen.

SHEILA DE BRETTEVILLE is a graphic designer, feminist artist, and educator. She is a faculty member of the Yale School of Art. De Bretteville created the first women's design program at the California Institute of the Arts in 1971.

CHARLES BUKOWSKI (1920–1994) was a Los Angeles-based poet and writer known for a dirty realist style of writing. Some of his major works include the semi-autobiographical novels *Ham on Rye* and *Post Office*.

DEZ CADENA is a musician and the former singer for Black Flag. Cadena also played guitar with the Misfits.

JUDY CHICAGO is a feminist artist best known for her large, collaborative creations, including *The Dinner Party* and the *Birth Project*. She co-founded the California Institute of the Arts Feminist Art Program with Mimi Schapiro.

ED COLVER is a photographer best known for his coverage of the greater Los Angeles punk rock scene. Colver's photographs, many of them iconic, have appeared on more than 250 record covers.

LIZA COWAN is a New York City-based feminist artist who is an influential figure in the lesbian-feminism and lesbian-separatism movements. In the 1970s, she created *DYKE: A Quarterly* magazine.

DARBY CRASH (1958–1980), also known as Bobby Pyn and Paul Beahm, was a musician and singer for the Germs. Crash appears in Penelope Spheeris's 1981 film *The Decline of Western Civilization*.

JACQUES DERRIDA (1930–2004) was a French philosopher and educator best known for his development of the theory of deconstruction.

DAVE DICTOR is a musician best known as the singer for MDC. Dictor is also known for his political activism related to human and animal rights.

DIRK DIRKSEN (1937–2006) was a music promoter known for his role in promoting punk rock bands at the Mabuhay Gardens club in San Francisco.

ALIX DOBKIN is a folk musician and singer-songwriter. Dobkin is a lesbian activist who co-produced the 1973 album *Lavender Jane Loves Women*, which was created for and about lesbians.

BETTY DODSON is a sex educator known for sex-positive feminism. Much of her work is related to advocating masturbation.

JOHN DOE is a musician, poet, and writer who is best known as the singer and bassist for X. He also sings and plays bass for the Knitters.

ROY DOWELL is a visual artist. In 1979, Dowell founded the Graduate Fine Arts Department at Otis College of Art and Design.

DAVE DRIVE is a musician and drummer for the Gears.

RICHARD DUARDO (1952–2014) was an artist and printmaker who was a significant figure in the Los Angeles Chicano art community. Duardo worked with Self-Help Graphics and co-founded the political art collective Centro de Arte Público in the late 1970s.

EL DUCE (1958–1997) was the singer for the controversial "rape rock" band the Mentors.

CHUCK DUKOWSKI is a musician and the former bass player for Black Flag. Dukowski has also played with FLAG, SWA, and other bands.

RON EMORY is a musician and the guitarist for TSOL.

KLAUS FLOURIDE is a musician and the bass player for the Dead Kennedys.

KIM FOWLEY (1939–2015) was a record producer and manager who managed several bands, including the Runaways.

PAOLO FREIRE (1921–1997) was an educator and philosopher associated with critical pedagogy, and best known for his book *Pedagogy of the Oppressed*.

HARRY GAMBOA is a Chicano performance artist, writer, and photographer. He was a founding member of ASCO, an East Los Angeles-based Chicano artist collective.

ELSA GIDLOW (1898–1986) was a poet, author, and philosopher known for her lesbian love poetry. Gidlow founded a rural retreat center, the Druid Heights Artists Retreat, in Marin County, California, in the 1940s.

GREG GINN is a musician best known as the guitarist for Black Flag. Ginn is also the owner of SST Records.

KIM GORDON is a musician, writer, and artist best known as the singer and bassist for Sonic Youth.

JACK GRISHAM is a writer and musician best known as the singer for TSOL.

NAT HENTOFF (1925–2017) was a columnist, historian, and music critic. Hentoff wrote for numerous publications and was the jazz critic for the *Village Voice* from 1958 to 2009.

WILLIE HERRON is a Chicano muralist and performance artist. Herron was one of the founding members of the punk band Los Illegals, as well as ASCO, an East Los Angeles-based Chicano artist collective.

ROBERT HILBURN is a music critic and writer who was the music editor at the *Los Angeles Times* from 1970 to 2005.

PENELOPE HOUSTON is a musician best known as the singer for the San Francisco band the Avengers.

BRUCE KALBERG (1949–2011) was the co-founder of *NO MAG* magazine with Mike Gira from the Swans.

CHRISTOPHER KNOWLES is a Brooklyn-based artist with a diverse practice that includes painting, sculpture, and performance art.

SUZANNE LACY is an artist and educator whose work includes video and photographic installations. She is a member of the faculty at the University of Southern California Roski School of Art and Design.

CRAIG LEE (1956–1991) was a musician and the former guitarist for the Bags and Catholic Discipline. Lee produced the Rock Against AIDS benefit and was also a music reviewer for the *Los Angeles Times*.

DICKEY LEE is a country singer and songwriter from Memphis, Tennessee.

EVE LIBERTINE is a musician and the former singer for Crass. Libertine performed on the band's feminist *Penis Envy* album.

ROBERT LOPEZ, also known as El Vez, is a musician and the former guitarist for the Zeros.

LYDIA LUNCH is a writer, poet, and singer. Lunch's career includes founding the no wave band Teenage Jesus and the Jerks.

DAVE MARKEY is a filmmaker whose work includes documenting the Southern California punk rock scene.

TOM MORELLO is a musician who is best known as the guitarist for Rage Against the Machine.

KEITH MORRIS is a musician who is best known as the former singer for the Circle Jerks and Black Flag.

BRENDAN MULLEN (1949–2009) was a music promoter and writer best known as the founder of the punk rock club the Masque.

TOM MURRIN (1939–2012) was a performance artist and playwright known for his work in experimental theater.

MIKE NESS is a musician best known as the singer and guitarist for Social Distortion.

CLAES OLDENBURG is a performance artist and sculptor. Oldenburg was a leading pop artist known for combining consumer culture into his work.

CATHERINE OPIE is an artist and photographer whose work focuses on a diverse array of subjects, including Los Angeles freeways, surfers, and tree stumps.

RAYMOND PETTIBON is an artist who is widely known for his creation of punk rock art in the 1980s, especially for bands on SST Records. He created the iconic four bars logo for Black Flag.

JEFFREY LEE PIERCE (1958–1996) was a musician and the former singer and guitarist for the Gun Club.

LARI PITTMAN is a painter known for his use of vivid color. Pittman is a faculty member in the University of California, Los Angeles Department of Art.

ARLENE RAVEN is an art historian, writer, and educator who co-founded the Feminist Studio Workshop with Judy Chicago and Sheila de Bretteville.

PAUL ROESSLER is a musician and the former keyboardist for the Screamers.

ZACK DE LA ROCHA is a musician best known as the singer for Rage Against the Machine.

MIKE ROCHE is a musician and the former bassist for TSOL.

HENRY ROLLINS is a musician, actor, and writer. Rollins is well-known as the former singer for Black Flag.

MIMI SCHAPIRO (1923–2015), also known as Miriam Schapiro, was a feminist artist who co-founded the California Institute of the Arts' Feminist Art Program with Judy Chicago.

PAT SMEAR is a musician best known as the former guitarist for the Germs and current guitarist for the Foo Fighters.

STEVE SOTO is a musician and a founding member of the Adolescents. Soto was also in the bands Agent Orange and Legal Weapon.

BILL STEVENSON is a musician and drummer for the Descendents who formerly played drums for Black Flag.

JOE STRUMMER (1952–2002) was a musician best known as the singer and rhythm guitarist for the Clash.

MARTHA SWOPE (1928–2017) was a photographer who started photographing New York dance and theater performers in the 1950s.

MIKE WATT is a musician best known as the bassist for Minutemen and Firehose.

BROCK WHEATON is a musician and the former drummer for Chinas Comidas.

MARK WHEATON is a musician and the former keyboardist for Chinas Comidas.

SHANNON WILHELM is a musician and the former singer for Castration Squad.

WOLFMAN JACK (1938–1995) was a disc jockey known for his raspy voice and howls.

JOE WOOD is a musician and the former singer for TSOL. He also formed the blues band Joe Wood & the Lonely Ones.

Z'EV is a percussionist, sound artist, and performance artist. Z'EV has been an influential figure in industrial music.

BILLY ZOOM is a musician and guitarist best known as the guitarist for X.

ACKNOWLEDGMENTS

I WANT TO THANK all the beautiful women who took the time to sit down with me or take my call and contribute to this project. Without you, this wouldn't have happened. The support, kindness, and friendship I've received have been overwhelming. Thank you also to the women I interviewed who are not included here. I'm grateful for your stories and the time you spent with me.

Thank you to the Voice of Witness foundation, especially Cliff Mayotte and the Amplifying Unheard Voices Oral History Training educators, for providing me with the inspiration and the ethical and practical tools I needed to complete this project. Thank you to Jeffrey Goldman at Santa Monica Press for believing in the project, providing help and guidance along the way, and giving me ideas that made it better. Thank you to my friends who spent so much time talking with me about this project, especially Renie, Annie Knight, Theresa Paulsrud, and Luis Pedroza. Thank you Sasha, Mr. Pipps, Little Bear, and Joni. Thank you to my brother, David Shotsberger, for providing encouragement of this project since the beginning. Thank you to Steven Soto for your support, ideas, love, and conversations about the book.

PHOTO CREDITS

INDEX

ABOUT THE AUTHOR

STACY RUSSO is a librarian and associate professor at Santa Ana College in Santa Ana, California. She has English degrees from UC Berkeley and Chapman University and a master's degree in library and information science from San Jose State University. She is a poet and writer. Stacy's writing has appeared in *Feminist Teacher*, *Feminist Collections*, *Library Journal*, *American Libraries*, *The Chaffey Review*, *Serials Review*, *Counterpoise*, and the anthology *Open Doors: An Invitation to Poetry* (Chaparral Canyon Press, 2016). Her other books are *The Library as Place in California* (McFarland, 2007) and *Life as Activism: June Jordan's Writings from The Progressive* (Litwin Books, 2014). She grew up in the 1980s Southern California punk rock scene, which has been a big influence on her life.

MIKE WATT is the son of a sailor. He was born in 1957 in Portsmouth, Virginia, but has lived in San Pedro, California, for the last fifty years. He's known mainly for starting the Minutemen with his buddy, D. Boon, but went on to later found Dos, Firehose, and, more recently, the Secondmen, the Missingmen, Cuz, and Il Sogno del Marinaio. He does bass, spiel, and writes songs. Watt also helped Porno for Pyros, Banyan, and J Mascis and the Fog, and had the huge honor of working for the Stooges during their reunion from 2003 to 2013.